KV-648-770

Palgrave Studies in European Union Politics

Following on the sustained success of the acclaimed *European Union Series,* which essentially publishes research-based textbooks, *Palgrave Studies in European Union Politics* publishes cutting edge research-driven monographs.

The remit of the series is broadly defined, both in terms of subject and academic discipline. All topics of significance concerning the nature and operation of the European Union potentially fall within the scope of the series. The series is multidisciplinary to reflect the growing importance of the EU as a political, economic and social phenomenon. We will welcome submissions from the areas of political studies, international relations, political economy, public and social policy, economics, law and sociology.

Submissions should be sent to Amy Lankester-Owen, Politics Publisher, 'a.lankester-owen@palgrave.com'.

Titles include:

Sebastian Krapohl
RISK REGULATION IN THE SINGLE MARKET
The Governance of Pharmaceuticals and Foodstuffs in the European Union

Katie Verlin Laatikainen and Karen E. Smith *(editors)*
THE EUROPEAN UNION AND THE UNITED NATIONS
Intersecting Multilateralisms

Esra LaGro and Knud Erik Jørgensen *(editors)*
TURKEY AND THE EUROPEAN UNION
Prospects for a Difficult Encounter

Paul G. Lewis and Zdenka Mansfeldová *(editors)*
THE EUROPEAN UNION AND PARTY POLITICS IN CENTRAL AND EASTERN EUROPE

Ingo Linsenmann, Christoph O. Meyer and Wolfgang T. Wessels *(editors)*
ECONOMIC GOVERNMENT OF THE EU
A Balance Sheet of New Modes of Policy Coordination

Hartmut Mayer and Henri Vogt *(editors)*
A RESPONSIBLE EUROPE?
Ethical Foundations of EU External Affairs

Lauren M. McLaren
IDENTITY, INTERESTS AND ATTITUDES TO EUROPEAN INTEGRATION

Philomena Murray *(editor)*
EUROPE AND ASIA
Regions in Flux

Daniel Naurin and Helen Wallace *(editors)*
UNVEILING THE COUNCIL OF THE EUROPEAN UNION
Games Governments Play in Brussels

Frank Schimmelfennig, Stefan Engert and Heiko Knobel
INTERNATIONAL SOCIALIZATION IN EUROPE
European Organizations, Political Conditionality and Democratic Change

Justus Schönlau
DRAFTING THE EU CHARTER

Angelos Sepos
THE EUROPEANIZATION OF CYPRUS
Polity, Policies and Politics

Marc Weller, Denika Blacklock and Katherine Nobbs *(editors)*
THE PROTECTION OF THE MINORITIES IN THE WIDER EUROPE

Palgrave Studies in European Union Politics
Series Standing Order ISBN 978–1–4039–9511–7 (hardback) and
ISBN 978–1–4039–9512–4 (paperback)
(outside North America only)

You can receive future titles in this series as they are published by placing a standing order.
Please contact your bookseller or, in case of difficulty, write to us at the address below with
your name and address, the title of the series and one of the ISBNs quoted above.

Customer Services Department, Macmillan Distribution Ltd, Houndmills, Basingstoke,
Hampshire RG21 6XS, England

EU Cohesion Policy after Enlargement

Edited by

Michael Baun

and

Dan Marek

First published 2008 by
PALGRAVE MACMILLAN

Palgrave Macmillan in the UK is an imprint of Macmillan Publishers Limited, registered in England, company number 785998, of Houndmills, Basingstoke, Hampshire RG21 6XS.

Palgrave Macmillan in the US is a division of St Martin's Press LLC, 175 Fifth Avenue, New York, NY 10010.

Palgrave Macmillan is the global academic imprint of the above companies and has companies and representatives throughout the world.

Palgrave® and Macmillan® are registered trademarks in the United States, the United Kingdom, Europe and other countries.

ISBN-13: 978–0–230–52472–9 hardback
ISBN-10: 0–230–52472–9 hardback

This book is printed on paper suitable for recycling and made from fully managed and sustained forest sources. Logging, pulping and manufacturing processes are expected to conform to the environmental regulations of the country of origin.

A catalogue record for this book is available from the British Library.

Library of Congress Cataloging-in-Publication Data

EU cohesion policy after enlargement / edited by Michael Baun and Dan Marek.
p. cm.—(Palgrave studies in European Union politics)
Includes bibliographical references and index.
ISBN-13: 978–0–230–52472–9 (alk. paper)
ISBN-10: 0–230–52472–9 (alk. paper)
1. European Union. 2. Regional disparities – European Union countries – Case studies. 3. European Union countries – Economic policy. I. Baun, Michael J. II. Marek, Dan, 1969–

JN30.E817 2009
341.242′2—dc22   2008030140

10 9 8 7 6 5 4 3 2 1
17 16 15 14 13 12 11 10 09 08

Printed and bound in Great Britain by
CPI Antony Rowe, Chippenham and Eastbourne

Contents

Illustrations

Maps

Tables

Abbreviations

AC	Autonomous Community
AKČR	Association of the Regions in the Czech Republic
ASEP	Higher Council for Personnel Recruitment (Aνώτατο Συμβούλιο Επιλογής Προσωπικού)
BMW	Border, Midlands and West (Ireland)
B-W	Baden-Württemberg
CAP	Common Agricultural Policy
CEC	Commission of the European Communities
CED	Community Economic Development
CEEC	Central and Eastern European Country
CF	Cohesion Fund
CI	Community Initiative
COR	Committee of the Regions
COREPER	Committee of Permanent Representatives
CSF	Community Support Framework
CSG	Community Strategic Guidelines on Cohesion
DAHR	Democratic Alliance of Hungarians in Romania
DG	Directorate-General
EAFRD	European Agricultural Fund for Rural Development
EAGGF	European Agricultural Guidance and Guarantee Fund
EC	European Community
ECU	European Currency Unit
EEC	European Economic Community
EFF	European Fisheries Fund
EGTC	European Grouping for Territorial Cooperation
EMU	Economic and Monetary Union
ENPI	European Neighbourhood and Partnership Instrument
EQUAL	Employment and Social Inclusion Programme
ERDF	European Regional Development Fund
ERP	European Reconstruction Programme
ESF	European Social Fund
ESPEL	External Consultant for Quality Control of Infrastructure Projects
ETC	European Territorial Cooperation
EU	European Union
EUROSTAT	EU Statistics Office

FDI	Foreign Direct Investment
FIFG	Financial Instrument for Fisheries Guidance
GDP	Gross Domestic Product
GVA	Gross Value Added
ICT	Information and Communications Technology
IDA	Industrial Development Agency (Ireland)
IMPs	Integrated Mediterranean Programmes
INTERREG	Interregional cooperation programme
IROP	Integrated Regional Operational Programme
ISPA	Instrument for Structural Policies for Pre-Accession
IOP	Integrated Operational Programme
IT	Internet Technology
JSC	Joint Steering Committee
JROP	Joint Regional Operational Programme
LEADER	Rural Development Programme
LMA	*Land* Ministry of Agriculture
LME	*Land* Ministry of Economics
LMSA	*Land* Ministry of Social Affairs
LTL	Lithuanian *litas* (currency)
MA	Managing Authority
MC	Monitoring Committee
MDPH	Ministry for Development, Public Works and Housing (Romania)
MoPARLA	Ministry of Public Administration Reforms and Local Authorities (Lithuania)
MOU	Managing Organization Unit
MP	Member of Parliament
MRD	Ministry of Regional Development
NCRD	National Council for Regional Development (Romania)
ND	New Democracy (Greece)
NDP	National Development Plan
NDS	National Development Strategy
NGO	Nongovernmental Organization
NPTD	National Plan for Territorial Development
NRP	National Reform Program
NSDP	National Strategic Development Plan
NSRF	National Strategic Reference Framework
NSS	National Spatial Strategy
NUTS	Nomenclature of Statistical Territorial Units
ODS	Civic Democratic Party (Czech Republic)

OP	Operational Programme
PA	Paying Authority
PASOK	Pan-Hellenic Socialist Movement (Greece)
PFI	Private Finance Initiative
PHARE	Poland, Hungary Assistance for Economic Reconstruction
PHARE CBC	PHARE, Cross-Border Programme
PP	People's Party (Spain)
PPPs	Public-Private Partnerships
PSOE	Spanish Socialist Party
R&D	Research and Development
RA	Regional Authority
RCE	Regional Competitiveness and Employment
RDA	Regional Development Agency
RDC	Regional Development Council
RDF	Regional Development Fund
RDP	Regional Development Plan
RES	Regional Economic Strategies
ROP	Regional Operational Programme
RTDI	Research and Technological Development and Innovation
S&E	South and East (Ireland)
SAPARD	Special Accession Programme for Agriculture and Rural Development
SEA	Single European Act
SME	Small and Medium-Sized Enterprise
SMIS	Single Management Information System
SOP	Sectoral Operational Programme
SPD	Single Programming Document
SPP	Special Preparatory Programme
STRUDER	Structural Development in Selected Regions
TENs	Trans-European Networks
URBAN	Urban Development Programme
VAT	Value Added Tax

Preface

Reducing economic and social disparities in Europe is a key goal of the European Union, which it seeks to achieve through cohesion policy. This task has become even more important as a consequence of EU enlargement in 2004 and 2007, which added a dozen mainly poorer member states and greatly increased intra-EU disparities, and more complicated as a result of the EU's decision to link cohesion policy to the achievement of its Lisbon Agenda growth and competitiveness goals. Both enlargement and the 'Lisbonization' of cohesion policy, therefore, raise important questions about how cohesion policy is being implemented and its implications for multilevel governance in a larger and more diverse EU.

This book examines the implementation of EU cohesion policy after enlargement and the 2006 cohesion policy reform. It does so by examining cohesion policy implementation in ten EU countries – five old (pre-2004) and five new member states. This balanced selection of cases enables us to assess how both old and new member states, and relatively wealthy and less wealthy countries among the old member states, have implemented cohesion policy and responded to Lisbonization and other changes to cohesion policy introduced by the 2006 reform. Each of the case studies is written by national experts who in many cases have been directly involved in the implementation of EU cohesion policy in their own countries.

The book's chapters are structured as follows. Chapter 1 discusses the key questions posed by enlargement and the 2006 reform for cohesion policy implementation in both old and new member states, thus providing a conceptual and analytical framework for the country case studies which follow. Chapter 2 provides an historical overview of the development of EU cohesion policy and reviews the debate on cohesion policy reform in the context of enlargement. It thus sets the policy context and provides important background information for the examination of cohesion policy implementation in specific national settings.

The next ten chapters are the country case studies that comprise the core of this book. Chapters 3–7 examine cohesion policy implementation in five old member states – the United Kingdom, Germany, Spain, Ireland and Greece – while Chapters 8–12 examine how cohesion policy is being implemented in five new entrants – Poland, the Czech Republic,

Hungary, Lithuania and Romania. Each of these chapters discusses how specific member states have responded to the challenges posed by enlargement (or membership, as the case may be) and the 2006 reform of cohesion policy, as well as the various factors influencing this response. Chapter 13 sifts through the findings of the previous chapters and attempts to draw some general conclusions about the implementation of EU cohesion policy after enlargement and the factors accounting for national variation in cohesion policy implementation.

Completing this book was a definite, although enjoyable, challenge and we could not have done it without the help and advice of many people. We would like to give special thanks to the Prague Office of the Friedrich Ebert Stiftung, and to Project Manager Kristina Larischová in particular. Financial support from the FES enabled a May 2007 workshop in Olomouc, Czech Republic that brought together many of the book's contributors and allowed us to discuss first drafts of the chapters.

We would like to thank the editors of Palgrave-Macmillan's *Studies in European Union Politics* series, Neill Nugent, William Paterson and Michelle Egan, for their valuable advice and suggestions and for agreeing to include the book in their excellent series. We are also grateful to Amy Lankester-Owen, Gemma d'Arcy Hughes and the editorial team at Palgrave-Macmillan for their patience, guidance and advice. Thanks also to our contributors for their efforts to adhere to our timetable and guidelines, as well as their responsiveness to our many suggestions and requests.

Michael Baun would like to thank the family of Col. Vernon Pizer, whose generous financial support of the Marguerite Langdale Pizer Chair in International Politics at Valdosta State University has provided him the time and resources to work on this book. He would also like to thank Valdosta State University and the VSU Center for International Programs for research grants that funded work on this book.

MICHAEL BAUN
DAN MAREK

Contributors

David Allen is Professor of European and International Politics and Head of the Department of Politics, International Relations and European Studies (PIRES) at Loughborough University in the United Kingdom. His most recent publications include contributions on cohesion policy to the latest edition of *Policy-Making in the European Union* (edited by Wallace, Wallace and Pollack), on Britain to *The Member States of the EU* (edited by Bulmer and Lequesne) and on the Europeanization of UK foreign policy and the UK Foreign and Commonwealth Office in *The Europeanization of British Politics* (edited by Bache and Jordan). In December 2007 he co-edited with Borja Garcia a special issue of the *Journal of Contemporary European Research* entitled 'The EU and Sport'.

Michael Baun is Marguerite Langdale Pizer Professor of International Politics at Valdosta State University. He has published widely on the EU and European politics, including several journal articles on EU cohesion policy. He is co-editor with Katja Weber and Michael E. Smith of *Governing Europe's Neighborhood: Partners or Periphery?*

Jozsef Benedek is Professor of Geography at the Babes-Bolyai University of Cluj-Napoca and Vice Dean of the Faculty of Geography. He was a Humboldt Fellow in 2002–03 at the University of Würzburg, Germany. His research activity focuses on local and regional development and territorial planning.

Rachael Chapman is a Senior Research Fellow at the Local Governance Research Unit, De Montfort University, Leicester. Her expertise and research interests focus on multilevel governance, the EU structural funds, democratic legitimacy and civil society participation. She is currently finalizing a joint publication with Ian Bache entitled 'Democracy through Multi-Level Governance? The Implementation of the Structural Funds in South Yorkshire'.

Grzegorz Gorzelak is Professor of Economics and Director of the Centre for European Regional and Local Studies at the University of Warsaw. He has published many books, chapters, articles and research papers on regional development and regional policy in Poland and abroad. He has managed numerous projects financed by the Polish Committee for Scientific Research and the Polish Government and an international project financed by the European Commission. He has participated in the EC-coordinated LEDA programme as well as projects financed by the World Bank, USAID, UNDP, UNESCO and other international institutions. He managed one of the first PHARE programmes in Poland (1990–91), directed at Polish municipalities.

Gyula Horváth is Professor in Regional Economics and Policy at the University of Pécs and Director-General of the Centre for Regional Studies, Hungarian Academy of Sciences. He is a member of the Academia Europaea (London) and president of the Hungarian Regional Science Association. His areas of expertise are European regional policy and restructuring and regional transformation in Central and Eastern Europe. He is author, editor and co-editor of 30 books and over 300 articles and papers (in both Hungarian and other languages). He is a member of the Evaluation Board of the Framework Programme of the European Commission and an external expert for the RIS, RITTS, PHARE and TACIS projects of the EU.

Réka Horváth is Lecturer in the Faculty of Economics and Business Administration at Babes-Bolyai University, Cluj, Romania. She has a PhD in political science from the Free University of Brussels. Her main research interests are regional development and ethnic parties.

Marek W. Kozak is Assistant Professor at the Centre for European Regional and Local Studies at the University of Warsaw. From 1993–02 he was President and CEO of the Polish Agency for Regional Development (PARR), in charge of PHARE regional development programmes in Poland. He has advised the Ministry for Regional Development and other ministries and taken part in numerous project evaluations. He is a member of the Committee for Spatial Economy and Regional Planning of the Polish Academy of Sciences and member of the board of the State Council for Spatial Economy. He is the author of over 70 publications on regional development, cohesion policy, evaluation, socioeconomic aspects of transition and tourism in Poland.

Dan Marek is Jean Monnet Lecturer in European Politics at the Department of Politics and European Studies, Palacký University, Olomouc, Czech Republic. He is the author of several books and numerous academic journal articles, including publications in the *Journal of Common Market Studies*, *Regional and Federal Studies* and *Publius*.

Irene McMaster is a Research Fellow in the European Policies Research Centre at the University of Strathclyde, in Glasgow. She specializes in regional economic development and policy in Europe, with emphasis on Ireland and Central and Eastern Europe. She has undertaken a range of research projects and evaluation studies of EU territorial and spatial development policies, including the evaluation of the spatial and urban dimensions of the 2000–06 Objective 1 and 2 programmes on behalf of DG REGIO, the *ex ante* evaluation of structural fund and pre-accession programmes and evaluation methodologies in Ireland.

Francesc Morata is Professor of Political Science at Universitat Autònoma de Barcelona (UAB) and holds a Jean Monnet Chair Ad Personam in European Integration. He is also director of the University Institute of European Studies in Barcelona, and director of the Masters programmes in European Integration and European Policies of International Cooperation for Development of UAB. His main research areas are Europeanization, European public policies, multilevel governance and environmental studies. He has published extensively.

Vitalis Nakrošis is Associate Professor in the Institute of International Relations and Political Science at Vilnius University and a partner in the Public Policy and Management Institute in Vilnius. He was previously employed in the Ministry of Public Administration Reforms and Local Authorities and the National Regional Development Agency. He has been involved with many research, evaluation and technical assistance projects dealing with EU cohesion policy and its implementation in Lithuania.

Christos J. Paraskevopoulos is Assistant Professor of Political Science and European Public Policy at the University of Macedonia, Thessaloniki, Greece and Visiting Research Fellow at the LSE/European Institute. He has written on social capital, institutions, local economic development and EU structural policy in various academic journals and edited volumes in the United Kingdom, United States and Greece. He is the author of *Interpreting Convergence in the European Union: Patterns of Collective Action, Social Learning and Europeanization*. His most recent publications are *Learning from Abroad: Regionalization and Local Institutional Infrastructure in Cohesion and Accession Countries*, 2004 Special Issue of *Regional and Federal Studies* (co-editor), and *Adapting to EU Multi-Level Governance: Regional and Environmental Policies in Cohesion (Greece, Ireland, Portugal) and CEE (Hungary, Poland) Countries* (co-edited with P. Getimis and N. Rees).

Lucia Alexandra Popartan is a PhD student in European Integration at the Universitat Autònoma de Barcelona. She is research fellow of the University Institute of European Studies in Barcelona, member of the research group in Multilevel Governance of IUEE (EUgov) supported by the Generalitat de Catalunya and member of CONNEX (Connecting Excellence on European Governance – EU VI Framework Programme). Her research interests include Europeanization, multilevel governance, EU enlargement and cohesion policy.

Ingo Schorlemmer is a Research Assistant and PhD student at the Department of Political Science, University of Erlangen-Nürnberg.

Roland Sturm is Professor of Political Science at the University of Erlangen-Nürnberg and Director of the Centre for Area Studies. He has published widely in the fields of European integration, comparative politics and comparative public policies.

1
Introduction

Michael Baun and Dan Marek

Cohesion policy is one of the European Union's (EU) most important activities, currently accounting for more than a third of the EU budget. Through the structural funds – the main financial instruments of cohesion policy – the EU seeks to reduce economic and social disparities in Europe by providing assistance to disadvantaged regions and localities. Cohesion policy is not only important for what it does but for how it does it. Structural funds are provided to EU member states on a regionalized basis to help fund multiannual development programmes. These Operational Programmes (OPs) are planned and implemented according to the principle of 'partnership', which requires the European Commission and national governments to cooperate with appropriate subnational (regional and local) and nongovernmental actors. Because of the partnership principle and its emphasis on decentralization and subsidiarity, some scholars have argued that EU cohesion policy has promoted the development of multilevel governance in Europe (Bache, 2008).

Both because of what it is – a programme to provide development assistance to poorer regions and countries that is redistributive in effect – and its budgetary status, cohesion policy was bound to be affected by the 2004 and 2007 enlargements of the EU.[1] Most of the new member states are relatively poor Central and Eastern European countries (CEECs), with per capita incomes far below the EU average. Thus, economic disparities within the EU have grown considerably as a result of enlargement. In 2004 the wealthiest member state, Luxembourg, had a per capita GDP that was 226 per cent of the EU average, while the poorest (at that time prospective) member states, Bulgaria and Romania, had per capita incomes that were only around 30 per cent of the EU norm (European Commission, 2006a). The gap between the wealthiest and poorest regions, most of which are in the CEECs, has also grown as a result of enlargement, while many of the new member states also feature sharp internal disparities between rapidly-growing and more prosperous capital-city metropoles and poorer outlying regions. Enlargement, therefore, has made the traditional cohesion policy task of reducing economic and social disparities even more necessary and important. However, because of the reluctance of wealthier member states to increase the size of the EU budget and their own contributions, enlargement has not been accompanied by a corresponding expansion of funding for cohesion policy; in fact, cohesion policy spending is declining as a percentage of EU GDP, from a high of about 46 per cent in 1999 to a projected 35 per cent in 2013 (European Commission, 2007a, pp. 173–4). One consequence has been a reduction of cohesion policy allocations for relatively wealthier countries that were member states before 2004.

Enlargement has also coincided with a profound thematic re-orientation of cohesion policy. In March 2005 the European Council decided to relaunch the stagnant 'Lisbon Agenda' to promote economic growth and competitiveness in the EU and it accorded cohesion policy a key role in achieving the Lisbon goals. The decision to link cohesion policy to achievement of the Lisbon goals (and the 'Gothenburg' goal of environmental sustainability) was subsequently confirmed by the European Council in December 2005 and incorporated into the new Regulation governing the structural and cohesion funds that was approved by the Council in July 2006 (OJEU, 2006a). As a consequence, a certain percentage of EU funding under each of the main objectives of cohesion policy – 'Convergence' and 'Regional Competitiveness and Employment' – must now be used for projects which contribute to achievement of the Lisbon goals. While the Lisbon 'earmarking' requirements have been waived for new member states in the 2007–13 programming period, they are nevertheless expected to adhere to them on a voluntary basis. The 2006 cohesion policy reform also makes some important changes to programming and implementation procedures, most notably the drafting of strategic frameworks at both the EU and national levels and provisions for further simplification and decentralization of cohesion policy.

Both enlargement and 'Lisbonization' raise important questions about the implementation of cohesion policy in a larger and more diverse EU. Some of these questions pertain specifically to old or new member states: How have reduced levels of funding after 2006 affected the implementation of cohesion policy in old member states? How have new member states performed in implementing cohesion policy? Have their administrative and institutional structures been up to the task?

What has been the impact of cohesion policy on multilevel governance in the new members? Other questions pertain to all member states in common: How have member states, both old and new, responded to the Lisbonization of cohesion policy? What impact have the new implementation rules and policy governance requirements for cohesion policy introduced in 2006 had on multilevel governance? Are there significant differences between member states in implementing cohesion policy, and if so, how can these be explained? These are some of the key questions which this book seeks to answer.

Before proceeding to the country case studies which make up the core of this book, however, the remainder of this chapter discusses these questions in greater detail. The next section examines specific questions for old and new member states when it comes to implementing EU cohesion policy, followed by a discussion of the challenges posed for all member states by Lisbonization and the 2006 cohesion policy reform. The chapter then briefly discusses the literature on Europeanization, drawing from this to identify various 'domestic mediating factors' which might affect the implementation of cohesion policy in different national settings.

Old and new member states: different challenges and questions

The distinction between old and new member states will undoubtedly fade and eventually disappear, as it has following previous enlargements. For the moment, however, these two groups of countries face very different challenges when it comes to implementing cohesion policy that result from their different economic and political situations.

A challenge for most old member states is dealing with reduced levels of cohesion policy funding, the inevitable consequence of the accession of relatively poor CEECs who are needier claimants for a limited amount of EU assistance. It also results from the 'statistical effect' of enlargement, which has lowered the average per capita GDP of the EU and raised many of the original 15 member states' (EU15) regions and countries above the eligibility thresholds for structural and cohesion fund assistance.

Most of the EU15 began dealing with the problem of reduced funding before the 2004 enlargement. The March 1999 'Agenda 2000' agreement aimed at consolidating structural funds spending and concentrating it on fewer, more needy regions and priority areas. As a result, the proportion of the EU population receiving structural funds assistance in 2000–06 fell from 51 to 42 per cent. Generous transitional arrangements and financial packages for regions losing EU assistance were agreed to as compensation, however (European Council, 1999; OJEC, 1999).

The December 2005 European Council agreement on the financial perspective for 2007–13 saw a major shift of cohesion policy spending in favour of the new member states; in the current programming period these countries will receive about 51 per cent of all cohesion policy spending, even though they account for less than one-third of the total EU population. The shift of cohesion policy spending eastwards would have been even greater if not for the efforts of major EU15 beneficiaries to maximize their share of funding and the agreement to generous transitional arrangements for regions losing assistance because of enlargement.

Each of the old member states examined in this book faces a significant loss or reduction of EU assistance. In the current programming period relatively wealthy Ireland will receive 80 per cent less than in 2000–06, while the United Kingdom (46 per cent) and Germany (19 per cent) will also see a decline in cohesion policy funding. Spain also suffered a sharp drop in funding (42 per cent), in fact the largest in absolute terms (€23 billion) of the EU15, but all of its regions will continue receiving cohesion policy support in 2007–13. Relatively poor Greece suffered a 26 per cent reduction of funding, but remains a major beneficiary of the structural and cohesion funds for now.[2]

The reduction of EU funding raises a number of important questions for old member states regarding the impact on cohesion policy implementation: What is the impact of diminished funding on structural programming in these countries – has it led to an increased concentration of resources and an emphasis on certain types of projects and priorities? How has reduced funding affected implementation and management structures for cohesion policy – has it resulted in the rationalization or centralization of implementation systems? How has reduced funding affected application of the partnership principle – has it increased or decreased the importance of partnership, and what kinds of partners and partnership arrangements does it favour? And, finally, what is the impact of reduced funding on the relationship between EU cohesion policy and national regional policies – has it led to a closer alignment or a decoupling of EU and domestic policies?

New member states face a very different set of problems and questions. Chief among these is whether they will be able to effectively utilize and absorb increased amounts of EU assistance. As a precondition of

ession, each of the candidate states had to create the institutional
administrative capacity to effectively manage cohesion policy,
uding mechanisms for inter-ministerial coordination at the national
l, regionalized administrative structures, and systems for financial
itoring and control. As evidenced by the Commission's criticisms
in its annual progress reports for each country, however, this was an
aspect of pre-accession preparations that proved problematic for most of
the CEECs. Considerable doubts about the institutional and administrative capacity of the CEECs remained even as these countries were
formally admitted to the EU in 2004 and 2007.

How have the institutional and administrative structures of the new
member states – at both the national and regional levels – performed
since accession? Have they been adequate to the task of implementing
and managing cohesion policy? Have they functioned well enough to
allow the full use of available EU assistance, or have there been major
problems and inefficiencies that have limited the 'absorption capacity'
of the CEECs? If there have been problems, what is their source or
nature, and what steps have been taken to deal with them? Problems
with institutional and administrative capacity were behind the
European Council's decision in December 2005 to modify the 'automatic de-commitment' rule for the new member states, giving them an
additional year to use EU funds; however, this step provides only a temporary respite, with the usual 'n+2' rule applying from 2010 (European
Council, 2005, p. 22).

Also affecting absorption capacity is the ability of new member states
to provide adequate co-financing for EU-funded projects. On this score
too, the European Council approved some temporary concessions for
the new member states in 2007–13, allowing VAT to be counted as part
of national contributions to funding EU-supported projects, and increasing the percentage of EU-funded projects that can be co-financed by the
structural funds from 75 to 85 per cent (European Council, 2005,
pp. 20–2). These conditions did not apply in 2004–06, however. Even
with these concessions, have new member states been able to provide
the necessary co-financing for EU-funded projects in the current
programming period?

Another set of questions concerns the impact of EU cohesion policy
on multilevel governance in the new member states. The concept of
multilevel governance has attracted growing scholarly attention in
recent years, since being initially applied to analyses of EU regional policy in the early 1990s (Bache and Flinders, 2004). At its core, it describes
how decision-making authority is increasingly diffused and exercised

jointly by governmental and private actors at different territorial levels, with the boundaries between state and society becoming increasingly blurred as a result. The initial focus of the multilevel governance literature was on territorial governance, with some scholars asserting that the partnership requirement of EU cohesion policy was mobilizing regional actors and empowering them (and supranational actors) at the expense of national governments, leading to the emergence of a 'Europe of the regions' (Marks, 1992, 1993; Jones and Keating, 1995; Caporaso, 1996; Hooghe, ed., 1996; Kohler-Koch, 1996; Marks et al., 1996; Hooghe and Marks, 2001). Others disputed this assertion, however, pointing to the 'gate-keeping' capacity of national governments and the role of national political conditions and constitutional arrangements in limiting or mediating the governance effects of EU policies (Pollack, 1995; Jeffery, ed., 1997; Börzel, 1999; Benz and Eberlein, 1999; Laffan, 2004; Allen, 2005).

More recently, the concept of multilevel governance has been refined to incorporate a non-territorial dimension. Thus, Marks and Hooghe (2004) define two main types of multilevel governance: type I, which refers to the dispersion of decision-making authority among different territorial levels of government; and type II, which refers to the exercise of public authority within 'task-specific jurisdictions' with intersecting memberships that may operate at numerous territorial levels. In other words, type I multilevel governance concerns the 'vertical' redistribution of power between different governmental levels (in the EU context: supranational, national, regional and local), while type II multilevel governance concerns the 'horizontal' transfer of state authority to functional governmental arrangements involving non-governmental or private actors. According to Bache (2008, 2007), the governance effect of EU cohesion policy can perhaps best be seen in its promotion of type II multilevel governance in many member states, including those which have been more successful in limiting its impact on territorial governance.

The debate about cohesion policy and multilevel governance generated considerable scholarly interest in the impact of EU conditionality on territorial governance in the CEECs, with many studies focusing on the adaptation of these countries to EU cohesion policy requirements and the administration of EU structural assistance in the pre-accession period. What these studies found was that before 2004 most CEECs administered EU pre-accession assistance in a very centralized manner, allowing only limited participation by regional and local actors; indeed, this was the case even for those countries – Poland, the Czech Republic and Slovakia – that had created new structures for regional self-governance after the end of communism. This pattern of centralized administration reflected many factors, including long traditions of centralized government and the weakness of new regional institutions. Also playing a role was the attitude of the Commission, which after 2000 abandoned its previous emphasis on decentralization and instead encouraged the centralized administration of EU assistance by the CEECs in order to ensure the efficient utilization of allocated funds. In this manner, the accession process appears to have reinforced centralized government in the CEECs rather than encouraging decentralization and regionalization as some advocates of devolution may have hoped (Brusis, 2001a, 2001b, 2003; Grabbe, 2001; Hughes, Sasse and Gordon, 2001, 2003, 2004a, 2004b; Marek and Baun, 2002; Keating, 2003; Jacoby, 2004).

How has cohesion policy been implemented since accession, however? Have the new member states continued with centralized systems for administering EU structural funds, or have they decentralized the implementation and management of cohesion policy to any significant degree, thereby giving a greater role to regional and local actors? What has been the impact on implementation systems of both increased experience with cohesion policy (at all territorial levels) and increased levels of funding after 2006? Is there a notable difference, for example, in the way that cohesion policy is being implemented in 2007–13 compared to the first years after accession? In addition to regional and local authorities, how successful have governments in the new member states been in involving nongovernmental and civil society actors in cohesion policy implementation? What kinds of 'vertical' (territorial) and 'horizontal' (involving nongovernmental, private sector and civil society actors) partnership arrangements have been established in these countries and how effective and influential have they been? In other words, is there any evidence that EU cohesion policy has contributed to the growth of multilevel governance – both types I and II – in the new member states, even though their experience with EU membership is relatively brief?

Lisbonization and the 2006 reform

In December 2005 the European Council approved far-reaching changes to EU cohesion policy, including a redefinition of the main objectives of the structural funds. Among the three new objectives – Convergence, Regional Competitiveness and Employment, and European Territorial Cooperation – it allocated the great majority (81.5 per cent) of cohesion policy funding for 2007–13 to the Convergence objective, with most of this money going to regions meeting the old Objective 1 criterion of per capita GDP less than 75 per cent of the EU average, or to 'Phasing-out' regions in old member states that slightly exceeded the 75 per cent threshold because of the statistical effect of enlargement. Special allocations were also made under the Competitiveness objective for 'Phasing-in' regions which formerly held Objective 1 status (European Council, 2005; OJEU, 2006a).

EU leaders also approved a fundamental thematic re-orientation of cohesion policy by linking cohesion policy spending to achievement of the Lisbon Agenda goals. Accordingly, they agreed that 60 per cent of spending under the new Convergence objective in 2007–13, and 75 per cent under the Competitiveness objective, should be 'earmarked' for programmes which contribute to achievement of the Lisbon goals. In recognition of their economic situation and development needs, new member states were exempted from these earmarking requirements (European Council, 2005, p. 7). The first 'Community Strategic Guidelines on Cohesion' (CSG), drafted by the Commission and approved by the Council in October 2006, further specified that cohesion policy spending should be targeted at the following Lisbon-oriented objectives: improving the attractiveness of member states, regions and cities; encouraging innovation, entrepreneurship and the growth of the knowledge economy; and creating more and better jobs (OJEU, 2006b, p. 14).

The 2006 reform of cohesion policy, so-called because the new structural funds Regulation was approved in July 2006, also introduced significant changes in implementation rules and procedures, including the requirement that governments draft National Strategic Reference Frameworks (NSRFs) in line with the Community Strategic Guidelines to guide the use of EU assistance in the seven-year programming period. Governments are also now required to make annual and three-year reports on the contribution of EU-financed programmes to the achievement of cohesion policy and Lisbon goals (OJEU, 2006a, p. 44). The 2006 reform also introduced new measures to ensure greater 'simplification' (reduced number of objectives, single-fund OPs, streamlined eligibility rules for expenses, etc.) and 'decentralization' (strengthened subsidiarity, greater involvement of regional and local actors in the selection and preparation of OPs) of cohesion policy, and it extended the definition of partnership to place even greater emphasis on the role of nongovernmental and civil society actors and 'horizontal' partnership arrangements (OJEU, 2006a).

The Lisbonization of cohesion policy presents a significant challenge for both old and new member states, prompting some important questions: What has been the impact of Lisbonization on structural programming in the member states? How successful have they been in meeting the new Lisbon earmarking requirements in their NSRFs and OPs for 2007–13? To what extent does structural programming for 2007–13 reflect the new growth and competitiveness approach of the Lisbon Agenda, with its focus on developing human resources and the knowledge economy, rather than the more traditional 'equity' approach to economic development aimed at alleviating regional disparities and focused on large-scale infrastructure projects? Have the new earmarking requirements affected the ability of governments to deal with specific national and regional needs? In this regard, has Lisbonization affected relatively wealthy and poor member states differently? For the latter in particular, it could require a major shift in spending priorities from the previous programming period, from infrastructure and regional development to education, employment and other human-capital projects.

While new member states are not formally bound by the new earmarking requirements, they are expected to adhere to them on a voluntary basis. Thus, to what extent have these countries incorporated the Lisbon goals into their structural programming? Have the new member states welcomed or resisted the Lisbonization of cohesion policy, and how has Lisbonization affected their views on national economic development planning?

Another set of questions concerns the new strategic planning requirements of cohesion policy, including the preparation of NSRFs in alignment with the Community Strategic Guidelines: How have member states responded to these new requirements? What has been the impact of strategic planning for cohesion policy on national economic planning more broadly? What processes were put in place in different countries to prepare the NSRFs, and how was the partnership principle applied in drafting these documents? While the new strategic orientation of cohesion policy affects all member states, it is perhaps of special relevance for the new members. In the rush to accession most of these countries emphasized meeting the basic requirements of EU membership and fully utilizing available EU assistance within a short period of time (the remaining two-plus years of the 2000–06 programming period for the 2004 entrants); the focus, therefore, was very much on the short term. Has the new strategic orientation of cohesion policy, along with increased EU funding over a longer period of time, enabled the new member states to begin thinking more strategically about national economic development? A final set of questions concerns the impact of the new policy governance requirements of cohesion policy. The 2006 reform extends the definition of partnership to emphasize the role of 'horizontal' partners (nongovernmental, private and civil society actors), and it places even greater emphasis on decentralization and subsidiarity in the implementation of cohesion policy, including the selection and preparation of programmes. What has been the impact of these changes on cohesion policy implementation and multilevel governance in the member states? Have the new requirements led to increased decentralization and the greater involvement of nongovernmental and local actors in cohesion policy implementation? What impact has the thematic re-orientation of cohesion policy towards the Lisbon goals had on partnership networks and arrangements? To what extent, in other words, have Lisbonization and the new governance requirements of cohesion policy promoted the further development of multilevel governance in the EU, and in what directions?

Europeanization and 'domestic mediating factors'

As the previous discussion makes clear, all member states, whether old or new, face difficult challenges in adjusting to Lisbonization and the new requirements of cohesion policy introduced in 2006. Old and new member states also face similar challenges when it comes to dealing with reduced levels of funding or absorbing and utilizing EU funds, as the case may be. If past experience is any guide, we can expect considerable variation in how member states deal with these challenges and adapt to new EU policy requirements. To the extent that we find such variation among the countries examined in this book, how can we explain it?

Explaining differential adaptation to EU processes and requirements is a key focus of the literature on Europeanization, which generally deals with the EU's impact on domestic policies, politics and institutions.[3] Recent years have seen a veritable flood of Europeanization studies examining the impact of EU integration on different national policies, domestic institutions and aspects of politics, most of them adopting a 'top-down' perspective.[4] Among the key findings of this literature is that Europeanization does not necessarily lead to convergence across member states or even within countries across different aspects of politics and policy areas; instead we find a complex pattern of differential adaptation, or what Risse, Cowles and Caporaso (2001, p. 1) refer to as 'domestic adaptation with national colors'.

A key concept in Europeanization studies is the 'goodness of fit' between EU policy requirements and domestic institutions and practices; the better the 'goodness of fit', the weaker the adaptational pressures faced by national institutional structures and *vice versa* (Börzel, 1999, 2002; Risse, Cowles and Caporaso, 2001). Differences in 'goodness of fit' thus help account for the varying need for and extent of policy and institutional change in different national settings, although as Paraskevopoulos and Leonardi (2004, pp. 316–7) point out high adaptational pressure is not by itself a sufficient condition for bringing about such change. A good place to start when comparing the implementation of cohesion policy in different member states, therefore, is how well national institutions and practices fit with EU requirements and expectations.

Beyond 'goodness of fit' the Europeanization literature also emphasizes the role of other domestic factors in shaping national adaptation to EU policies. Thus, in step three of their three-step approach for studying Europeanization (step one identifies the relevant Europeanization processes implying the need for domestic change; and step two the 'goodness of fit' between EU policy requirements and national arrangements) Risse, Cowles and Caporaso (2001, pp. 6–12) identify the key 'domestic mediating factors' that intervene to shape or affect the pattern of domestic change: multiple veto points, facilitating institutions, political and organizational cultures, the differential empowerment of domestic actors, and learning (defined as the capacity of Europeanization to promote fundamental changes in the preferences and interests, even identities, of domestic actors). Borrowing from this approach, we can identify several domestic mediating factors that might affect the implementation of EU cohesion policy in different member states.

One such factor is *established governmental structures and arrangements*, which previous studies have found to be a key factor explaining variation in the impact of cohesion policy on territorial (type I) multilevel governance in EU countries. These studies have found that subnational governmental actors are generally more fully involved in structural funds implementation in federal or decentralized political systems, such as Germany, Belgium and Spain, while in more centralized systems, such as France or Greece, their role is more limited (Hooghe, ed., 1996; Marks, 1996; Bache, 1998). There are interesting exceptions to this rule, however, for example the role of local actors in cohesion policy implementation in centralized Ireland (Adshead, 2002), and studies have also shown variation in the level of regional engagement within countries like Italy and France (Smyrl, 1997) and Spain (Bache and Jones, 2000) in accordance with differing regional capacities.

Governmental and administrative traditions are another factor affecting cohesion policy implementation, especially when it comes to applying the partnership principle. As Bache (2008, pp. 55–85) has argued, countries with consensual political styles (e.g., Ireland and Sweden) are more amenable to the horizontal partnership requirements of cohesion policy than those with highly statist governmental traditions, such as Greece or the CEECs, and are thus more likely to involve nongovernmental and civil society actors in cohesion policy implementation. In another example of how governmental traditions can affect cohesion policy implementation, previous studies of cohesion policy implementation in Germany have shown that the national tradition of 'cooperative federalism', featuring close cooperation between the federal government and the governments of the 16 *Länder*, has inhibited the inclusion of sub-regional and nongovernmental actors in cohesion policy management (Kelleher, Batterbury and Stern, 1999; Thielemann, 2000; Bache, 2008, pp. 63–5).

Political-cultural values also affect cohesion policy implementation. For instance, Paraskevopoulos et al. (2006) argue that the depth of social capital in a country, including levels of social and political trust, affects not only the strength and functioning of partnership networks but also the learning capacity of domestic governance structures. High levels of social capital are also linked to strong civil societies, which are required to provide governmental actors with competent social and nongovernmental partners.

Domestic politics and partisan contestation is another important factor, which Bache (2008, pp. 16–17) argues can greatly affect the Europeanization process in particular countries even though its impact is often neglected in Europeanization studies. In the case of cohesion policy, the potential for domestic politics to play a role would seem to be greatest in countries with severe regional disparities or strong regional identities and territorially-based ethnic cleavages. Regional actors in such cases are more likely to mobilize and contest the national management of cohesion policy, in the effort to gain a larger share of resources or more decision-making power. New member states, where political systems are still developing or consolidating, could also offer opportunities for political actors to exploit regional issues. We might also expect that cohesion policy is more likely to become a political issue in less wealthy countries, where EU assistance is relatively more important. In all member states, of course, the temptation for political actors to favour more highly-visible 'hard' projects (e.g., roads and other basic infrastructure), which are more objectively measured and show shorter-term results, over 'soft' investments such as education and human-resource development, which strengthen the conditions for future economic growth and competitiveness yet take longer to yield demonstrable results, will play a role. The partisan composition of government could also affect cohesion policy implementation in countries where political parties hold divergent views on decentralization and the inclusion of nongovernmental actors in public policymaking.

While it is easy to identify the domestic factors affecting cohesion policy implementation, it is more difficult to explain just *how* they do so, and how such factors interact with EU-level processes and non-EU factors (e.g., globalization) to produce policy outcomes and institutional change. It is much more difficult, in other words, to establish causality. Indeed, this is an area of Europeanization theory that remains relatively weak and underdeveloped (although see Börzel and Risse, 2003). Particularly in cases of 'good fit' between national practices and EU requirements, it is often difficult to determine the extent to which domestic political change reflects mainly national policies, practices and preferences rather than EU-level processes. Disentangling the relative impact of national and EU factors in the implementation of cohesion policy will be a key challenge in the country case studies which follow.

In this chapter we have discussed some of the main questions concerning the implementation of EU cohesion policy after enlargement and the 2006 reform. We also discussed a number of 'domestic mediating factors' that might affect the way that member states implement EU cohesion policy and address the challenges posed by Lisbonization and new cohesion policy requirements. In the following chapters, these questions will guide our examination of cohesion policy implementation in the ten countries we have selected as case studies. First, however, we take a closer look at the recent development of EU cohesion policy and the debate about cohesion policy reform in the context of enlargement.

Notes

1. In May 2004 ten countries acceded to the EU: Cyprus, the Czech Republic, Estonia, Hungary, Latvia, Lithuania, Malta, Poland, Slovakia and Slovenia. In January 2007, Bulgaria and Romania joined.
2. Calculated from European Commission (2006d–g) and CEC (2006a).

3. In contrast to this essentially 'top-down' definition, Europeanization can also be viewed from a 'bottom-up' perspective, as the process by which member states seek to 'upload' their policy preferences to the EU level, with domestic politics being a factor promoting EU-level change (Bache and Jordan, 2006, p. 14; Bulmer and Radaelli, 2005, p. 340). For a discussion of the various meanings and definitions of Europeanization, see Bache and Jordan (2006, pp. 17–33); also Olsen (2002) and Radaelli (2000).

4. For prominent examples of Europeanization studies adopting this approach, see Cowles, Caporaso and Risse eds (2001); Goetz and Hix, eds (2001); Héritier et al. (2001); Knill, ed (2001); Anderson (2002); Börzel (2002a); Featherstone and Radaelli, eds (2003); and Bulmer and Lequesne (2005).

2
Cohesion Policy Pre- and Post-Enlargement

David Allen

Introduction

Since 1988 expenditure on cohesion policy via the structural funds has grown steadily and has now stabilized at around one-third of the total EU budget, or about 0.46 per cent of EU GDP. In recent years what used to be described simply as regional policy has been specifically linked to the promotion of 'economic and social cohesion' – an objective extended to 'economic, social and *territorial* cohesion' in the Reform Treaty agreed by the European Council in June 2007. Cohesion policy, in turn, has been progressively associated with a growing number of broader EU objectives such as economic growth, competitiveness, employment, sustainable development, subsidiarity, regionalism and good governance, including the participation of civil society. It is argued here that cohesion policy funding has been mainly used to compensate member states for both enlargement and the 'deepening' of European integration, and that this has been rationalized in terms of the EU objectives mentioned above. As we shall see in the conclusion, ambiguity about the fundamental purposes of EU cohesion policy and its financial support make it difficult to assess its effectiveness over time. It is also argued that the European Commission has sought over time to exploit the implementation of cohesion policy expenditure to further the cause of multilevel governance in the EU by encouraging the participation of regional and local governments as well as representatives of civil society. The Commission's early success in developing a supranational policy in association with subnational governments has been progressively countered by the determination of the member states' governments to retain a 'gatekeeping' role (Allen, 2005), although this view has recently been challenged (Bachtler and Mendez, 2007).

The 2004 enlargement of the EU presented a series of challenges to cohesion policy as it has evolved since 1985, with the original 15 member states (EU15) significantly divided over whether expenditure on this policy area should be expanded, maintained or renationalized. As in the past, a compromise was agreed in 2005–06 to maintain cohesion policy finance for the 2007–13 period along broadly the same lines as before. New regulations were introduced to govern the implementation of cohesion policy expenditure (but see Taylor, 2006b) with a much greater emphasis being given to the contribution of that policy towards the EU's overall objective of becoming the world's most competitive economy (the Lisbon Agenda). The compromise meant that a considerable enlargement of EU membership (this time to include a large group of states with significant 'regional' problems) had been achieved without either significantly altering the fundamentals of cohesion policy or changing the relative size and structure of the EU budget (until 2014 at least). This means that we will have to wait until 2013–14 before we will be able to fully understand EU cohesion policy after enlargement.

Since the mid-1980s cohesion policy has focused on disparities in GDP per capita and has therefore privileged the macroeconomic and the territorial over the social, and it can be criticized for its failure to address significant disparities of income which can occur within a region even when that region is itself converging with others in the EU (De Rynck and McAleavey, 2001).

Since 1988 the structural funds, which underpin cohesion policy, have grown to become a significant part of the EU budget, although they still only represent around 0.46 per cent of the EU's GDP – a figure that many feel is far too small to make any serious macroeconomic impact on EU disparities, either regional or national, let alone seriously impact on EU competitiveness, growth, employment or ability to achieve sustainable development. Instead, the most important role that cohesion policy expenditure has played is to provide compensation to help facilitate both EU enlargement and the development of ambitious integrative packages such as the Single Market programme, the Economic and Monetary Union (EMU) and the Lisbon and Gothenburg programmes. Thus cohesion policy spending has always been inextricably intertwined with high-level inter-state bargains. It is the member state governments who call the overall tune when it comes to cohesion policy, although the Commission and a variety of regional and local actors make much of their particular roles in determining and implementing the detailed rules under which the agreed sums of cohesion policy spending are dispersed.

This essentially intergovernmentalist explanation of cohesion policy is contested by those (for instance Marks, Hooghe and Blank, 1996) who see the manner of its implementation supporting the notion that a system best described as 'multilevel governance' is developing. In this view the 'gatekeeping' (Bache, 2004) power of the member state central governments is challenged by a combination of supranational (Commission) and subnational (local and regional authorities and representatives of civil society) actors. This argument about the relative power with regard to cohesion policy of the member states and supra- and subnational actors is ongoing, with Bachtler and Mendez (2007) challenging the 'renationalization thesis' expressed in this chapter and elsewhere (Allen, 2005), but with Blom-Hansen (2005) arguing that studies of the way that cohesion policy is implemented do indeed confirm the need to focus on national rather than EU actors.

Regional (or territorial) policy has always been seen within the EU as the best means of achieving cohesion, which in turn is rationalized as a means to achieve other EU goals such as growth, competitiveness, sustainable development and employment. No mention is ever made in Commission literature about the compensation role that cohesion policy plays, although there are occasional references to the positive integrative effect that might be gained from the visibility of structural intervention in the poorer regions of the Union. Cohesion policy is also a policy area characterized as one of 'mixed competence', with the member states supporting EU policies whilst at the same time continuing to develop their own national regional policies. This raises the possibility of conflict with EU policy towards state aids, and it is significant that the reforms proposed by the Commission in its Third Report on Cohesion (European Commission, 2004) advocate both better coordination and EU strategic direction of national policies designed to enhance cohesion and a radical overhaul of EU state aids policies.

The biggest challenge to the EU's cohesion policy came from the 2004 and 2007 enlargement. In the past cohesion policy funding had always been used to facilitate enlargement and the developments leading up to May 2004 and beyond were no exception to this rule. During the 2000–06 programming period significant structural funds were made available (along with the Poland, Hungary Assistance for Economic Reconstruction [PHARE] aid) as pre- and post-accession aid to those who eventually joined in 2004 and 2007. The EU15 are all agreed that significant cohesion policy funding should continue to be advanced to the new members, but they disagreed at first about whether they too should continue to benefit from cohesion policy funding or not, suggesting that some of them at least saw this funding as essentially transitory even if the transition period was perceived as potentially lengthy. Although the fourth financial perspective agreed at the end of 2005 retained the notion that all EU member states should continue to benefit from cohesion policy funding in the period up to 2013, the possibility that it might be limited after that period to the newer member states has at least been raised.

Cohesion policy pre-enlargement

In the early days a regional policy was developed partly because the Treaty of Rome provided for it, but mainly because following the 1973 enlargement there was a determination to reduce the dominant role of the Common Agricultural Policy (CAP) in the evolving Community budget by developing other areas of expenditure. In particular it was perceived as important to develop policies that the United Kingdom, a major contributor to that budget, might be able to benefit from. Thus, from the beginning, cohesion policy was related to enlargement and was perceived as playing a significant facilitating role when it came to trying to establish a balanced and equitable EU budget. Also, in these early days regional development funds were allocated to the member states using a quota system rather than one informed by the comparative evaluation and weighting of specific regional needs.

As policy developed throughout the 1980s the 'facilitating' driver remained significant even though it was accompanied by moves to impose at least the veneer of economic rationality on regional funding by the introduction of concepts such as additionality, concentration, programming and partnership (Allen, 2005, p. 218). After 1988 regional policy was rationalized in terms of cohesion and the reduction of regional disparities was to be achieved predominately by structural funds expenditure (the territorial approach) but also by loans from the European Investment Bank to improve the workings of the internal market (the competitive approach) and by the coordination of member state regional policies, although not every member state possessed a national regional policy framework.

The use of cohesion policy funding to facilitate further EU developments, first seen with the Integrated Mediterranean Programmes (IMPs), was repeated with the complex bargain that saw the supposed financial 'costs' of the Single Market programme 'compensated' by the first financial perspective, which saw a doubling of cohesion policy funding. It was then repeated again in the early 1990s when the EMU package was agreed at Maastricht in December 1991 and then effectively financed by the second financial perspective agreed in Edinburgh in December 2002. The mini enlargement, which saw the five eastern *Länder* incorporated into a unified Germany in 1990, was also facilitated by an additional allocation of 3 billion European Currency Units (ECUs) of cohesion policy funding for the 1991–93 period.

A similar, albeit less direct, link can be seen between the Treaty of Amsterdam agreed in June 1997 and the 'Agenda 2000' proposals (European Commission, 1997a) launched in July 1997 and further consolidated in the third financial perspective, agreed in Berlin in March 1999. This compensation saga was then repeated once again at the end of 2005 when a fourth financial perspective, which included complex plans for cohesion policy funding for the EU27 up to 2013, was agreed by the EU25 and thus made possible the implementation of plans for further cohesion policy reform laid out in the Commission's Third Cohesion Report (European Commission, 2004) and further discussed in the Fourth Cohesion Report (European Commission, 2007a).

Throughout this period both the secondary 'distributive' arrangements and the primary 'historic' decisions were dependent on high-level bargaining. It was only subsequently, as the implementation process began, that other actors began to play a role. Thus the process of implementation does provide some scope for a challenge to the powers of the central governments of the member states, although some care needs to be taken in specifying which central powers are being challenged. It may be that the member state governments have little interest in the implementation stage once they have secured guarantees of a certain level of cohesion policy expenditure, and it may be that the budgetary net contributors do have an interest in a degree of Commission oversight over the spending habits of the net recipients. It may also be the case that the member state governments are either able to control, manipulate or even cooperate with newly enfranchised subnational actors so as to consolidate, rather than weaken, their central authority.

Although the admission of Sweden, Finland and Austria in 1995 did not disturb cohesion policy arrangements (other than to stimulate the invention of Objective 6 to ensure that the new members themselves were eligible for regional benefits), the prospect of further enlargement to the east and south necessarily led to a debate about the future of EU cohesion policy. Decisions on this were postponed while the member governments negotiated the Amsterdam Treaty but immediately afterwards the Commission delivered, as requested, its proposals for managing further enlargement. The 'Agenda 2000' documents (European

Commission, 1997a) made proposals for the third financial perspective and proposed that overall spending on cohesion policy, in both the EU15 and the enlarged membership, be frozen at 0.46 per cent of EU GDP. The Commission proposed a total expenditure on structural operations within this ceiling of €275 billion, at 1997 prices, between 2000 and 2006. This sum was broken down into €230 billion for the EU15, and €45 billion, to be ring-fenced, for both pre-accession aid for all the applicants and post-accession aid for the six states (the Luxembourg Six) that were assumed at that time to be likely to join the EU by 2006. In proposing that cohesion policy funding should remain a high priority, but that its growth should be curtailed, the Commission was constrained by the member states who were committed to freezing the overall budget at a maximum of 1.27 per cent of EU GDP up to 2006, with little prospect that they could agree any significant reductions in other areas of expenditure such as agriculture.

The Commission proposed that cohesion policy funding should be further concentrated and that implementation should be simplified. To this end it suggested reducing the number of Objectives to just three and reducing the coverage of funding from over 50 per cent of the EU population to between 35 and 40 per cent. It was also proposed that unemployment should become the major criterion for allocating funds in the newly created Objective 2 regions. The new rules for determining aid in Objective 2 regions and the proposed stricter application of the rules for Objective 1 eligibility would mean that many regions that had received aid between 1988 and 1999 would no longer be eligible in the period up to 2006.

Following tough negotiations on these proposals, in March 1999 the European Council agreed a deal which reduced the Commission's proposed expenditure from €275 billion (at 1999 prices) to €258 billion with €45 billion ring-fenced for pre-accession aid and post-accession benefits. To reach agreement the Commission was forced to concede that special transitional arrangements would be tolerated for those regions likely to lose out, that no region would lose no more than one-third of its population previously covered by EU funding, and that the Cohesion Fund would continue to be available for the 'poor four' (Greece, Spain, Portugal and Ireland) even though three of them had apparently 'converged' enough to join the single currency.

The Berlin agreement was facilitated by acceptance of the principle of providing something for everybody which seemed to leave the member governments, especially the net recipients, in a stronger position than before. This appears to confirm the renationalization of control of structural funds expenditure and the weakening of the Commission's four implementing principles that has been apparent since the 1993 reform. Formally, the 1999 reforms dealt with the immediate problem of enlargement in terms of budgetary allocations, but they had little serious impact on the problem of regional disparities. Politically, the new proposals served the function of facilitating agreement between the member governments, and the Commission may have been wise to respond to the new atmosphere with its proposals to simplify the implementation procedures and to step back from some of its contacts with subnational actors. All of these tendencies seemed to take the policy process further and further from the concept of multilevel governance and much closer to the modified intergovernmentalism that Bache (1999, pp. 37–42) has described as 'extended gatekeeping'.

In the early years of the enlargement process PHARE was used for funding individual projects and involved direct dealing between the Commission and the applicant central governments. As such it was much criticized for its excessive bureaucracy and for the fact that it was based on annual rather than multiannual programming and as such did little to prepare the new members for the structural funds. In the 2000–06 funding period, in response to this criticism, the EU introduced two new programmes which ran alongside PHARE, Instrument for Structural Policies for Pre-Accession (ISPA) and Special Accession Programme for Agriculture and Rural Development (SAPARD). Bailey and De Propris (2004, p. 83) note that the idea was for PHARE (€1.5 billion) to prepare the new members for general regional funding, for ISPA (€1 billion) to prepare them specifically for the Cohesion Fund and for SAPARD (€500 million) to prepare them for the Guidance section of the European Agricultural Guidance and Guarantee Fund (EAGGF). Nevertheless, at a time when the 1999 reforms were devolving budgetary control down to the member state governments, the Commission maintained its own tight control over pre-accession funding – not the best way to prepare the new members for 2004. Similarly, whilst efforts were made to build institutional capacity in the new members, doubts were expressed about the likelihood of institutional capacity being turned into capability in the short time that was available before enlargement. (Bailey and De Propris, 2004, p. 90)

Cohesion policy post-enlargement

The 2004 enlargement was certainly partially facilitated by the use of the structural funds to provide pre- (and post-) accession aid and the new member states clearly expected that they would be significant beneficiaries of cohesion policy funding under the 2007–13 financial perspective. Whilst this assumption was not contested by the EU15 there were fundamental disagreements about how exactly this enlargement should impact on cohesion policy funding. In particular there was a significant dispute between those (mainly the net contributors) who wanted to restrict future cohesion policy spending to the new members and those who would wish to see such funding continue to provide 'something for everybody'. However, the budgetary arithmetic was such that, given an agreed limit of 4 per cent of GDP on what any new member could receive, the EU25 were effectively left with a choice between maintaining the present system of funding (albeit reformed), as the Commission had proposed, or halving the anticipated costs by restricting funding to the new member states. Thus, because of the 4 per cent rule, had the member states gone for the option of restricting cohesion policy spending to the new members the EU total for such funding would have dropped from 0.46 of EU GDP to only 0.16 per cent.

The context for planning the fourth financial perspective and thus the funds available for cohesion policy up to 2013 was significantly altered by the 2004 and 2007 enlargements (Crosbie, 2006). Enlargement to EU25 increased the population of the EU by 20 per cent but its GDP by only 4–5 per cent, with the result that the EU's average per capita income fell by 10 per cent. By the time the EU had 27 member states more than one-third of the EU population were living in member states with a per capita income of less than 90 per cent of the EU average (the criteria for Cohesion Fund assistance) compared to just one-sixth in the EU15. In the EU27 the poorest 10 per cent of the population earn just 31 per cent of the EU27 average compared to the 61 per cent of the EU15 average income earned by the poorest 10 per cent in the EU15.

Nearly all the regions of the new member states qualified for EU funding under the old Objective 1 criteria (GDP per capita of less than 75 per cent of the EU average). In 2004 around 70 per cent of the structural funds were allocated to this Objective and under the new arrangements, which retain the same criteria, this figure is lifted to just over 80 per cent. The reduction in the average per capita income in the EU27 means that most of the regions in the EU15 which qualified for Objective 1 funding no longer do so because their relative, but not their absolute, prosperity has changed – they are victims of what is known as the 'statistical effect' – but the EU has once again applied its classic criteria of compensation to ensure that everybody gets something (and thus agrees to the funding package). Thus the new Convergence funding goes to those Nomenclature of Statistical Territorial Units (NUTS) regions whose GDP per capita is less than 75 per cent of the EU average. They are as follows:

Bulgaria	All regions
Czech Republic	7 regions
Germany	7 regions
Estonia	All regions
Greece	9 regions
Spain	4 regions
France	4 regions
Hungary	6 regions
Italy	4 regions
Latvia	All regions
Lithuania	All regions
Malta	All regions
Poland	All regions
Portugal	All regions
Romania	All regions
Slovenia	All regions
Slovakia	3 regions
United Kingdom	2 regions

In addition, the following member states have regions that benefited from Objective 1 regional funding in 2000–06 and will continue to benefit from 'phasing-out' or transitional funding despite the fact that their GNP per capita is above 75 per cent of the EU average.

Belgium	1 region
Germany	4 regions
Greece	3 regions
Spain	4 regions
Austria	1 region
Portugal	1 region
Italy	1 region
United Kingdom	1 region

The ultimate impact of enlargement on EU cohesion policy remains to be determined. Whilst enlargement has created an increased regional problem by increasing the diversities it is by no means clear that cohesion policy, which at best will represent 0.46 per cent of EU GDP, is the best means to bring about convergence. Opinions are divided about the effectiveness of the present arrangements for significantly reducing divergence with some commentators inclined to leave it to the workings of the market supported by competition policy and others convinced that diversity within and between regions is best rectified at the national rather than the EU level. The problem with this approach is that the new member states have the least developed national regional policies to fall back on should the EU fundamentally change its approach after 2013. Finally, as we discuss below, there is the question mark about both the capacity and the capability of the new member states to implement structural spending either under a system in which subnational partnerships with the Commission are encouraged or one that places more weight on the activities of the central governments of the member states.

Although ten member states joined the EU in May 2004 there were serious doubts about their capacity to 'absorb' all aspects of the structural funds that they became entitled to (Keating and Hughes, 2003). They of course immediately became involved in negotiations with the other member states and the Commission over the fourth financial perspective as well the detailed arrangements for the dispersal of cohesion policy funding in the next programming period. The new arrangements will remain in place until 2013 but, before they began at the start of 2007, an adjustment of the 1999 accords provided for regional aid as well as ongoing pre-accession aid for the new members of just under €25 billion.

Despite the fact that the new members received considerable amounts of pre-accession aid as well as assistance from the PHARE programmes, doubts have been expressed about their capacity to manage EU assistance and in particular about the existence of capacity below the national governmental level. Bailey and De Propris (2004) argue that the new members are just not in a position to properly participate in multilevel governance partnership schemes partly because the local and regional institutional capacity does not exist and partly because of the conscious and effective 'gatekeeping' of the new member state central governments. Even where a degree of subnational activity can be detected in the new members it is clear that, as noted above with regard to the EU15, there is a significant distinction to be made between activity and participation and the sort of influence that might be regarded as governance. In the battle to establish multilevel governance in the new member states via the pre- and post-accession funding procedures the Commission seemed, to this observer at least, to be losing out to the newly acquired 'gatekeeping' skills of the central governments. However, with regard to cohesion policy Bachtler and Mendez (2007, pp. 554–5) contest this assessment and argue instead that the Commission's new programming arrangements (discussed below) make the member states more accountable for their implementation activities because they are now required to draw up a national policy framework and report regularly to the Commission on their progress towards meeting EU strategic objectives.

Nevertheless most of the new members lacked effective regional policies at the national level and this raised doubts about their ability to effectively participate in the national regional development planning process resulting in National Strategic Reference Framework (NSRFs), which are a vital aspect of the new arrangements. Doubts about the 'absorption capacity' of the new members were responsible for the EU decision to set (at least until 2013) a cap of 4 per cent of GDP on the total amount of structural assistance that any member state can receive. Whilst the sums involved are relatively small, there is at least the possibility that by 2013 regional and national disparities might increase, as the richer new members with higher GDPs will continue to qualify for high levels of assistance.

In February 2004 the Commission published its proposals for the 2007–13 financial perspective and the incoming Barroso Commission presented its fully-fledged budgetary proposal in the spring of 2005. After much haggling the European Council, meeting at the end of the British presidency in December 2005, finally reached a deal (Taylor, 2006a), which was effectively the second instalment of the 'bill for enlargement' (the Berlin accords being the first). Although the Commission at the same time created the necessary legislation to introduce the reforms proposed in 2004, the ultimate shape of EU cohesion policy until 2013 was decided by a process of intergovernmental bargaining leading to yet another 'history-making decision'. Before agreement was reached there was a real choice to be made between the Commission's proposal that around €336 billion (compared with €257 billion in 2000–06) be allocated for cohesion policy over the period and the British counter proposal for approximately half that figure, although both sides of course adopted opening positions that they knew they would have to bargain over. The British proposal was also a reaction to the fact that the United Kingdom supported the idea of a smaller EU budget but was unable to achieve this by its preferred method of cutting CAP spending because France and Germany had already agreed that there would be no significant cut in such spending at least until 2013. Maybe the British thought that the threat of reduced cohesion policy spending, which delivers identifiable and measurable resources to each member state, would force the others to think again about the freeze on agricultural spending reform, but if that was the case they were wrong. In the event, the European Council reduced the overall size of the Commission's proposed budget and agreed that in 2007–13 the EU would allocate €308 billion rather than the €336 billion originally proposed by the Commission. This nevertheless represented an 11.5 per cent increase in cohesion policy spending, distributed mainly to Convergence and transitional regions as detailed above, and a 74 per cent increase in the Cohesion Fund, which is now made available to those member states whose GDP is less than 89 per cent of the EU average. The eligible countries are Portugal and Greece plus all 12 new members with transitional funding for Spain.

In February 2004 the Commission published its Third Report on Economic and Social Cohesion, in which it presented its proposals for regional structural funding in 2007–13 along with an unsurprisingly positive assessment of the impact of the current programmes (European Commission, 2004), although the Third Progress Report on Cohesion (European Commission, 2005a) did note that whilst disparities across the EU had been falling overall, the fall had been more rapid between member states than between regions with internal regional disparities in several member states increasing. The Commission, of course, sees this as evidence of the need for an active EU cohesion policy and this is apparent in the Fourth Report on Cohesion (European Commission, 2007a), which is aimed at the 2008 EU expenditure review and is rather defensive in its attempt to prove value added. It is, of course, enthusiastic in its stress on the contribution of cohesion policy towards achievement of the Lisbon goals and in its emphasis on the new focus on cities (Crosbie, 2007). It also includes a series of questions designed to kick off the debate within the European institutions and beyond on the future of cohesion policy; this debate was formally initiated at the Cohesion Forum held in Brussels in September 2007 and attended by just under 1,000 national and regional representatives.

However, this essentially positive evaluation presented by the Commission conflicts with other assessments (Boldrin and Canova, 2001) and those commissioned by the British government or parliament (ECOTECH, 2003; UK House of Commons, 2004) which suggest that cohesion policy spending in the richer member states is now producing diminishing returns with no visible added value over what might be achieved with national regional programmes. There are also those who are concerned about the links that are now made between the Lisbon Agenda and EU cohesion policy. It certainly suits the Commission to control what is effectively now seen as the Lisbon Agenda spending instrument, giving it more control and ownership of a process that is seen as favouring the intergovernmental over the supranational. However, there are also fears that the 'Lisbonization' of cohesion policy is likely to prove premature for the new members who need basic assistance before they move on to focus on becoming competitive.

The Sapir report (Sapir et al., 2004) noted the compensation function of cohesion policy funding but could find no hard evidence to either support the argument that the funds had made a significant difference to the performance of lagging regions or the argument that they had not. Sapir went on to state that a national (as with the Cohesion Fund, whose success especially in Ireland and Spain is universally acknowledged) was preferable to a regional approach (European Regional Development Fund [ERDF]) to determine eligibility for funding and recommended that, in future, cohesion resources would be best spent on building institutional and physical capacity as well as developing human capital. However, these recommendations do not seem to have had much influence on the Commission's new arrangements for implementing cohesion policy in 2007–13.

The Commission has reduced the six priorities or objectives of the 2000–06 programming period to just three: Convergence, which now receives 81.54 per cent of overall cohesion policy funding, Regional Competitiveness and Employment (RCE) (15.94 per cent) and European Territorial Cooperation (2.52 per cent). Under these new arrangements, which came into force at the beginning of 2007, all the previous Community Initiatives, INTERREG, EQUAL, LEADER and URBAN have been integrated into the three mainstream programmes and the Commission is making increased efforts to involve city authorities in the planning and implementation of structural programmes to a greater extent than before. Cities are of course problematic for those who seek to eliminate disparities because their aggregate data tend to disguise extremes of wealth and poverty in what is a very small 'region'. Within the three objectives the Commission has given indicative annual sums per member state with each deciding how to divide this between eligible regions. Until 2013 the new member states will get 166 per cent of what they got in the previous period and the EU15 will collectively get 30 per cent less, but the principle of everybody getting something from cohesion policy spending has been maintained.

Programming, partnership, additionality (although this will prove difficult with cross-border programmes between member and non-member states) and concentration remain as the key principles of implementation. As noted above, programming has also been made more strategic and implementation simplified, but with enhanced transparency and financial accountability.

Under the new arrangements the European Council agreed on the Strategic Guidelines for EU cohesion policy in October 2006. The new generation of structural programmes are deemed to be at 'the heart of the Lisbon strategy' (Taylor, 2006b; European Commission, 2008a) and as such are now rationalized in terms of the promotion of investments that will stimulate growth and employment, the growth of the knowledge economy by promoting research and innovation capacities, new information and communication technologies, and human capital and entrepreneurship. The so-called Lisbon restraints are applied more rigorously to structural spending by the EU15 than by the new member states (a concession that British Prime Minister Tony Blair argued mitigated the impact of the overall reduction by the Council of the Commission's original spending plans for 2007–13).

Within these strategic guidelines the member states now draw up NSRFs followed by a list of Operational Programmes. The new rules, allowing for the 'Blair dispensation' for the new member states, require that 60 per cent of the Convergence Objective Operational Programmes (OPs) and 75 per cent of the RCE Objective OPs must relate to the Lisbon goals. By the end of 2007, although some member states were at first slow to draw up their NSRFs and OPs, all 27 NSRFs had been approved and the Commission had formally adopted 302 OPs, which represented 96 per cent of the programmes planned for 2007–13 (European Commission, 2008a). Also, in December 2007 the Commission (2007b) adopted a Communication, snappily entitled 'Member States and Regions delivering the Lisbon strategy for growth and jobs through EU cohesion policy, 2007–2013', which set out an overview of the results of the negotiations on the NSRFs and OPs. This Communication attempted, in anticipation of the spring 2008 European Council, to reflect on the role that cohesion policy-funded programmes would play in taking the renewed Lisbon Strategy forward during its next three year cycle, all of which seems a long way away from the time in the mid-1970s when the ERDF was invented in order to find a way of enabling the United Kingdom to benefit from the EU budget!

Now that the Commission has validated the majority of the OPs, it will keep an eye on their implementation to ensure that economic and social partners as well as civil society bodies are able to fully participate in their ongoing management. As the member states begin to implement projects within the OPs the Commission will commit the expenditure and hand it over to the member states, and it will then monitor progress and produce further strategic reports which will doubtless be increasingly optimistic as the cohesion policy cycle approaches the time when further reforms and the next financial perspective become the subject of internal EU negotiation. Before that happens around 2011–12 the EU is also committed, as a concession to British frustrations about their inability to reform the financing of the CAP, to consider in 2008–09 the long-term future of EU financing, although no decisions taken then (if indeed any meaningful decisions are possible) will alter what is already agreed up to 2013.

Day-to-day financial control of EU cohesion policy spending is now said to be more 'proportionate' and devolved downwards as much as possible to deal with the charge of excessive bureaucracy on behalf of the Commission. The decision to continue funding for all member states has prevented a further concentration of resources, whereas limiting such funding to the new members would of course have had a significant concentration impact. There is an increased emphasis on partnership, with proposals for further decentralization to 'partnerships on the ground' underpinned by 'tripartite' contracts between the member states, the regions and local authorities. The aim is clearly enhanced multilevel governance but the actual impact will depend on the extent of central government 'gatekeeping' in each member state. Much the same caution needs to be expressed about the Commission's plans to further involve the social partners and civil society.

Finally, it has been agreed that there will be new, more formal arrangements to promote cross-border, transnational and regional cooperation. Although the idea of cross-border cooperation is not new a new legal entity was established – the European Grouping for Territorial Cooperation (EGTC) – whose members can be member states, regional or local authorities, associations or other public bodies. The EGTC is designed to enable the grouping together of authorities from various member states without the need for prior international agreements ratified by national parliaments. The relevant structures and legal requirements were put in place by August 2007, but Commissioner Hübner expressed her frustration at the time that no new bodies had been established under these procedures. By March 2008 this remained the case as far as the United Kingdom was concerned, although some projects such as a hospital on the Dutch-German border at Limburg and another on the Spanish-French border were being considered.

The 2007 Reform Treaty did not introduce much that was new in regard to cohesion policy, but it was nevertheless welcomed by Michel Delabarre, the President of the Committee of the Regions (COR), who said that it preserved 'most of the institutional rights for local and regional authorities contained in the draft Constitutional Treaty' (*European Voice*, 2007). The amended Treaties on the European Union and the Functioning of the European Union along with two Protocols (dealing with the Application of the Principles of Subsidiarity and Proportionality and with Economic, Social and Territorial Cohesion [FCO, 2008]) provide for: the structural funds; economic, social and territorial cohesion; subsidiarity, including a new definition which, if not respected by the member states or the EU institutions, gives the COR the right to take the matter to the European Court of Justice; the recognition of and respect for local and regional self-government; the granting of special status for the most remote EU regions; participative democracy and the recognition of the role of civil society and the protection of cultural and linguistic diversity.

Conclusions

The Reform Treaty makes it clear that the EU will continue to pursue the objective of economic, social and territorial cohesion. The structural funds are most clearly directed at the territorial aspect in pursuit of a logic that assumes that regional and national convergence will deliver cohesion, which in turn will deliver growth, competitiveness, employment and sustainable development (the Lisbon and Gothenburg objectives).

Post-enlargement, a number of problems associated with EU cohesion policy remain. The determination to maintain co-financing as a principle begs the question as to how relatively poor states can afford to accept EU money even if they have been able to develop the sophisticated governance institutions to successfully devise and manage structural programmes to the administrative standards required by the Commission (Hughes, Sasse and Gordon, 2004a) and the accountability and transparency standards that should be required by the European Parliament and the Court of Auditors.

Other questions remain about the exact role that cities will play in the evolution of EU cohesion policy and about the appropriate role for the COR. It remains to be seen whether the new arrangements do provide anything more than lip service to the principles of democracy, accountability and legitimacy that continue to concern some observers of cohesion policy. The idea is that cohesion policy will play its part in bringing the EU closer to its citizens, particularly in those new member states where the long wait for EU membership has given rise to a more sceptical view of its advantages. During the pre-accession period there was little chance for the applicants to do anything other than receive instructions and possibly be confused and intimidated by the Commission bureaucracy. There was little chance to shape policy but there was a general raising of expectations that incomes would rise in the short term with little understanding of the fact that cohesion policy is designed to change structures for less obvious gain over the longer term. On the other hand, enlargement has given a huge boost to the academic 'Europeanization' industry (see for example Mendez, Wishlade and Yuill, 2006) and it will be interesting to see what the literature has to say in the future about cohesion policy and its impact on the new member states. To what extent, for instance, will we be able to observe transformation, absorption, accommodation, retrenchment or inertia? Is the impact of regional funding predominately economic, financial, political or administrative?

What remains in doubt are the overall size and beneficiaries of cohesion policy spending in an enlarged EU. The sums allocated to this policy area for 2007–13 reflect the degree of compensation for enlargement that the member states agreed to pay themselves as well as the amount that was deemed appropriate and acceptable to the new members. It appeared as though the consensus required to agree the future of EU cohesion policy required that, as before, all member states received something tangible from the funding allocation.

It is argued here that the process of renationalizing the means of delivery, financial management and evaluation of cohesion policy funding will continue. In addition, some member states already see the pursuit of best practice and benchmarking with regard to national regional policies as being an attractive alternative to a more interventionist EU-level policy. The Commission has already made concessions to this tendency with its proposals for the coordination and standardization of national regional programmes as part of its recent cohesion policy reforms. On the other hand the regions, in the new member states as well as the old, that benefit from EU financial support may, as suggested above, come to value cohesion policy support and financing partly for its medium-term economic reliability (when national expenditure might be more likely to be cut at short notice) and partly for its symbolic political support for areas and actors which might otherwise be neglected.

There is an increased emphasis on the role of national regional policies, which already account for over 75 per cent of regional spending in the EU, although there is also some evidence to suggest that national regional policy has to a minor extent been Europeanized over the years. Involvement in EU cohesion policy has impacted the way that the member states define their regions and has also led to a greater awareness within the member states of the need to attend to regional divergence. EU programmes may have enhanced the visibility of the EU in those regions and localities that have benefited from structural funding, but does this amount to evidence that this has enhanced the popularity of the EU in the public imagination? Opinion remains divided about the precise extent of the impact of EU funding on regional and national convergence because of the immeasurable impacts of other factors such as national regional programmes, other national macroeconomic policies and globalization. Whilst the structural funds to date have taken up a significant percentage of the EU budget the absolute sums remain small at under 0.46 per cent of EU GDP.

Attempts to evaluate the impact of EU policy to date have not produced clear results. There has been a great deal of economic modelling and survey data gathering but these have not produced any outstanding evidence of EU cohesion policy having a discernible impact. Instead cohesion policy is judged more by political than economic criteria, possibly because whilst the economic evidence of positive impact is unconvincing, survey evidence about the visibility and popularity of the policy is more positive although still rather nebulous, which is probably why it continues albeit underpinned by a constantly changing set of strategic rationalizations of which the Lisbon goals are but the latest. Even the Commission, which is good at finding evidence of reductions in national and regional disparities, struggles to link this evidence directly to its own cohesion policies, although it might be argued that EU cohesion policy is at least not as hard to justify as the CAP where positive evidence of its failure is constantly available and relatively easy to gather.

The relationship between cohesion policy and regionalism is also potentially problematic in the EU, with regional identity increasingly challenging the nature and existence of the member states such that the aspiration to create a 'Europe of the Regions' may not always be shared by member states anxious to preserve their current national identity. The EU and its enthusiasm for partnerships with subnational actors in the pursuit of eliminating regional disparities increasingly serves to give meaning and an alternative potential framework for those who aspire to detach Scotland from the United Kingdom, Bavaria from Germany, Northern Italy from the rest of Italy, Flanders, Wallonia (and Brussels!) from Belgium, the Basque country from Spain and northern Cyprus from southern Cyprus – all within the all-embracing haven of the EU. It remains to be seen what the impact of receiving significant cohesion policy funding will be on the new member states in the longer term.

This chapter also takes issue with the argument that the manner in which the structural funds have been implemented has had a significant impact on the development of multilevel governance. Despite the initial thrust of the 'partnership' provisions of the 1988 reform, the central governments of both the old and the new member states have either retained or learned for the first time 'gatekeeping' skills so as to effectively allow public and private, regional and local interests to participate but no more than that; multilevel participation should not be confused with multilevel governance. Regional and local actors are no more effective individually in relation to cohesion policy and EU governance than they are collectively within the COR or the Economic and Social Committee. In general, the degree of subnational participation in EU cohesion policy governance remains primarily a product of the nature of the constitutional arrangements within particular member states.

If these final conclusions are correct, then EU cohesion policy may over time have less of a role to play in the hierarchy of EU budgetary expenditure and policy competences. The British have already played devil's advocate by proposing (albeit unsuccessfully in 2005) that in future cohesion policy funding could and should be limited to the new members on the assumption that disparities between the regions of the old member states can now be dealt with as effectively at the national rather than the EU level. This assumes that structural assistance at the EU level should be seen as transitory and that once it has done the job it can and should be stood down. This is a logic which in time could also be applied to cohesion policy assistance to the new member states, but it tends to assume that cohesion policy mainly serves the purpose of eliminating regional disparities, whereas we have tended to argue in this chapter that the way that cohesion policy has evolved suggests that its role in facilitating major changes either of EU strategic objectives (Single Market, EMU, Lisbon, etc.) or EU membership provides its most significant rationale – in which case it is likely to survive well beyond 2013.

3
The United Kingdom

Rachael Chapman

Introduction

The UK allocation of EU cohesion policy funding has fallen considerably in the wake of the 2004 EU enlargement, which resulted in a major shift of structural spending in favour of the new member states. This has created major political and administrative challenges in the 2007–13 programming period, which together with the 2006 cohesion policy reforms and domestic developments have significant implications for programme development and delivery. This chapter explores the implications of such developments for the United Kingdom. Drawing upon existing literature and documentary evidence, it undertakes a preliminary review of how EU cohesion policy is being implemented in the new programming period, and explores key factors shaping this. The chapter begins by reviewing trends and challenges surrounding cohesion policy implementation in the United Kingdom, both past and current. Three key aspects of implementation in the 2007–13 programming period are subsequently examined: strategic programming, programme management and partnership. Key changes and/or developments in these areas are identified and potential explanations for these offered. The chapter concludes by arguing that UK cohesion policy implementation has been rationalized, reflecting national policies and preferences, alongside EU factors. This brings into question the prospect of a partial renationalization of EU cohesion policy in the United Kingdom. The evidence to date, however, suggests that substantial renationalization has not taken place, at least in ways that are contrary to policies, practices and preferences advanced through the EU system of governance.[1]

Cohesion policy in the United Kingdom: key trends and challenges

As stated in Chapter 1, the implications of EU cohesion policy for domestic politics and territorial governance have prompted considerable academic interest and debate. In the UK context, debates focused on the extent to which national government lost or retained control over the formulation and implementation of cohesion policy in light of new opportunities open to the European Commission and subnational actors following the 1988 cohesion policy reform; with some studies alluding to the emergence and/or deepening of multilevel participation and governance (Marks, Hooghe and Blank, 1996; Marks, 1993), and others emphasising the 'gate-keeping' role of central government (Anderson, 1990; Pollack, 1995; Bache, 1999; Allen, 2000).

Prior to 1989, the implementation of cohesion policy was generally acknowledged to be a top-down process in which central government made decisions and local government implemented them. The 1988 cohesion policy reform sought to invoke a step change through the introduction of programming, additionality, concentration and partnership. The EU partnership principle, however, met with initial resistance in the United Kingdom. In the period between 1989 and 1993, partnership composition was seen to be narrow, societal partners (trade unions and employers' representatives) and elected local authority members were generally excluded, and research pointed to the dominance and gate-keeping powers of the UK central government (see Bache et al., 1996). The latter was evident, for example, in debates on the additionality principle, in which the then Conservative Government was seen to play a 'gatekeeper' role by controlling the financial impact of EU funds on domestic public spending. The Conservative Government's non-compliance of the requirement to ensure EU funding was additional to planned domestic expenditure was criticized by the opposing Labour party as well as the Commission and UK local authorities (see Bache and Bristow, 2003).

Although some improvements were evident in partnerships between 1993 and 1996 (e.g., local councillors were finally accepted on partnership bodies), it was not until the 1997 general election, which brought a change of government from Conservative to Labour, that significant progress was made towards more inclusive and effective partnerships. An immediate improvement was the inclusion of trade unions onto partnerships and, in the years to follow the concept of partnership became deeply embedded in the policy process across Britain. This contributed to the further development of multilevel governance, particularly at the local and sub-local levels (Bache, 2008, p. 147). As part of this, third sector engagement became increasingly widespread in cohesion policy partnerships (see below). The election of the Labour government and resulting process of devolution (see below) also raised potential for changes in the government's approach to additionality. A study by Bache and Bristow (2003) concluded, however, that while there was increased local scrutiny of funding flows from the centre, Treasury accounting procedures continued to obscure the extent to which the government had moved towards providing full additionality and, despite devolution, there was no change in the mechanisms by which central government dealt with additionality. In other words, the UK government retained control over key features of additionality implementation.

These shifts towards more inclusive partnership arrangements reflect EU-level developments associated with the partnership principle. However, the mediating role of central government is regarded as being crucially important. Changing actor preferences at the national level, brought about by the 1997 Labour election victory, and regional level help explain the broadening of partnerships and improved partner relations (Bache, 2003). Chapman (2006) also highlights the importance of domestic factors in mediating third sector engagement. In this case, EU-level pressures arising from the EU partnership principle and inclusion of Community Economic Development (CED) in programmes (which was encouraged by the European Commission), helped open windows of opportunity for third sector participation; but domestic actors and their preferences were key to explaining the role and extent of their involvement.

In addition to the above are UK trends towards greater decentralization and regionalization in the management and administration of cohesion policy. Of particular relevance is devolution to Scotland, Wales, Northern Ireland and the English regions in 1999. Variable powers were transferred to devolved administrations in these regions. In Scotland, for example, the Scottish Parliament was granted powers to undertake primary legislation in some areas and has limited tax-varying powers, whereas the National Assembly in Wales was granted powers to pass secondary legislation only and has no tax-varying powers. This, together with block grants arrangements, effectively means that Scotland, Wales and Northern Ireland have freedom over policy design and associated allocation of resources in support of regional development and regeneration (HM Treasury/DTI/ODPM, 2003). It also meant that the devolved administrations would take over day-to-day management of cohesion policy in their territories in 2000. In England, devolution entailed the creation of nine Regional Development Agencies (RDAs), who are directly accountable to government ministers and Parliament and have a remit to promote economic development and regeneration at the regional level. Since their creation, RDAs have been given increasing flexibility to allocate funding in support of regional priorities. They have also played a key role in cohesion policy partnerships, and look set to take on an even bigger role in the management of the 2007–13 programmes (see below). Many of these developments, such as formal political devolution of powers to Scotland, Wales and Northern Ireland, have been largely explained by domestic, as opposed to EU-level processes (see Smith, 2001, 2006; Bulmer et al., 2002; Bulmer and Burch, 2002; Sloat, 2002). However, Burch and Gomez (2006) and Bache (2008) have suggested that EU cohesion policy, together with the 1994 creation of Government Offices which represent central government at the regional level, have helped strengthen the English regional tier through promoting networks and partnerships.

Trends towards increased devolution and decentralization, together with EU enlargement, provided impetus for UK Government calls for a partial renationalization of EU regional policy in the negotiations leading up to the 2006 cohesion policy reform. As part of this call, the Labour Government published proposals for a 'devolved framework' for EU regional policy in a consultation document entitled 'A Modern Regional Policy for the United Kingdom' (HM Treasury/DTI/ODPM, 2003). This proposed the concentration of structural and cohesion funds on the poorest member states, with wealthier member states (i.e., those with GNP per capita greater than 90 per cent of the EU average) taking responsibility for financing and delivering regional development in their own countries in accordance with broad policy objectives established at the European level. The proposals were the subject of domestic political debate, and were opposed by Welsh Plaid Cymru Party Members of Parliament in Westminster on the basis of their potential implications for Wales. They did, however, find some resonance among other net contributor countries, such as the Netherlands, Denmark and Sweden. Even so, the final outcome was such that cohesion policy would cover all EU member states. Had the UK calls for a partial renationalization been successful, most UK regions would not have received EU regional policy funding in the 2007–13 period, with the exception of some possible transitional community support over a period of time (HM Treasury/DTI/ODPM, 2003, p. 27). Instead, the government pledged to increase national spending on regional policy so that UK regions would not have received less funding than they would based on eligibility criteria of an enlarged EU.

Whilst the United Kingdom continues to receive EU cohesion funding in the 2007–13 programming period, it is not without its challenges. Among these are reduced levels and scope of funding resulting from EU enlargement, budget negotiations and the Lisbon Agenda (see Chapters 1 and 2). As can be seen from Table 3.1, UK cohesion policy assistance has fallen by 46 per cent, from €17.6 billion in 2000–06 to €9.4 billion (at 2004 prices) in 2007–13. Of this, Convergence funding represents approximately 28 per cent (€2.6 billion). Qualifying regions include Cornwall and Isles of Scilly and West Wales and The Valleys, with Scotland Highlands and Islands receiving phasing out assistance. Regional Competitiveness and Employment funding represents approximately 66 per cent (€6.2 billion) of the budget. This covers all UK regions not receiving Convergence funding, with Merseyside and South Yorkshire being allocated transitional 'phasing-in' assistance. A further €0.6 billion (6 per cent approximately) has been allocated to the United Kingdom as Cooperation funding for cross-border and transnational cooperation activities. The programme financial allocations can be seen in Table 3.2 and Map 3.1.

In the context of reduced funding, the United Kingdom is presented with specific challenges including: what strategies to adopt that meet EU and domestic requirements and make best use of the more limited resources, and how best to manage and deliver such strategies in the context of the UK's complex and devolved governance framework.

Table 3.1   Cohesion policy allocations in the United Kingdom

Allocations 2000–06 (€ mn, 2004 prices)		Allocations 2007–13 (€ mn, 2004 prices)	
Cohesion fund	NA	Cohesion fund	NA
Objective 1	5,200	Convergence	2,430
		Statistical phasing out	158
Phasing out	1,192	Phasing-in	881
Objective 2	5,184	Regional competitiveness	5,336
Objective 3	5,043	and employment	
Community initiatives	1,003	European territorial cooperation	640
Total	17,622	Total	9,444

Source: CEC (2006a).

Table 3.2 Indicative annual allocation of UK cohesion policy funding

Operational programme	%	EU contribution (in €)
Convergence objective		
Highlands and Islands of Scotland ESF	1.79	52,150,195
West Wales and the Valleys ESF	28.62	833,585,460
England and Gibraltar ESF	6.74	196,433,940
Highlands and Islands of Scotland ERDF	4.18	121,862,392
West Wales and the Valleys ERDF	42.93	1,250,378,189
Cornwall and the Isles of Scilly ERDF	15.73	458,056,615
Total ESF convergence funds	37.16	1,082,169,595
Total ERDF convergence funds	62.84	1,830,297,196
Total 2007–13 All convergence funds	–	2,912,466,791
Competitiveness and employment objective		
East Wales ESF	0.91	63,597,452
Lowlands and Uplands of Scotland ESF	3.87	269,920,942
Northern Ireland ESF	2.38	165,777,300
England and Gibraltar ESF	41.46	2,893,452,439
Lowlands and Uplands of Scotland ERDF	5.39	375,957,844
South East England ERDF	0.34	23,706,375
Northern Ireland ERDF	4.40	306,833,439
East of England ERDF	1.59	110,994,719
North East England ERDF	5.38	375,698,920
London England ERDF	2.61	181,889,213
West Midlands England ERDF	5.73	399,899,930
North West England ERDF	10.83	755,754,611
Yorkshire and Humberside England ERDF	8.36	583,580,959
East Midlands England ERDF	3.85	268,495,983
South West England ERDF	1.79	124,658,086
East Wales ERDF	1.04	72,451,721
Gibraltar ERDF	0.08	5,800,739
Total ESF competitiveness	48.62	3,392,748,133
Total ERDF competitiveness	51.38	3,585,722,539
Total 2007–13 All competitiveness funds	–	6,978,470,672

Source: CEC (2007a).

Lessons learnt from the previous 2000–06 programmes are important in meeting these challenges. According to a mid-term review of Objective 1 and 2 programmes in England, the 2000–06 programmes were generally performing efficiently (DfT, 2005). Whilst there was considerable variation in progress towards outputs and results targets, the expectation was that the majority of output targets would be met by the end of the programmes, with a number being exceeded. Slower

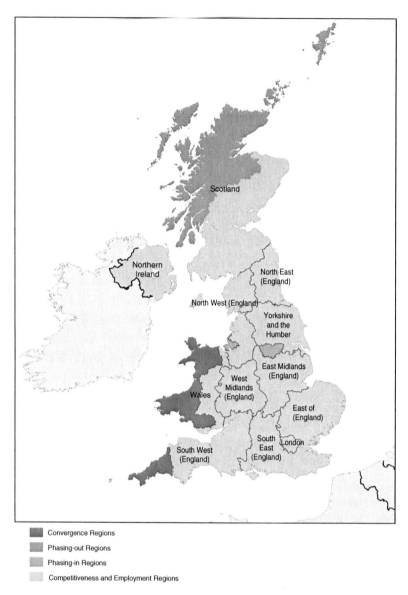

Map 3.1   Cohesion policy funding in the United Kingdom, 2007–13
Source: European Commission, DG Regional Policy.

performance was reported towards result and impact targets, although it was suggested that significant progress in these areas would not be observed until the end of the programmes. The effectiveness of the 2000–06 UK programmes is, however, debated and has been acknowledged as being difficult to quantify (see Open Europe, 2005). Even so, various elements of good practice and/or lessons for the new programming period have been identified through programme evaluations (see DfT, 2005; Regeneris, 2006; Davis et al., 2007). These highlight the importance of: leadership and close partnership working; strategic planning, including the identification of bottlenecks to development; managed risk taking; close monitoring of projects; flexibility in management systems; and complementing domestic policy frameworks and strategies. The remainder of this chapter examines how these challenges are being met and discusses key factors shaping this.

The implementation and impact of EU cohesion policy

Strategic programming

The UK National Strategic Reference Framework (NSRF) sets out the strategy underpinning the delivery of the 2007–13 Structural Fund programmes (see DTI, 2006). This document was finalized in October 2006, following a nationwide consultation process. It outlines the Government's central economic objective to ensure sustainable growth, increased prosperity and better quality of life with economic and employment opportunities for all, and specifies separate priorities for the four nations and Gibraltar in line with the devolved UK governance framework. The NSRF, alongside the Community Strategic Guidelines on Cohesion (CSG), provides the context for 22 Operational Programmes (OPs), which have been approved by the European Commission. A review of these documents and existing literature enables initial observations to be made concerning member state responses to the current cohesion policy climate. Studies by Polverari et al. (2005) and Bachtler et al. (2007), for example, identify various shifts in the current strategies. Of relevance to the United Kingdom include: a strong focus on Lisbon objectives and interventions and a stronger alignment of cohesion policy programmes with domestic regional policy goals and strategies. These are examined in turn.

Focus on the Lisbon agenda:
competitiveness, growth and jobs

The greater focus on activities supporting Lisbon objectives and interventions in the United Kingdom and elsewhere clearly reflects EU-level
agreements and regulations, which specify that member states are
required to direct a substantial amount of structural funding towards
such activities. The new constraints on how Structural Funds can be
spent means, however, that there will be less EU assistance for some
activities traditionally funded by the cohesion policy. It also raises the
possibility that Lisbon-targets may be promoted at the expense of other
domestic regional policy needs and preferences. In Scotland, for
example, it is anticipated that there will be less support for large-scale
infrastructure projects in transport, tourism and economic development more generally and greater focus on activities such as workforce
development, encouraging enterprise, business growth, support for
innovation and commercialization of research and development
(Scottish Executive, 2006). It is also expected that there will be less
scope for funding the same volume of projects as in 2000–06, and that
various project eligibility principles will be put in place to promote the
best use of reduced funds. For the Scottish Lowlands and Uplands programme, this includes setting a minimum size for projects based on
minimum annual average total project costs, placing a greater emphasis
on strategic fit and sustainability of projects and encouraging projects
that are explicitly partnership-based in design.

Bache (2008, pp. 50–1) also raises concerns that activities associated
with more bottom-up approaches to development might be marginalized in favour of more top-down, higher profile projects. According to
one Commission official: 'some of these local projects are very important but in terms of creating sustainable jobs and the economic growth
of the region the benefits are not so easily captured' (Interview, 2006 in
Bache, 2008, p. 51). The NSRF, in connection with ERDF in England,
and the Scottish Executive (2006) also place emphasis on larger, higher
value added and more strategic projects, bringing with it concerns that
this might exclude the participation of smaller organizations as beneficiaries (see Bachtler et al., 2007, p. 74). Similarly, there is some indica-
tion of a change in focus relating to CED approaches, which were
included (and endorsed by the European Commission: see CEC, 1996)
in many of the UK 2000–06 programmes. The CED approach entailed
targeting resources on the most disadvantaged communities, with the
eventual aim of linking them back into mainstream social and economic
activity. It emphasized 'bottom-up' economic and social development

based on engaging and empowering communities in capacity-building and tackling social and economic exclusion. CED does not appear to feature so prominently in the new programming period, and where it does, more emphasis appears to be on economic objectives associated with Lisbon as opposed to social inclusion and capacity-building activities. CED is not identified, for example, as a *main* priority goal in the NSRF, although community regeneration is identified as a priority in Scotland. The NSRF indicates targeted support for disadvantaged communities can still be provided in the new period, but that it should be incorporated in sustainable communities and/or other priorities (such as the English European Social Fund (ESF) 'tackling barriers to employment' priority), and must illustrate how it contributes to the Lisbon Agenda (see DTI, 2006, p. 47). The Department for Communities and Local Government ERDF and ESF good practice guide (Regeneris, 2006, pp. 38–9) also signals a potential shift in focus towards more economic, Lisbon-related objectives. It states:

> If the objective is to encourage greater rates of entrepreneurship amongst residents of deprived communities then we doubt whether the past Community Economic Development focus of programmes and support is the best way forward. Community Economic Development and what it is associated with in terms of enterprise support (social and community enterprises) has its place. But it should not be the main focus of support.

In broad terms, the United Kingdom is responding to the current cohesion policy climate by taking a relatively narrow and focused approach orientated towards competitiveness, growth and jobs (see HM Treasury/DTI/ODPM, 2003; Polverari et al., 2005; Scottish Executive, 2006). This contrasts with new member states and those with considerable Convergence funding (e.g., Germany, Greece, Italy, Portugal and Spain), which 'have a much wider set of goals' including: human resources development and/or societal modernization and social cohesion (Polverari et al., 2005, pp. 31–5). Even so, some variation across the UK regions is evident. According to Polverari et al. (2005, p. xii), OPs in North East England are adopting a 'narrow' interpretation of the Lisbon themes, whereas Scotland and West Wales are continuing to fund a broader range of interventions, including transport, business start-up and development and community development.

Whilst these shifts reflect EU-level agreements and regulations, it remains unclear as to the extent to which change is more attributable to, or at least in keeping with UK domestic preferences. The twin focus on employment and productivity of the Lisbon Agenda is seen as complementary to the UK Government's domestic policy objectives emphasizing sustainable growth and rising prosperity through employment creation (HM Treasury/DTI/ODPM, 2003, p. 17). The Scottish Government (2006) also emphasizes the close fit between its domestic priorities and the CSG, particularly in connection to the Lisbon Strategy for Growth and Jobs. In other words, EU pressure for change may be weak due to a 'good fit' between EU and domestic UK policies and practices. Additional confirmation of this is provided by Bachtler and Wishlade (2004, p. 46) who state: 'the thrust of the European Commission's proposals is regarded as representing a good 'policy fit' with the trend in their [United Kingdom, Netherlands and Sweden] national regional policies', which are increasingly concentrating on growth and competitiveness objectives. A study by Polverari et al. (2005) takes this further, suggesting that the narrower focus of some OPs is being driven more by reduced funding than by the new Lisbon requirements. In North East England, for example:

> The feeling is that Lisbon is already embedded in the current programme, certainly since the Mid-Term Evaluation. As the new programme will be very closely aligned with the RDAs Regional Economic Strategies (RES), and Lisbon is embedded in the RES, by implication it will also be embedded in the new OP. (Polverari et al., 2005, p. 62)

Finally, O'Donnell and Whitman (2007, pp. 263–4) also raise the potential for 'uploading' of national ideas and practices to the EU by highlighting parallels between British Government proposals for European economic reform and the Lisbon Agenda.

Alignment with domestic policies

As with other member states experiencing reduced funding, the UK strategy for implementing cohesion policy is closely aligned with domestic regional policy. In England, this is currently defined by a Public Service Agreement target to 'make sustainable improvements in the economic performance of all English regions by 2008 and over the long term reduce the persistent gap in growth rates between the regions, demonstrating progress by 2006' (DTI, 2006). This target is shared across several British government departments. Close alignment of OPs and Regional Economic Strategies is also expected (DTI, 2006). Developed by

RDAs, these strategies establish broad frameworks for economic development intervention based on analysis of economic strengths and weaknesses in each region. In doing so, they highlight the importance of urban areas, including city-regions, as drivers of economic growth, which the government again expects to be taken into account in the development of OPs. Consistency and alignment with other regional and local domestic strategies is also expected in relation to Regional Skills Strategies, Regional Spatial Strategies, Neighbourhood Renewal Strategies and Local Area Agreements (DTI, 2006, pp. 48–9). In Scotland closer alignment is expected with Scottish Executive priorities, as set out in strategies such as the Framework for Economic Development in Scotland, Smart Successful Highlands and Islands and the Scottish Sustainable Development strategy (see Scottish Government, 2006).

So far, this discussion suggests that domestic mediating factors (i.e., domestic regional policies and preferences) are highly significant in shaping EU cohesion policy implementation strategies. Such factors appear more significant in the current programming period than in previous rounds. Bachtler and Wishlade (2004, p. 50), for example, observe a closer alignment of national and EU strategies in the new period, and state:

> There have often been significant differences in the past between the strategic objectives and priorities of national and EU regional development programmes and strategies. Indeed, EU programme priorities tended to determine national funding priorities rather than vice versa. This is now changing, partly because of the maturity of devolved or deconcentrated arrangements for regional development.

The Scottish case appears to support this, as well as indicating the significance of reduced funding and close fit between domestic and EU priorities. As noted on the Scottish Government's website (2006):

> It is important that the [OP] priorities are aligned with existing domestic policy in Scotland which, in many respects, closely follows EU priorities. With reduced levels of Structural Funds and a new policy environment in Scotland following devolution it is necessary to ensure that Structural Fund programmes are closely aligned with domestic funding streams so that full use can be made of the reduced EU funding available to Scotland. This is a new opportunity, as previous Structural Fund programmes were developed before many of the Executive's key common strategies were in place.

The so called 'policy-driven' approach adopted in the United Kingdom also contrasts with the more 'needs-driven' approach adopted by other member states with substantial levels of funding, such as Greece, Italy and the EU10 (Polverari et al., 2005, p. 29). Rather than relying on alignment with existing domestic policies, these member states are 'tending to root their strategies in an ex novo reflection of development disparities, problems, challenges and needs' (Polverari et al., 2005, p. 30).

Programme management

In the United Kingdom, responsibility for cohesion policy implementation spans across a complex array of organizations at various territorial levels. Its management, however, is characterized by a regionalized approach, a feature that has been shaped by devolution, agencification and partnership. Whilst this approach is maintained in the new programming period, rationalization in the range and functions of regional bodies is evident in the context of reduced funding. In Scotland, for example, the 2000–06 programmes were managed by five Programme Management Executives (with the Scottish Government acting as the Managing Authority), whereas in the new programming period this will be undertaken by two intermediate administration bodies: one covering ESF and ERDF in Lowlands and Uplands Scotland and one in the Highlands and Islands. These bodies will undertake functions similar to the Programme Management Executives, for example, administering the programmes, supporting management and partnership structures and facilitating access to European funding for partner organizations. There will also be a move away from a purely challenge-funding system (where organizations are invited to submit bids to run projects for which they have to find match funding from a public sector partner organization) to a hybrid approach involving commissioning elements of the new programmes through existing domestic delivery organizations or Intermediate Delivery Bodies (see Scottish Government, 2006; and Bachtler et al., 2007). In England, there will be a shift in management responsibilities from the Government Offices, who will play a less 'hands-on' and more strategic role in programme delivery, to RDAs, who will be designated as intermediary bodies.

Trends towards rationalization of management arrangements in the United Kingdom appear to reflect a complex mix of domestic and EU factors. The reduced level and scope of EU cohesion funding, and the resulting impact on programme strategies as mediated at the domestic level, are particularly significant in justifying rationalization.

Political devolution to Scotland, Wales and Northern Ireland, a domestic factor that has taken place in relative isolation from the EU (see Bache, 2008), is also important to the extent that it has provided scope for programmes and delivery mechanisms to be aligned more closely with devolved institutional arrangements and policies in the new programming period. As the Scottish Government points out (2006, paragraph 32):

> A revised, more strategic approach to Structural Funds delivery would reflect both the reduction in the scale and scope of future funding and the changed policy environment in Scotland post-devolution. It is necessary to modernise the delivery mechanism to make it more cost-effective, more closely integrated with the wider strategic objectives of Scottish domestic policy and in line with Scottish Executive Efficient Government reforms.

In England, the transfer of management responsibilities to RDAs can be seen as part of UK Government strategies to devolve and rationalize regional policy decision-making (see DTI, 2006; and HM Treasury/ODPM, 2006), facilitate closer alignment of cohesion policy with domestic policy (e.g., through improved alignment with Regional Economic Strategies developed by RDAs) and develop more streamlined processes for project commissioning, decision-making and programme management. According to a government review of subnational economic development and regeneration (HM Treasury/DBERR/DCLG, 2007), improved alignment between ERDF and domestic funding streams (e.g., the RDAs single pot) will help ensure that European and domestic regional development funds are managed on a consistent basis. The review also alludes to the potential for further devolution of cohesion policy responsibilities to the sub-regional and local levels. More specifically, it states that RDAs will be expected to 'delegate responsibility for spending to local authorities or sub-regions wherever possible, unless there is a clear case for retaining spending at the regional level'. Finally, there is some evidence suggesting that the shift in management responsibilities has been indirectly influenced, or at least justified, by the shift in focus towards a Lisbon competitiveness agenda. A committee paper for the East of England Development Agency (EEDA, 2007), for example, suggested that the government linked the emphasis on Lisbon to Regional Development Agency (RDA) economic development priorities and indicated that cohesion policy delivery responsibilities should reflect this.

Partnership

The 2006 cohesion policy reform brought about a further widening of the partnership principle to include nongovernmental and civil society organizations, among others. As far as the involvement of nongovernmental organizations is concerned, it seems reasonable to suppose that this element of reform is unlikely to have a significant impact in the United Kingdom. Third sector engagement had already become widespread in the 2000–06 programmes, particularly in connection with CED (Chapman, 2006). In South Yorkshire, for example, the third sector played a significant role in shaping the Objective 1 Programme strategy (Armstrong, Wells and Woolford, 2002) and was designated lead partner on the partnership established to deliver CED. In West Wales and the Valleys, the composition of the Programming Monitoring Committee and several local partnerships was established on a 'three-thirds' principle, with equal representation from the public, private and third sectors (see CRG, 2003). In fact, there are indications that the United Kingdom has gone further than other countries, and arguably the Commission's requirements, in partnership working with the third sector (Kelleher, Batterbury and Stern, 1999; Chapman, 2004; Bache, 2008). Some confirmation of this was provided in an interview with a Commission official, who stated: 'voluntary and community participation in the United Kingdom is well ahead of other member states' (Interview with author, 2004). In short, the United Kingdom is already 'ahead of the game' as far as third sector engagement is concerned.

Perhaps of greater significance will be changes in the level of funding available, territorial coverage and thematic focus of programmes and domestic administrative reforms, which Bachtler et al. (2007) highlight as key factors set to influence partnership arrangements. The substantial fall of assistance available to the United Kingdom suggests some rationalization of partnerships might be expected, which may in turn have implications for the prevalence and nature of multilevel participation and governance. To elaborate, the scaling down and re-focusing of programmes may initiate narrowing or streamlining of partnerships, as well as changes in their composition. Thematic reorientation towards the Lisbon Agenda, for example, may mean greater emphasis is placed on representatives of industrial sectors and the business community (see Bachtler et al., 2007, p. 72). The narrowing of partnerships may result in the loss of some previously engaged partners, and with them expertise. The shift in focus relating to CED, for example, may lead to a loss of partnership working with some local voluntary and community sector organizations, especially those previously involved in capacity-building and more social aspects of CED delivery. The Lisbon Agenda is clearly implicated in the future role of the third sector. As the NSRF (DTI, 2006, p. 47) states, third sector organizations will continue to have a role, but 'will need to demonstrate how they contribute to the economic objectives of the programme'.

Changes in management arrangements whereby RDAs are given a greater role in programme administration may also have implications for partnership, as well as the balance of power among partners. Previous research, which highlights the significant role and influence of actors involved in day-to-day programme administration (Chapman, 2005; Bache, 2008), suggests this could enhance the influence of RDAs in programme implementation. Whether this would be at the expense of other partners remains to be seen.

Yet, whilst some changes are anticipated, many existing partnership relations could be maintained. This was alluded to in the UK NSRF, which states that 'across the UK, Programmes will be expected to maintain and build upon existing successful arrangements for involving partners in Structural Funds spending' (DTI, 2006, p. 16). It goes further to specify appropriate liaison and coordination is expected with local authorities, the higher and further education sector, the voluntary and community sector and the private sector. The continued involvement of existing regional, sub-regional and local partnerships is also mentioned in England, as well as in Welsh OPs (see WEFO, 2007a, 2007b).

The discussion so far suggests that the 2006 extension of the EU partnership principle is unlikely to have a significant impact on partnership in the United Kingdom. The United Kingdom is already ahead of the game as far as third sector engagement is concerned and has embraced the notion of partnership more generally, particularly following the 1997 election of the Labour Government. Even then, domestic mediating factors are likely to remain as important as ever in shaping the role and extent of participation. Reduced funding and shifts in the thematic focus of programmes, on the other hand, may be significant in shaping partnerships in the new period through the scaling down of partnerships and in changing the type of partners most appropriate to effective programme delivery. Changes in implementation arrangements may also have an impact on the nature of partnerships and balance of power. With the exception of reduced funding, which has been affected by EU enlargement and budget negotiations, these factors highlight the importance of domestic factors. As argued above, adaptational pressure arising from the EU Lisbon requirements, for example, appears relatively weak in the new programming period, in part due to strong domestic policies and preferences already favouring Lisbon objectives and interventions.

Conclusion

This chapter highlighted various challenges facing the United Kingdom in the 2007–13 programming period associated with reduced funding, cohesion policy reforms and the domestic context. These challenges have provided the context and have helped trigger, or at least justify, rationalization in UK cohesion policy implementation strategies. Rationalization has taken a number of forms, including: a stronger and narrower focus on activities associated with the Lisbon Agenda, closer alignment with domestic policies, and changes in programme management responsibilities and arrangements at the regional level. There is also potential for shifts in the number and composition of partnerships involved in programme delivery.

These changes reflect a complex combination of EU and domestic factors. At the EU level, the Lisbon Agenda, cohesion policy reforms and reduced funding have had a significant impact, thereby indicating some degree of Europeanization. The impact of these factors has been heavily mediated at the domestic level. Domestic regional policies and preferences have, for example, played a crucial role in determining outcomes. In some cases, it remains unclear as to the extent to which change is more attributable to, or at least in keeping with UK domestic preferences. The fact that domestic regional policies and governmental preferences closely match Lisbon objectives suggests that associated EU-level pressure for change, and therefore Europeanization, is relatively weak as far as strategic programming is concerned. It also suggests that whatever Europeanization is taking place is likely to be voluntary, as opposed to, coercive. The fact that political devolution to Scotland, Wales and Northern Ireland has taken place in relative isolation from the EU system of governance also suggests some degree of nationalization[2] has taken place, to the extent that it has provided scope for programmes and delivery mechanisms to be aligned more closely with devolved institutional arrangements and policies. Such developments do not, however, appear contrary to policies, practices and preferences advanced through the EU system of governance. They also fall far short of UK led calls for partial renationalization of EU cohesion policy in the negotiations leading up to the 2006 reform, which proposed wealthier countries take full responsibility for financing and delivering regional development within their own territories, albeit in accordance with broad policy objectives established at the European level.

Notes

1. I would like to thank Michael Baun, Dan Marek, Ian Bache, John Chapman and Irene McMaster for their helpful comments. The usual disclaimers apply.
2. Understood here as the reorientation or reshaping of politics in the domestic arena to reflect national policies, practices and preferences advanced through the domestic system of governance in relative isolation to the EU system of governance.

4
Germany

Roland Sturm and Ingo Schorlemmer

Introduction

For a number of reasons regional policy has always had major implications for Germany. On the one hand, there has been general political support for a relatively homogenous economic and social development throughout the country, and on the other a constant worry that the subsidization of industry or infrastructure might distort economic competition and become so widespread that, in the end, it would no longer channel private investment exclusively into the poorest regions (Jákli, 1990; Sturm, 1991).

When the European Economic Community (EEC) was founded in 1957 Germany's Economics Minister, Ludwig Erhard, distrusted the new Community because he feared it would limit economic competition and thereby stifle economic growth (Brunn, 2002, p. 103). At the time regional policy, which embodies the belief that markets fail and need politically motivated corrections, was not yet on the European agenda. In Germany, while no objections were raised against selective periodical support for the country's less-developed regions, especially those bordering the 'iron curtain' and West Berlin – a political island in those days – more systematic efforts to overcome regional disparities were not made.

In the mid-1960s, with a new Keynesian Economics Minister, and after a constitutional reform which prepared the ground for close cooperation between the German *Länder* and the federal government in regional policymaking, it became a constitutional requirement to draw up plans for regional economic development. This national planning process has been in place up to the present day. After creation of the European Regional Development Fund (ERDF) in 1975, and especially after 1988 when the EU began to define general objectives for regional policy, the organization and results of regional development planning in Germany had to be reconciled with the instruments of EU cohesion policy and the control of state aid implied by EU competition policy.

Another dimension of cohesion policy for Germany has always been the fact that Germany is a net contributor to the EU budget, in fact the biggest one. The funding of EU cohesion policy used to be a convenient, though expensive, method for oiling the integration machinery and securing political success on the European stage for Germany's supra-nationally-minded leadership. Party politics never played a role here, not least because European integration was the accepted route back to an international role for Germany in the postwar years. Germany's ability to increase her contributions to the EU budget has decreased over the last two decades, however, and the redistributive character of cohesion policy has become more apparent. The German *Länder* resented the loss of funding which resulted from the end of financial status quo plus-x allocations at the European level. They tried to convince the federal government that their share of EU funding should be protected and that, if this was not an option, generous phasing-out arrangements should be guaranteed.

Germany's unification in 1990 has also had broad implications both for the logic of Germany's interest representation on the European level and the political and economic balance of interests in Germany when it came to securing funds for its less-developed regions. In the European context, Germany now had regions that were among Europe's poorest, with a per capita GDP less than 75 per cent of EU average. In the German context, the challenge was to integrate the poor East German *Länder* in a financial mechanism of regional aid which was originally designed for regions that were developing fairly homogeneously. Not surprisingly, some East German politicians do not see regional aid as a resource-dependent policy, but as a financial obligation of West Germany. When in 2007 the federal government reduced its contributions to the funding of regional policies in East Germany, the East German MPs protested (Deutscher Bundestag, 2006a).

And there was a parallel unease regarding the statistical effect of EU enlargement, which was to affect the poorer East German *Länder* much more than the richer West German ones. This has to be seen in perspective, however. Gross financial transfers to East Germany totalled €189 billion in 1998, to which the EU contributed only €7 billion (Deutscher Bundestag, 2007a, p. 9). Still, as Table 4.1 shows, whereas Germany as a whole has only had to cope with a moderate loss of cohesion funding

Table 4.1 Cohesion policy allocations in Germany, 2000–06 and 2007–13

Allocations 2000–06 (€ mn, 2004 prices)		Allocations 2007–13 (€ mn, 2004 prices)	
Cohesion fund	na	Cohesion fund	na
Objective 1	17,594	Convergence	10,527
		Statistical phasing-out	3,761
Phasing-out	667	Phasing-in	NA
Objective 2	3,875	Regional competitiveness and employment	8,349
Objective 3	5,058		
Community initiatives	1,639	European territorial cooperation	754
Total	28,833	Total	23,391

Source: European Commission (2006d).

(19 per cent) as a consequence of enlargement, the poorest regions suffer from much higher levels of funding cuts.

This loss of funding did not lead to a redesign of cohesion policy in Germany, however. What gives cohesion policy after 2006 its new direction is Lisbonization, irrespective of the volume of funding. Not even with regard to the number of specific targets defined in the Operational Programmes (OPs) for 2007–13 do we find a correlation with the level of funding. In some *Länder*, such as Saxony or Mecklenburg-West Pomerania, new funding priorities were defined even though ERDF funding was reduced, whereas North Rhine-Westphalia reduced its specific targets although its funding was increased.

In the remainder of this chapter the implementation of EU cohesion policy in Germany is examined more closely. The next section briefly discusses the goals of German regional policy and the coordination of national and EU regional policies. The implementation of EU cohesion policy at the *Land* level is then discussed, with a focus on the case of Baden-Württemberg in 2000–06. The chapter then examines the drafting of Germany's National Strategic Reference Framework (NSRF) and OPs for 2007–13 in order to assess the impact of reduced funding and Lisbonization on cohesion policy in Germany. It concludes by arguing that Lisbonization has caused problems for Germany by limiting the flexibility of the federal and *Länder* governments when it comes to addressing regional needs, while the new efficiency philosophy of cohesion policy also presents a challenge for Germany's bureaucratic culture.

Elements of German regional policy

Common task 'improvement of regional economic structures'

German regional policy rests on two pillars: a joint federal-*Land* subsidy, the so-called Common Task 'Improvement of Regional Economic Structures', and the EU structural funds. For Small and Medium-Sized Enterprises (SMEs) additional funding from the European Reconstruction Programme (ERP) is possible. The ERP is a postwar left-over, also known as the Marshall Fund, which is today used as a source of indirect state aid by means of cheap credits, especially to SMEs.

The Common Task has as its primary aim the creation and protection of jobs in less-developed regions of Germany. Its major instrument is state aid for private sector investments and for local infrastructure development. The yardstick for successful subsidization is additional regional income created as a result of regional policies. Regions in the national definition are different from the EU's Nomenclature of Statistical Territorial Units (NUTS) categories. Whereas the latter are defined by size of territory, the former are based on an elaborate mix of indicators. From 2007 the 'labour market regions', on which regional funding in Germany is based, are defined by four regional indicators which have different impacts on the final measurement: average unemployment rate over the last three years (50 per cent impact); gross wage levels (40 per cent); expected future employment rate (5 per cent); and infrastructure (5 per cent). Altogether, 35.84 per cent of the German population lives in areas which receive Common Task regional funding (Deutscher Bundestag, 2007b, pp. 19–20).

Similar to EU cohesion policy, national regional policy is selective. The least developed *Länder* or regions are all situated in East Germany, whereas the West German *Länder* of Baden-Württemberg and Hamburg are too well-off to qualify for any kind of state aid.

Coordination of national and EU policies

German regional policy is fully controlled by the European Commission. The Commission grants permission for the amount of money spent, and also for the territorial allocation of funds and the purposes for which they are used. Even with regard to the definition of key reference points for German regional policy, the Commission has the last word. Since 2005, for example, ERP funds have only been given to SMEs which fit the definition of such companies provided by the Commission. Commission control is not always restrictive, however.

In December 2006, for example, the EU approved German legislation to attract companies to East Germany (*Investitionszulagegesetz*). The new law guarantees companies which invest in East Germany until 2011 state support for their investments in industry, industrial services and tourist accommodations.

The EU's negative coordination (permission and control) of national regional policy is just one way that it affects regional development policy in Germany. Another is the positive coordination or integration of national and EU structural programming. Since 1988 in West Germany, and 1994 in East Germany, EU funding has been fully integrated with national programming. The goals of regional policy are defined nationally and co-funding for EU cohesion policy, required by the principle of additionality, is taken from the federal-*Land* regional development programme, the Common Task Regional Economic Development (Conzelmann, 2002, p. 146ff.).

However, with the conceptual enrichment of EU cohesion policy in the 1990s it became much more difficult to argue that the aims of national regional policy and EU cohesion policy were compatible. Whereas Germany's idea was, and still is, to offer state aid and wait for companies to take it and set their own priorities, the EU has a much more specific, but at the same time wider and richer concept of regional development. The EU has always been much less interested in subsidizing the specific investments of companies, among other things because it feared market distortions. EU cohesion policy concentrates instead on aggregate indicators, such as economic growth or infrastructure development.

For the *Länder*, the broader approach of EU cohesion policy was not only attractive because the partnership principle gave them the possibility of bypassing the federal government to some extent when it came to the definition of development goals (Bauer, 2006); the *Länder* also liked the idea that there were now funds available in new fields. Even wealthy *Länder* such as Baden-Württemberg, who could not expect state aid from German sources, qualified for Objective 2 support, for example. The logical consequence of the growing incompatibility of EU and national regional policies, and the differences in the delimitation of national and EU funding regions, was a decoupling of national and EU policies (Sturm and Pehle, 2005, p. 328). This was politically plausible in the German context, where the *Länder* were seeking more control over their own resources. The direct contact with the Commission has given the *Länder* more room to manoeuvre *vis-à-vis* the federal government. The 2006 cohesion policy reform and Lisbonization did not change the rules of the game. *Land* autonomy is in this context not a party political issue, but one affecting the internal balance of power in German federalism and economic policymaking. For the Commission, East Germany was also a test case to find out how EU cohesion policy worked in postcommunist transition countries.

Implementing EU cohesion policy in 2000–06: the *Land* level

Germany was allocated €29 billion (at 2004 prices) in cohesion policy funding for 2000–06. Most of the money (€17.6 billion) had to be spent in the Objective 1 regions, that is in East Germany. For Objective 2 regions €3.9 billion was allocated, and for Objective 3 regions €5 billion was available (see Table 4.1).

The experience of *Länder* decisionmakers with the advantages and disadvantages of EU cohesion policy, especially with regard to implementation, has not found broad scientific interest. In our analysis, therefore, we rely to some extent on interviews[1] in *Land* Economics Ministries, which have the role of policy coordinators in cohesion policy. What can be observed in general is that, although Germany is a federal system, variation in cohesion policy implementation between the *Länder*, which might have stimulated greater research interest, has been rather limited. This is the case for two reasons. One is the German brand of federalism, which is strongly coordinated and operates in a dense political culture of consensus. The second has to do with the actors involved; these are civil servants, mostly trained in law and with a very similar approach to policy implementation and conflict management.

We will take Baden-Württemberg (B-W) as an example for our arguments regarding the way funds provided by the European Social Fund (ESF) and the ERDF were used in 2000–06. This is because the relatively modest amount of money allocated to this *Land* allows us an almost complete overview of all programmes run in the funding period. In addition, the regional concentration of programmes leads one to expect a maximum impact. The extent to which this was or was not the case is a good illustration of the consequences of EU cohesion policy, which also makes it easier to draw lessons for 2007–13.

The impression of those involved in the *Land* programmes was that the 2000–06 programmes were definitely less goal-oriented than is the case for 2007–13. In the past, funding was directed towards five policy goals, which the Commission had defined and for which funding was provided: an active labour market policy; avoiding social exclusion; improving vocational training; education and lifelong learning; developing an entrepreneurial culture; and better chances for women in society. In the eyes of those civil servants responsible for the implementation of regional programmes, all of these goals were fairly vague. What was meant by support for the development of an entrepreneurial culture, for example? For the German *Länder* the lack of clarity was, however, not necessarily negative because it implied greater flexibility for regional decisionmaking. The handling of funds in B-W shows that flexibility was used to cope with the short-term political challenges that influenced policymaking on the *Land* level. It also facilitated cooperation of the two *Land* ministries involved in policymaking, the Economics Ministry (LME) and the Ministry for Social Affairs (LMSA). As always the drawback of flexibility was an inflation of demands, because many interests saw an opportunity to get activities funded which were often rather marginal to the original intent of cohesion policy.

Cohesion policy implementation was less oriented towards the co-financing of policies than of projects. Applications for funding had to come from institutions planning projects in various regions of the *Länder*. On this sub-*Land* level, a regional working group pre-selected the project applications and the approved projects were then sent to the two ministries involved. The working groups involved in the selection process for the LMSA were organized on the level of local government districts (*Landkreis*), while those for the LME were organized on the level of regional chambers of commerce.

This was not without problems. Regarding the implementation of goals defined by the ESF in B-W, for example, 400 projects had to be evaluated in the Economics Ministry alone, though it was less involved than the LMSA. This consumed a considerable amount of work hours for decisionmaking and the evaluation and monitoring of projects. In the LME, ten-to-fifteen staff members were concerned with project administration and paid out of the technical aid funds. The LME concluded that the procedures in place produced inefficiencies and looked for alternatives. Thus, in the second half of the funding period they decided to reduce the administrative workload. To this end, they standardized the kinds of programmes for which applications could be made; instead of accommodating a wide variety of interests, the choice of programmes was pre-defined and the selection process lost some of its flexibility.

This new strategy is also being used in 2007–13. The LME's decisionmaking on programmes has also been centralized. It is now the responsibility of the *L-Bank*, a *Land*-owned bank, to handle applications.

Furthermore, regional chambers of commerce are no longer involved in project selection; instead the LME decides at first instance. The LMSA, however – notwithstanding programme standardization – still utilizes the same pre-selection process that it used in 2000–06. However, one should not interpret the reduced flexibility of a standardized process as the end of innovative initiatives originating from outside the *Land* bureaucracies. Standardized programmes often have their origins in such initiatives and build on them. Of course, standardization means that the comprehensive goals of programmes are defined in the OPs, and the ministries provide a choice of alternatives as to how these goals can be achieved. Whoever wants to apply has to work within this framework, with the freedom to choose a project alternative which suits their needs.

Whereas the change in implementation strategies for the ESF in 2000–06 took some time to complete, new implementation procedures for the ERDF were already in place at the beginning of the programming period. For the first time, in addition to rural areas and former Objective 5b areas, urban areas were entitled to apply for funding. This meant that the implementation of ERDF goals in B-W was no longer only the responsibility of the *Land* Ministry of Agriculture (LMA), but also the Economics Ministry. This necessitated a greater degree of inter-ministerial coordination, which in the new programming period has become more problematic: Lisbonization means support for innovation and new technologies, which are rarely to be found in rural areas. In planning for 2007–13, for example, the LMA initially insisted on an OP which favoured voters in rural areas. This met stiff resistance from the Commission, which did not accept first versions of the programme that were presented. In the long run, this conflict may be solved either by shifting responsibilities from the LMA to the LME – which is, however, difficult because the ministries are held by different parties of the *Land* coalition – or by finding a way that connects aspects of innovation and new technology with needs in rural areas.

To get the most benefit from the limited amount of funding available, the decision was made to concentrate resources. In economically less-developed regions funds were reserved for clusters of growth-oriented companies, with the idea of developing these into 'beacons of excellence' which serve as growth poles that stimulate economic development in the regions where they operate. Ideas for clusters are developed in the economically weak regions themselves, and are defined after a consultation process between the regions and the Economics Ministry. The clusters concept was initially applied in the city of Mannheim in

2000–06, and extended to additional urban areas in 2007–13. ERDF-funded projects in Baden-Württemberg must also have a broader range of positive effects regarding structural social and economic deficits, such as employment opportunities for women and other disadvantaged groups, as a means of maximizing their impact.

The National strategic reference framework for 2007–13

Planning process and the national reform programme

On January 23, 2007 the German Economics Ministry sent the German NSRF for 2007–13 to the Commission for approval. Once approved, the NSRF would provide the guidelines for the OPs developed by the *Länder* and the federal government for the new programming period. The intention was to develop the NSRF in a bottom-up process that involved the regions affected, the *Länder* and civil society. Such a process was organized, but the German public took little notice and the core decisionmaking process was reduced to the well-known mechanism of federal-*Land* negotiations. The exercise in deliberative democracy, which was behind efforts to organize a bottom-up planning process, was supposed to be repeated on the *Land* level when the OPs were prepared.

The NSRF is based on the National Reform Programme (NRP) to which the federal government agreed on 7 December 2005. It interprets the aims of the Lisbon Agenda process in the German context and concludes that Germany faces four challenges: technological change; globalization; an aging society; and the consequences of German unification, for which 4 per cent of GDP will still have to be spent annually in the foreseeable future.

The NRP defines six strategies to meet these challenges: (1) investing in the knowledge society; (2) liberalizing markets and improving the competitiveness of industry; (3) improving conditions for the private sector and private sector investments; (4) sound public finance and social security systems; (5) taking advantage of the innovation potential of environmental technologies; and (6) labour market reforms to achieve more flexibility and better conditions for female career planning. In addition to the NRP strategies, less-developed regions also benefit from national regional policy as part of the Common Task described above, with some new instruments such as the management of regional clusters of industry and special advice for SMEs. A new situation has developed regarding the financial support provided by the ESF to local government, which was used for local initiatives to fight unemployment. After the reform of German unemployment policy, anti-exclusion policies have been centralized so that ESF money can now be used for other strategies to develop human resources.

The limited time available for the preparation of OPs, however, did not allow a strict adherence to the step-by-step approach for implementing EU cohesion policy. The NSRF did not in all aspects precede the OPs. In the fall of 2006 the federal government decided, in contrast to procedures in place for 2000–06, not to work out a joint document with the *Länder* on the implementation of EU cohesion policy. The consequence was that the federal government and the *Länder* developed their OPs for the structural funds independently, and on short notice. Preparation of the OPs took place parallel to development of the NSRF; because of time pressure, the *Länder* could not wait for the final NSRF version, as was originally intended, in order to base their programmes on this document.

Efficient coordination was achieved less by sequencing in the planning process than by informal coordination and the tradition of civil-servant networks with their specific decisionmaking cultures. One can distinguish three strategies of consensus-building which allowed a high degree of congruence between the OPs of the federal government and the *Länder*, on the one hand, and between the *Länder* OPs and the NSRF, on the other: (1) coordination; (2) political culture; and (3) vagueness.

(1) The first mechanism is coordination. German policymakers are embedded in a broad and closely-knit network which organizes policy learning and the exchange of ideas. For example there is a permanent committee of the federal government and the *Länder* which shadows the ESF. Here, the civil servants representing the *Länder* and the federal government informally coordinated the respective parts of their OPs concerning the ESF. With regard to the ERDF, informal consultation was possible in the framework of regular consultations of the federal government and the *Länder*. Some *Länder*, such as Bremen, presented in this context the current status of their operational planning; other *Länder* took from the discussions what they needed to improve their own planning documents.

In addition, there were a number of bilateral contacts between the *Länder* themselves at an early stage of the planning process. *Länder* which were behind schedule in their planning took the opportunity to learn from other *Länder* whose planning was more advanced.

For example, a delegation of civil servants from the B-W Agriculture and Economics Ministries travelled at an early stage of their own planning to North Rhine-Westphalia to inform themselves about progress there.

No actor involved in the planning process had the idea, however, that these informal contacts should lead to a fine-tuning of every detail in drafting the OPs. Two aspects played a role here. First, it was argued that that the political responsibility for the economic development of regions was not a common task. It was always the case that one could clearly define which *Land* was responsible; so *Land* autonomy should prevail. Second, coordination with the federal government had obvious limits, because the federal government had opted for programmes which were in principle different from those of the *Länder*. For example, regarding ESF funding the federal government did not, as the *Länder* do, concentrate on specific projects, but instead tried to define programmes that are attractive nation-wide.

The difference between *Land* and federal programmes reduces the need for cooperation and explains to some extent why time pressures and parallel working did not produce spectacularly negative effects. For example, in its first reaction to the way B-W wanted to spend ESF funds in its OPs, the Commission did not criticize a lack of clarity with regard to the respective competences of the federal and *Land* governments. It is the case that federal and *Land* programmes are often complementary. For example, ESF funding by a *Land* finances start-ups and the initial years in business, while the federal government finances a training programme for young entrepreneurs. It seems to be the case that the special way Germany coordinates the implementation of EU cohesion policy is more problematic with regard to the *Land* level than to federal-*Land* relations. The Commission criticized B-W, for example, because its OPs for the ESF and the ERDF were not sufficiently separate from each other.

(2) A second mechanism of consensus-building between the federal government and the *Länder* in cohesion policy implementation is the political culture, which expresses itself in trust, administrative routines and a common understanding of problems and possible solutions among the civil servants involved. Attitudes, beliefs and feelings converge. In addition, the representatives of the federal government and the *Länder* share a common understanding of the relevant challenges society faces. The challenges identified in the NRP – technological change, globalization, an aging society – are

also strategic landmarks for *Länder* policies. B-W, for example, addresses all of these issues in its OP for the ESF. Thus, convergence between the programming exercises on the federal and the *Land* level emerges without having to be negotiated.

(3) Consensus-building between the federal and the *Land* level is also facilitated by the fact that the goals defined in the NSRF are relatively vague. Coherence with *Land*-level programmes is therefore rarely a problem. There seems to be a trade-off between consensus-building and the specificity of the NSRF, as decisionmakers confirm.

In addition, it is possible from a *Land* point-of-view to be selective. The NSRF defines six strategies in the context of the Regional Competitiveness and Employment (RCE) objective: support for knowledge-based, innovative developments; strengthening the competitiveness of firms; reducing regional disparities and strengthening regional advantages; improving labour force flexibility; investment in human capital; and integration into the labour market of marginalized groups (Bundesministerium für Wirtschaft und Technologie, 2007, p. 78).

In B-W, for example, the Ministry of Agriculture and the Economics Ministry agreed to use ERDF funding for only two purposes. The first has a regional orientation and aims at the competitiveness of companies, the reduction of regional disparities and strengthening the endogenous potential of regions. The general aim is to provide for an environment which creates new jobs and secures existing ones. Resources will be concentrated on rural areas, as defined by the *Land*, and four urban regions – Mannheim, Heilbronn, Pforzheim and Villingen. The most important instruments will be investments in infrastructure and a greater diversity of the regional economy. The argument is that the rural areas still rely too heavily on industry and are too weak with regard to the service sector (Ministerium für Ernährung und Ländlichen Raum, 2007, p. 105ff.). The second purpose of ERDF funding is issue-oriented, and aims at support for a knowledge-based, innovative and sustainable development of the *Land* (Ministerium für Ernährung und Ländlichen Raum, 2007, p. 111ff.). Here again, the investment of resources is focused. Some resources, for example, will be given to research institutes, which plan important investments that will advance knowledge but which they cannot finance out of their own budgets. Others may go into new technologies and clusters in order to stimulate companies and research institutes to engage in joint research efforts. The *Land* plans to invest 69 per cent of its available funds for the RCE objective in the first strategy.

Other strategic aims of the NSRF are covered by the *Land* OP that is funded by the ESF. The Ministry for Social Affairs and the Economics Ministry defined in this context four 'axes of priority'. The first is increasing the flexibility and competitiveness of companies and their staff. This should be achieved through support for the training of employees (the concept of lifelong learning), support for the restructuring of companies, and support for start-ups. The second priority axis is human capital development. This has two major aims: to improve opportunities for young people looking for vocational training; and to keep older employees in the job market as long as possible. A third priority is to improve access to the job market for disadvantaged segments of the labour force (women, job seekers with insufficient qualifications, long-term unemployed). The goal is to improve the employability of such groups, for whom integration into the job market also means social integration. This last priority is the most important of the four in terms of resources spent, absorbing 40.7 per cent of ESF funds. The fourth *Land* priority for ESF funding is support for transnational social investments (Ministerium für Arbeit und Soziales Baden-Württemberg, 2007, p. 66ff.).

The example of B-W illustrates that the *Länder* are able and willing to define their own strategic priorities when it comes to the implementation of cohesion policy. It also shows that the setting of priorities by the *Länder* does not lead them into conflict with the NSRF. When one looks at the OPs for 2007–13, all of the NSRF strategic objectives come into focus in one way or another.

The prepatory work in the *Länder* is often done by more than one ministry. One could ask whether this is not too burdensome and might lead to conflict, especially because one ministry may be responsible for a larger sum of money than the others, and because there is no official hierarchy of competences for the decisionmaking process. Here, as mentioned above, it is important not to underestimate the importance of informality and underlying routines. In addition, cooperation is mostly restricted to the programme planning period, at the beginning of the implementation process. It is of much less importance once the programmes are implemented. In this process additional ministries, such as the Science and the Environment Ministries, may also become involved. In our interviews, we found that no conflicts over resources and competences arose in connection with cohesion policy.

Regional disparities

The statistical effect of enlargement had, above all, consequences for the former Objective 1 regions, now Convergence regions. In the German context, these are the eastern *Länder*, most of whom massively lost EU funding as a consequence of enlargement, although in three of the five cases a generous phasing-out period has been granted. Germany's total cohesion policy support was reduced by about €5.5 billion (in 2004 prices) compared to the previous funding period, and the lion's share of this reduction is the result of reduced funding for East Germany.

This loss of funding has produced some worries in the East German *Länder*, which fear that they will now experience budgetary difficulties. The federal government has explained reduced levels of EU support as the inevitable price to be paid for enlargement. For Germany, however, it was important that funding for the new member states would not subsidize the relocation of companies.

Nearly two decades after unification, significant disparities between the West and East German *Länder* remain. In East Germany the annual income per capita in 2005 was one-third below the level of West Germany. In the same year, economic efficiency in East Germany, measured as GDP per employee, was €46,000, or 80 per cent of the West German level. The rate of unemployment (18.7 per cent) was twice as high in East as in West Germany. Unemployment was a problem for almost every region in East Germany. Women, youth and older workers were affected the most. The lack of positive economic prospects has triggered East-West migration, above all of young and well-educated people, a development which has accelerated the aging of society in the eastern *Länder* and their depopulation (all data in: Bundesministerium für Wirtschaft und Technologie, 2007). Inter-*Land* differences of such magnitude are reflected in the distribution of cohesion policy funding for 2007–13 (see Table 4.2) and define eligibility for cohesion policy, as shown in Map 4.1 below. All of East Germany, with the exception of Berlin, receives Convergence funding, which makes up the lion's share of EU assistance. Berlin and West Germany are funded in the context of the Regional Competitiveness and Employment objective (with the exception of the Lüneburg region of Lower Saxony, which receives Convergence funding).

Strategic reactions to Lisbonization and the problem of measuring success

The Lisbonization of cohesion policy did not find enthusiastic support in Germany. The federal government was not worried about the efficiency goals connected with this strategy, but about the possibility that new EU criteria might reduce national flexibility in the implementation of regional policy (Deutscher Bundestag, 2006b, p. 32). In addition, the

Table 4.2 Cohesion policy allocations by *Land*, 2007–13 (in € mn and percentage of EU funding in Germany)

Competitiveness and employment	Funding (in € mn)	%	Convergence	Funding (in € mn)	Phasing-out	%
Baden-Württ.	409.4	1.6	Brandenburg	1,107.4	1,011.5	8.3
			Lower Saxony			
Bavaria	885.9	3.5	(Lüneburg)	0.0	799.0	3.1
Berlin	1,211.6	4.7	Mecklenburg-W. Pomerania	1,669.9	0.0	6.6
Bremen	231.0	0.9	Saxony	3,089.2	873.8	15.5
Hamburg	126.4	0.5	Saxony-Anhalt	1,802.6	773.0	10.1
Hesse	450.2	1.8	Thuringia	2,106.7	0.0	8.3
Lower Saxony (except Lüneburg)	875.8	3.4				
Northrhine-West	1,967.4	7.7				
Rhineland-Palat	331.3	1.3				
Saarland	284.0	1.1				
Schleswig-Holst	473.0	1.8				

Source: Bundesministerium für Wirtschaft und Technologie (2007).

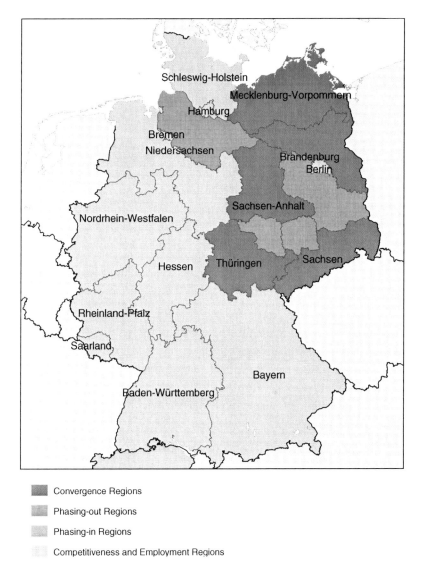

Convergence Regions

Phasing-out Regions

Phasing-in Regions

Competitiveness and Employment Regions

Map 4.1 Cohesion policy funding in Germany, 2007–13

Source: European Commission, DG Regional Policy.

budget committee of the German parliament at first voted to ignore the new globalization fund, because it feared a duplication of activities already organized as labour market policies in Germany (*Frankfurter Allgemeine Zeitung*, 8 April 2006, p. 12). Still, the German parliament approved the globalization fund in 2007. A third aspect which influenced German perspectives on the new strategic orientation of cohesion policy was the decision taken by governments on both the *Land* and federal levels to concentrate regional aid and support clusters of industry. While the EU is moving away from subsidizing territories without sufficient differentiation of specific needs, this approach differs from the targeting of regional aid envisaged by German policymakers.

In principle, it remains difficult to explain how market forces can be strengthened by a process which adds to market liberalization a number of mechanisms which correct assumed market failure. In the case of the Lisbonization of the cohesion policy, the idea seems to have been to avoid a conflict between market optimists and market pessimists by conceptualizing the objectives of cohesion policy in a way that is compatible with markets.

In response to the new EU aims in 2007–13 Germany has, as a first step, defined relatively vague or general strategic goals (the six strategies mentioned above), which are defined in the spirit of the Lisbon process but have no clear causal relationship to regional development policy. Germany will receive €26.3 billion (2006 prices) in cohesion policy support in 2007–13, of which €15.1 billion goes to the East German Convergence regions, and €991 million to the West German NUTS 2 region of Lüneburg (Büning, 2007, p. 31); €9.3 billion is available for regions which qualify for funding under the RCE objective. In accordance with the new spending rules for cohesion policy, 81 per cent of structural funds money spent on the Convergence objective in Germany will be earmarked for Lisbon-defined priorities, whereas 71 per cent of RCE funding will be used for this purpose.

The German government proposed, and the Commission eventually approved, a total of 36 OPs for 2007–13, including 34 Regional OPs – 12 funded under the Convergence objective, and 22 under the RCE objective. The OPs and their financial allocations are listed in Table 4.3 below.

One can see a bit clearer what cohesion policy now means when one takes a closer look at the OPs of the federal government and the *Länder*. Here, more concrete cohesion policy objectives are defined. For example, the federal government's OP for the ESF identifies output indicators, with the help of which the effects of programmes can be measured while they

Table 4.3 Financial allocations for German OPs, 2007–13

Operational programme	%	EU contribution (in €)
Convergence objective		
OP ESF federal government	8.24	1,325,569,051
OP Traffic federal government	9.57	1,520,319,639
Regional Operational Programmes (ROPs) – 12	82.30	13,233,306,635
ROP ESF Brandenburg	4.69	620,249,615
ROP ERDF Brandenburg	11.33	1,498,732,588
ROP ESF Mecklenburg-West Pomerania	3.15	417,473,463
ROP ERDF Mecklenburg-West Pomerania	9.46	1,252,420,390
ROP ERDF Saxony	23.36	3,091,139,706
ROP ESF Saxony	6.59	871,859,914
ROP ERDF Saxony-Anhalt	14.60	1,931,792,253
ROP ESF Saxony-Anhalt	4.87	643,930,752
ROP ERDF Thuringia	11.17	1,477,687,909
ROP ESF Thuringia	4.75	629,009,103
ROP ERDF Lower Saxony	4.45	589,000,000
ROP ESF Lower Saxony	1.59	210,010,942
Regional competitivness and employment objective		
OP ESF federal government	22.98	2,162,219,289
Regional Operational Programmes (ROPs) – 22	77.02	7,247,201,676
ROP ERDF Baden-Württemberg	1.98	143,400,068
ROP ESF Baden-Württemberg	3.67	265,998,586
ROP ERDF Bavaria	7.95	575,934,188
ROP ESF Bavaria	4.28	310,059,703
ROP ERDF Berlin	12.08	875,589,810
ROP ESF Berlin	4.64	335,976,031
ROP ERDF Bremen	1.96	142,006,631
ROP ESF Bremen	1.23	89,054,742
ROP ERDF Hamburg	0.49	35,268,791
ROP ESF Hamburg	1.26	91,152,890
ROP ERDF Hesse	3.64	263,454,159
ROP ESF Hesse	2.58	186,735,204
ROP ERDF Lower Saxony	8.81	638,769,613
ROP ESF Lower Saxony	3.27	237,090,765
ROP ERDF Northrhine-Westphalia	17.71	1,283,430,816
ROP ESF Northrhine-Westphalia	9.44	683,996,369

Continued

Table 4.3   Continued

ROP ERDF Rhineland-Palatinate	3.00	217,613,760
ROP ESF Rhineland-Palatinate	1.57	113,766,267
ROP ERDF Saarland	2.73	197,512,437
ROP ESF Saarland	1.19	86,490,338
ROP ERDF Schleswig-Holstein	5.16	373,888,769
ROP ESF Schleswig-Holstein	1.38	100,011,739
Total		25,488,616,290

Source: Data based on Operational Programmes 2007–13.

are implemented and *ex post*. For the goal 'Better opportunities for job seekers and for those employees threatened by unemployment', which is part of the strategy to increase the flexibility of companies and the labour force, the following indicator of success is used: An increase in the percentage of employees in training courses from 37 to 40 per cent. A further indicator is that 15,000 employees should participate. To measure success with regard to the goal 'Opening access to and sustainability of start-ups and entrepreneurship', the indicator used is the number of those supported by cohesion spending who are still in business after 12 months. At the moment the share is 70 per cent, which should increase to 75 per cent; in numbers this means 80,000 new start-ups (Bundesministerium für Arbeit und Soziales, 2007, p. 195).

The success of EU cohesion policy is measured in a similar way on the *Land* level. In the OP for Baden-Württemberg we find the strategic aim of 'better qualification of the skilled labour force and of those with insufficient education'. This is a programme which addresses the needs of those who went through vocational training, which means in Germany a combination of education in schools and on-the-job training. A second group which this programme targets are women and older employees, groups which are underrepresented when it comes to training those already in jobs. In addition, 200,000 employees of SMEs are in the same situation. The aim, according to the OP, is to mobilize 20,000 employees for additional training courses, of which one-quarter to two-thirds have the backgrounds mentioned. For these programmes, B-W earmarked €15 million in ESF funding for 2007–13 (Ministerium für Arbeit und Soziales Baden-Württemberg, 2007, p. 69).

Mecklenburg-West Pomerania has the aim of improving the access of its unemployed to the job market. Success is measured here by the share of co-funded start-ups which still exist after three years. The aim is to increase the current share of 60–70 per cent to 70 per cent. With regard to training programmes and micro-credits for small businesses, the goal is to enroll 4,000 participants (Ministerium für Wirtschaft, Arbeit und Soziales Mecklenburg-Vorpommern, 2007, p. 96).

Such concrete aims with clear indicators are an innovation of the 2007–13 programming period. In 2000–06, evaluation concentrated on policy areas which were relatively open with regard to their contents. There was no obligation to produce clearly measurable results in such a strict way. The new style of targeting in the 2007–13 OPs is the result of pressure from the Commission. OPs are now much clearer about who should be addressed by certain programmes and how to measure success; without this kind of clarity, the Commission would not approve them.

However, it is still up to the *Länder* or the federal government to choose the strategy by which they address the targeted audience or customers of cohesion policy and seek to achieve measurable success. The change of philosophy with regard to the accountability of the *Länder* and the federal government, which have to fulfil their obligations entered into with the Commission, has had at least two consequences: (1) both the federal government and the *Länder* have had to be very clear, and also very careful, when selecting the segment of society they target for support; and (2) evaluation has been facilitated by the use of quantitative indicators, with the disadvantage that a number of positive effects cannot be measured or cannot be measured adequately in this way.

Another aspect of the previous programming period was the greater range of specific targets compared to 2007–13. Most important was the development of infrastructure, to which every *Land* with the exception of small Schleswig-Holstein and the city-states of Bremen and Hamburg gave priority. Most of the *Länder* also supported the competitiveness of their SMEs as well as environmental protection policies. Not surprisingly, the East German *Länder* favoured labour market policies. Other targets were improvements in research and technology, tourism and industrial restructuring.

Conclusion

Cohesion policy in Germany is special in two ways: First, it has to take into account the federal constitution of the country, which means the competences of the *Länder* in regional policymaking; and second, Germany is a country which is economically divided. Though it would be too superficial to reduce the contrast between poorer and richer regions to the East-West divide, the latter is still very visible. EU cohesion policy has in general empowered the *Länder vis-à-vis* the federal government, although all levels of government in Germany have to accept that when it comes to the implementation of cohesion policy the Commission is in the driver's seat.

Cohesion policy is not a political or partisan issue in Germany. For the German public the making of regional policy is something that goes on behind the scenes. The policymaking process is dominated by networks of *Land* and federal civil servants, most of whom have the same background, a training in law. This facilitates intergovernmental compromise and the coordination of multilevel politics in Germany's federal system, but it does not improve the transparency of decision-making and democratic accountability, for example in the debates of the *Land* parliaments.

Reduced levels of funding in 2007–13 and the Lisbonization of cohesion policy have not changed the consensus-building mechanisms and policy routines in Germany. It certainly helped that the impact of the statistical effect was lessened, especially in East Germany, by the introduction of phasing-out periods for cohesion funding. Both the new efficiency philosophy and the use of indicators that increase formal accountability in cohesion policy are a challenge to the German bureaucrat, who is not used to thinking in economic categories. As always, the big question remains whether the rhetoric of such strategic ideas as Lisbonization will really lead to new thinking in cohesion policy. And even if this is the case for Germany, two more general questions remain: (1) Is there a chance to regain room-for-manoeuvre from the Commission to allow German governments to better address regional problems, with regard to both concepts for regional development and the allocation of funds? And (2), can Germany, as a net contributor to the EU budget, have the impression that cohesion policy serves its ends and is more than a financial equalization mechanism kept in place by the bargaining skills of national governments?

Note

1. The interviews were conducted in the Baden-Württemberg Economics Ministry on 4 May 2007.

5
Spain

Francesc Morata and Lucia Alexandra Popartan

Introduction

If we were to choose one country as the protagonist of EU cohesion policy, there would be no better candidate than Spain; not only did Spain determine the introduction of this policy and influence its successive reforms, but it is also the country that has most benefited from cohesion policy spending throughout the years.[1] In 2006 Spain celebrated its twentieth anniversary as an EU member state. These 20 years have been a period of profound political transformation and of structural and social maturation, but most of all it has been a period of spectacular economic growth. While in 1986 Spain was one of the poorest EU countries, 20 years later it is among the most well-off member states.[2] This positive evolution cannot be explained without looking at the significant financial input from EU cohesion policy.

However, the sheer numbers expressing Spain's economic success cannot fully encompass the diversity of changes attributed to interaction with the European sphere. Spain is an interesting subject of research for scholars of Europeanization or multilevel governance, and indeed it has been extensively studied, mainly with regards to the process of regional devolution that is deeply interlinked with the implementation of the cohesion policy (see Morata, 1995; Morata and Muñoz, 1996; Bache and Jones, 2000; Pasquier, 2005).

During budget negotiations for the 2007–13 programming period, it seemed very likely (and fair, some argued) that Spain's privileged relationship with EU cohesion policy should end. The new member states were countries with great economic needs and structural disparities; they required considerable financial assistance, which consequently should have been withdrawn from wealthier previous beneficiaries

(Navarro and Garrido, 2004). Yet, the Spanish negotiators managed once again to turn things in their favour, persuading European authorities to allow for a slow reduction of funds rather than an abrupt termination of support. Thus, Spanish regions will continue to qualify for EU structural assistance, although the amount will gradually but significantly decrease. Furthermore, the responsible authorities will have to adapt to the reformed guidelines of cohesion policy, which integrate an important reorientation towards the Lisbon Agenda priorities.

This chapter looks at how Spain has coped with these transformations, taking into account previous developments in the implementation and management of EU cohesion policy. We argue that Spain has witnessed a differential mobilization of the regions, and we look at how the Spanish regions have developed mechanisms for greater participation in EU decisionmaking, especially in areas that affect them such as cohesion policy. With the loss of EU funding, the introduction of more cooperative modes of governance – encouraged by the partnership principle and the reorientation of cohesion policy towards the Lisbon objectives – becomes essential for Spain. The regions will be confronted with the challenge of being able to use their experience to achieve a creative and more efficient use of resources.

We begin by looking at the domestic institutional arrangements that have influenced the implementation of cohesion policy, as the regionalized nature of Spain's governance system was expected to favour the participation of regional actors in the decision-making process. We then focus on how EU membership has encouraged regional mobilization in Spain, as regional authorities have attempted to build networks of cooperation and alternative channels of participation in EU policymaking, thereby fostering the emergence of innovative modes of governance. Subsequently, we analyze cohesion policy implementation in the current (2007–13) programming period, examining the strategies adopted by Spanish authorities in response to the 'Lisbonization' of cohesion policy.

Regionalization and cohesion policy in Spain: domestic variables

A brief history

Spain's entry into the EU in 1986 took place in the midst of a process of decentralization and democratization that began with the end of the Franco dictatorship in 1975. From an authoritarian, centralized system that was internationally semi-isolated, Spain became a country of political and territorial pluralism with ever-stronger links to Europe (Morata, 1995).

In 1978, under pressure from the Basque Country and Catalonia, the Spanish constitution introduced important territorial reforms, thereby beginning a process of regional devolution. The constitution's particular mix of flexibility and ambiguity on this issue reflected a political compromise; rather than establishing a precise delimitation of competencies for the new regions, it was decided to let each region take as much autonomy as it could manage within the limits of the constitution. The purpose was to neutralize Catalan and Basque specificities through a strategy popularly known as *'café para todos'* (coffee for everyone). Each of the new Autonomous Communities (ACs) would negotiate with the central government its own form of autonomy and the distribution of competencies between the state and region. Regional competencies can include such policy areas as regional development, industry, communications and transport, environment, banking, public works, agriculture and fisheries, tourism, housing and urban planning. If the region aspires to a higher degree of autonomy, it can also acquire competencies in education, health, local administration and police. The state and regions share competencies in some areas, such as culture and research policy. Besides its traditional areas of control, such as foreign policy, defence and monetary policy, the state also establishes basic legislation and principles.

The financial autonomy of the regions is limited by the fact that the state maintains control over revenues and organizes the process of redistributing funds between the regions. Regional funding comes from shared and assigned taxes, limited regional taxes and an equalization fund, with the state controlling the main sources of revenue.

Within this framework, and in order to maintain a territorial equilibrium challenged by the ambitions of the three 'historical nationalities' – the Basque Country, Catalonia and Galicia – the other 14 ACs, which had obtained an autonomy they never really asked for, were compelled by the very dynamics of the regionalization process to keep the level of negotiations high. From this multi-speed negotiation process, an asymmetrical type of regionalization resulted. Catalonia, Galicia and the Basque Country were recognized as nationalities, but shortly thereafter Andalucía obtained the same status as a region with full competencies. Later, Valencia, Navarre and the Canary Islands also joined this club. However, the bargaining was harsh, and not all ACs managed to obtain the same advantages. For example, in terms of financial competencies, Navarre and the Basque Country were given 'brandy with the coffee', in the sense that they enjoy quasi-sovereign fiscal and financial competencies. All-in-all, the result was a mixed regional map, consisting of ACs with a clear cultural identity (Catalonia, Galicia, the Basque Country), historical regions (Andalucía, Aragon, Asturias, Canary Islands, Valencia, Navarra, Extremadura, the Balearic Islands), improvised macro-regions (Castilla y León, Castilla-La Mancha), and regionalized provinces (Cantabria, La Rioja, Madrid, Murcia) (see Map 5.1).

In this framework, the integration of regional concerns in the governmental decision-making process was not an easy task. The absence of a genuine chamber for regional representation made institutional

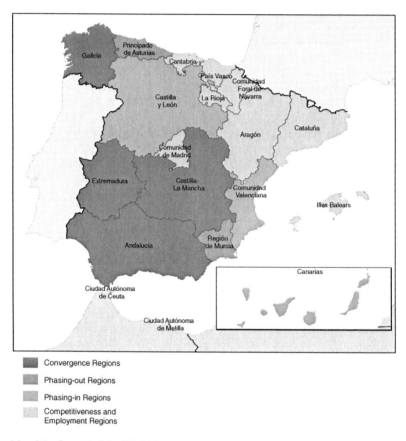

Map 5.1   Spanish ACs (NUTS 2 regions) and cohesion policy eligibility, 2007–13
Source: European Commission, DG Regional Policy.

cohesion more difficult: the Spanish Senate is elected on a majority basis at the provincial level, where national parties control the electoral sphere. Therefore, the representation of regional parliaments is generally low (Morata, 1995).

Cooperation between the different governmental levels is traditionally insured through bilateral negotiations and, since 1983, by the Sectoral Conferences. The latter are thematic forums of cooperation between the state and regional levels, and they are generally used by the regions in order to pressure the central government on specific issues, but the final say belongs to the state. In 1992, a special Sectoral Conference was created in order to deal with communitarian issues – CARCE (*Conferencia para Asuntos Relacionados con las Comunidades Autonómas*). In general, it was expected to be a framework of horizontal coordination between the Sectoral Conferences, a channel of information for the regions and a discussion forum on general or specific aspects of European integration (Pérez Tremps, 1999).

The need for horizontal (region-region) cooperation became acute after 2004, when the new Socialist government allowed the ACs to send a representative to certain EU Council Working Groups and the Committee of Permanent Representatives (COREPER). This forced the regions to further institutionalize their cooperation in order to aggregate the positions of all 17 ACs and to share relevant information obtained at the EU level. This step represented a qualitative leap forward, influenced undoubtedly by the outcome of the March 2004 national elections,[3] but also by the unprecedented cooperative approach to state-region relations adopted by the new government.

The Spanish regions in Europe

The regionalized institutional framework determined a twofold model of response by the Spanish regions to Europe, since EU accession was not perceived in the same way by all ACs. For Catalonia, the Basque Country and to a lesser extent Galicia, accession created the opportunity to affirm their national identities in the European arena, eluding as much as possible the central government. For other regions, it represented more a vehicle of modernization (Morata, 2004a).

The results, although differing in scale and intensity, were similar: enhanced administrative mobilization and institutional innovation. The ACs increased and diversified their presence in the European arena. Either through the intermediation of the Spanish government, in the framework of European regional organizations, through direct representation in Brussels, or simply by formalizing their cooperation with regions in other member states, the ACs managed to perform as independent actors, challenging the central government's exclusivity in external relations. Furthermore, in terms of administrative mobilization and institutional innovation, the profile of projects financed through EU funds confirms the creation of various instruments of cooperation between public and private actors, and between different levels of government, although progress in this area remains incomplete, as discussed below.

Although now a general practice of all ACs, the mechanism of regional representation in Brussels originated in the efforts of the 'historical nationalities', especially Catalonia and the Basque Country, to develop a direct bilateral relationship with EU institutions. The status of these regional representations has undergone a growing transformation, as they have passed from being mere administrative forums to gradually acquiring a political functionality; they have also gained in political importance, occasionally pressuring the decision-making process in a certain direction.

The Spanish regions are also among the most dynamic actors in European interregional organizations, such as the Committee of the Regions (COR), the Assembly of the European Regions, and the Council of Local and Regional Authorities of Europe.

Cross-border cooperation is another instrument used by the Spanish regions to achieve their interests in the European arena. The ACs are particularly active in this regard, and although regions with a strong identity created the first examples, the others followed rapidly in their steps. The first group, especially Catalonia and the Basque Country, viewed the possibility of strengthening their connections with foreign regions as a strategy to 'circumvent the state' (Börzel, 2002), and to build a channel of cooperation that would reinforce their statehood. The second group of ACs, with a weaker regional identity, nevertheless seized the opportunity to formalize and strengthen their relations with regions that were traditionally within their network of cultural and economic activity.

Thus, the Spanish regions joined with counterparts in neighbouring countries to form so-called Euroregions; these have a variety of formats and purposes, either aiming at solving specific local problems or pursuing more general cooperation goals.[4] Although the opportunities offered by EU cohesion policy are not the only thing encouraging cross-border cooperation (proximity, existing contacts and similar cultural identities are also essential in this sense) they do represent a strong factor moulding the development strategies these regions undertake.

Although European integration has offered a favourable context for establishing networks of interregional cooperation, the degree to which regions actually take advantage of it depends on their capacity to mobilize their internal resources, in terms of economy, political capacity and the strengthening of civil society (Radaelli, 2004).

Structural funds and regional mobilization: the partnership principle

Evolution of the principle across programming periods

The partnership principle represents one of the main elements of the governance model promoted by the European Commission. It seeks to create the conditions for close cooperation between different public, economic and social actors via policy networks. Partnership pursues the double objective of vertical (multilevel) and horizontal (public-private) cooperation in the elaboration and implementation of policies. The network connections among actors aim to bring together the ideas, interests, competencies and financial resources which are necessary for defining common problems and seeking their effective solution (Kohler-Koch, 2004). Spain, as one of the main beneficiaries of the structural funds, is expected to provide a comprehensive perspective on the effects of this policy, not only in economic terms but also regarding the transformations undertaken by regional administrations in order to comply with the principles and requirements of cohesion policy. The question is whether cohesion policy has indeed produced the expected modernization of administrative structures and introduction of new forms of governance, allowing it to become more of an arena of interest-aggregation and representation.

In practice the partnership principle required time and effort to be internalized, as centralized Spanish administrative structures were rigid and stubbornly resisted change. In the initial period following the 1988 cohesion policy reform (1989–93), the programming process for the structural funds was rather technocratic and centralized. Regional authorities were more involved in the project implementation phase. The main actor was the central government, which controlled the preparation of regional programmes through its Public Investment Committee, an informal organism under the State Secretary of Economic Planning. Regional authorities were invited to participate in the formulation of regional programmes but not in the final decisionmaking. The procedure adopted by the government for presenting the plans hindered the inclusion of regional input in structural interventions, as it retained a broad margin of manoeuvre in distributing and managing the funds (Morata, ed., 2004).[5] Moreover, the involvement of local representatives and social actors was almost nonexistent.

After 1994 the input of the regions improved slightly. The ACs participated in setting priorities, and enhanced coordination between central government and regional authorities was reflected in the increased flow of information between the two levels, especially on the distribution of multi-regional financing. At the same time, direct contacts between regional authorities and the Commission multiplied, concretized in a regular exchange of information (Bache and Jones, 2000).

For the 1994–99 programming period, a study conducted on the implementation of regional policies in Extremadura and Catalonia revealed that private actors were weakly organized; there were feeble synergies between civil society and public administration, a lack of information and insufficient diffusion of the projects. The main force in policy implementation was the regional bureaucratic techno-structure, which acted on its own amidst weakly-structured social networks with limited resources. By contrast, political representatives tended to be rather ignorant of the content of EU programmes. Nevertheless, cohesion policy did create incentives for the mobilization of public and private actors, especially in Objective 1 regions but not only there, and although their involvement is not yet firmly established or formalized the learning process is undeniable. Although established bureaucratic routines and traditional relations between the public and private sectors are not so easily changed, the mobilization of interests did take place even if outside the existing administrative framework (Barua and Morata, 2001).

For 2000–06 the empirical evidence is still scarce, yet existing reports conducted by the Commission on the implementation of the partnership principle in Spain indicate a trend towards more integrated networks of partnership (DG Regio, 2005). This evolution was facilitated by territorial restructuring conducted throughout the previous programming periods and the proliferation of regional networks of cooperation, within and outside state borders.

The Leader and Equal initiatives were among the most successful instruments in promoting the creation of partnership networks involving both public and private actors. The creation of new territorial units for planning and organization (*comarcas*) fostered the emergence of new forms of partnership between local actors and institutions, 'creating new spaces for local development' (Pasquier, 2005). The degree of institutionalization of partnership varies from one region to another, yet the common denominator remains the effort of regional elites to use these new structures, established as a base for Leader programme selection, as channels of communication with the EU level and as instruments for modernizing governance.

We have illustrated how, throughout the different programming periods the involvement of regional actors in cohesion policy implementation has grown, mostly due to the pressures they have exerted at the domestic and EU levels. This coincides with the multiplication of channels of influence developed by the ACs, both within and outside of the state.

Cohesion policy in Spain after the 2004 enlargement

Negotiating the 2007–13 financial perspective: the last victory

Negotiations for the 2007–13 financial perspective took place in a tense climate, as the EU was facing tremendous challenges: a constitutional deadlock, a general economic decline which ensured that the main budgetary contributors were in a less generous mood, and an unprecedented enlargement that added much poorer member states with high expectations of economic assistance from their better-off European partners. The result was harsh bargaining over how a limited EU budget was to be allocated.

After having experienced a long period of solid economic growth, and after having benefited more than any other member state from EU structural assistance, Spain entered the negotiations in a weak position, with the strong possibility of abruptly becoming a net contributor. The predicted loss of EU payments would result in an increased contribution to the budget which, considering the country's economic growth rate, was set to more than double, from €9.8 million in 2005 to €15.9 million in 2013 (Torreblanca, 2005a). Causing additional concern was the Commission's proposal to deny Spain transitional support from the Cohesion Fund, omitting completely any consideration of the statistical effect of enlargement in this case. In response, the Spanish government argued that an abrupt loss of EU funding combined with an increased national budgetary contribution created a situation that was both economically and politically unsustainable for Spain.

Thus, in the financial perspective negotiations Madrid focused on the so-called Spanish problem. First, it emphasized that Spain was one of the main contributors to the 'British Cheque', in fact the third largest after France and Italy, with a 13.6 per cent share of the total amount. It also claimed that Spain was among the member states destined to bear the heaviest financial burden of enlargement. Since the Spanish economy had grown twice as fast as the EU average in recent years, the loss of funding should have been a sign that Spain had 'done its homework' and reached a level where EU assistance was no longer needed. However, some of the Spanish regions had not actually achieved real convergence with the EU15, a fact obscured by the statistical effect of enlargement. Moreover, the statistical effect also applied to the country as a whole: if Spain's per capita GDP was 87 per cent of the EU15 average, in the context of EU25 or 27 it exceeded 90 per cent. While the Commission proposed offering affected regions 'phasing out' transition funding, Spain argued that such measures should also extend to the national level, resulting in the prolongation of its Cohesion Fund eligibility. Thus, after 2007 Spain would be able to continue with infrastructure and environmental projects financed by the Cohesion Fund which otherwise would be endangered. A similar argument was employed to sustain funding for 'phasing in' regions (achieving natural convergence with the EU15 in 2006), especially considering that half of the EU population in this situation was located in Spain.

Another aspect of the 'Spanish problem', not directly related to cohesion policy, was put forward by the Spanish government: the asymmetrical distribution of the macroeconomic benefits of enlargement. The main beneficiaries of the increased volume of commerce and investments triggered by enlargement were Germany, Austria and Italy. Spain, by contrast, would suffer the effects of the predicted delocalization of firms towards the new member states; Spanish products would also probably face enhanced competition in the European market due to the medium-level technology they incorporated (see Navarro and Viguerra, 2005; Torreblanca and Sorroza, 2006).

Consequently, in the negotiations Spain defended three key concepts: budgetary sufficiency, arguing against the idea of lowering the threshold of national contributions to the EU budget to 1 per cent of GDP; equity in the distribution of enlargement costs; and, the gradual reduction of funding for all regions, maintaining at the same time the special status enjoyed by the Canary Islands as an ultraperipheral area.

The agreement reached in December 2005 was indeed a victory for Spain. Despite a 42 per cent reduction in EU assistance, all Spanish regions would qualify for structural and Cohesion Fund support until 2013, even though they will have surpassed convergence levels by the end of the programming period. Moreover, a special Technology Fund was to be created especially for Spain in the framework of the European Regional Development Fund (ERDF), a measure without precedent in EU history (Torreblanca, 2005b). All-in-all, the outcome of the negotiations was satisfactory for Spain, as it remained a net recipient of EU funds with a positive balance for 2007–13 (see Table 5.1).

The domestic debate on the financial perspective

Unlike other member states, in Spain EU cohesion policy has become a matter of contention between the main political parties – the Spanish Socialist Party (PSOE) and the People's Party (PP). Already in 1992 the right-wing opposition leader, José Aznar, strongly criticized Socialist Prime Minister Felipe González when the latter threatened to block the 1994–99 financial agreement if Spain did not receive more funding, accusing him of behaving like an 'importunate beggar'.

Again, in December 2005 the agreement on the 2007–13 financial perspective negotiated by Socialist Prime Minister Zapatero was criticized by Rajoy, the new PP leader, as being 'a clamorous failure' and an 'unfair mockery' because Spain was unable to preserve its privileged financial position within the EU. Rajoy was immediately backed by the regional leaders of his party. The right-wing leader also insinuated an obscure deal linking the EU financial issue and the conflict between Spain and the Commission over the 'Endesa affair'. In fact, the Commission decided to open a procedure against Spain for giving the National Energy Agency competencies it should not normally have

Table 5.1 EU financial allocations for Spain, 2000–06 and 2007–13

Allocations 2000–06 (€ mn, 2004 prices)		Allocations 2007–13 (€ mn, 2004 prices)	
Cohesion fund	12,357	Cohesion fund	3,242
Objective 1	34,796	Convergence	18,680
		Statistical phasing-out	1,431
Phasing-out	325	Phasing-in	4,483
Objective 2	2,929	Regional competitiveness and employment	3,125
Objective 3	2,363		
Community Initiatives	1,904	European territorial cooperation	496
Total	54,671	Total	31,457

Source: European Commission (2006e).

had in the possible takeover of an electricity company, Endesa, by Gas Natural, a Catalan company, when the German company EON was also bidding for control. The government stated it had absolutely no intention of sending to Brussels requested information about a decree it had passed that effectively banned the German company from bidding for Endesa. The falseness of the PP's claims was later demonstrated when in March 2007 the Commission adopted a 'reasoned opinion' requesting the Spanish government 'to withdraw the illegal conditions it had imposed'.

The implementation of cohesion policy and the new programming period

In Spain the programming, implementation and monitoring of cohesion policy is coordinated by the central government, which cooperates with regional authorities and other actors in different phases of the process. However, the involvement of regional authorities in the administration of EU support is the result of a long and tedious process. It was in the 1989–93 programming period that the regional governments began to have a say in the programming of Regional Development Plans (RDPs), which were to be submitted through Community Support Frameworks (CSFs). The fact that the central government decided to submit only three CSFs, based on strategic rather that territorial criteria (one for each Objective), left the regions with little room for manoeuvre in terms of the allocation of resources. In spite of the creation of a monitoring committee involving regional representatives, the administration of funds was largely controlled by the central authorities. From 1993 onwards, the weight of the regions in the implementation process increased. The coordination mechanisms improved, while EU funding was transferred directly to regional and local authorities. Moreover, the Cohesion Fund was regionalized, allowing regions to participate in the administration of EU assistance in areas that were under their competence, such as environmental policy (Closa and Heywood, 2005).

The percentage of funds managed directly by the regional authorities is also an important measure of regional involvement in the implementation of cohesion policy in Spain. The degree of participation varies across regions and programming periods, although it has never been so great as to challenge central government supremacy in this respect. In the 2000–06 programming period, the ACs controlled 37.6 per cent of total funding. In 2007–13, this percentage has not changed much, with the regions managing 40 per cent of funds, and the central government the rest (Ministerio de Economia, 2007).

For 2000–06, Spain presented one CSF for each of the three Objectives. For Objective 1, the CSF was implemented through 12 Regional Operational Programmes (ROPs) and 10 Sectoral Operational Programmes (SOPs); for Objective 2, each region prepared a Single Programming Document (SPD) (see Table 5.2 for the list of Objective 1 and 2 regions). The responsible authority for managing the CSFs for Objectives 1 and 2 was the Ministry of Economy (Ministerio de Economía y Hacienda), through a specialized department (Dirección General de Fondos Comunitarios y Financiación Teritorial). Moreover, each fund was administered under the coordination of a Managing Authority (MA) at the national level: ERDF, Ministry of Economy; European Social Fund (ESF), Ministry of Labour; European Agricultural Guidance and Guarantee Fund (EAGGF-G) and Financial Instrument for Fisheries Guidance (FIFG), Ministry of Agriculture, Fisheries and Alimentation. The coordination between different levels of administration was ensured by monitoring committees, one for each Operational Programme (OP), composed of representatives of the central, regional and local levels together with relevant social and economic actors.

To look deeper into cohesion policy implementation in this programming period, we start from the assumption that a key indicator in assessing the success of this process is the degree of absorption of EU funds. The data provided by the evaluations performed of the various OPs (Table 5.2) show a variation of this indicator across the Spanish regions. This can be explained by a multitude of factors, economic and political, specific to each AC and the projects implemented. However, if we focus exclusively on the administrative mechanisms in charge of implementing the structural funds, we find relevant aspects that help us understand the conditions that might favour or undermine effective implementation. The participation of different levels of government in administering the structural funds, as well as the functioning of specific mechanisms of management, monitoring and especially coordination, are fundamental factors in this regard. As mentioned before, the central government is the main axis of the system of programming and management, performing also as a chain of transmission between regional authorities and the Commission. However, based on the principle of territorial decentralization, the ACs are also involved in the entire process as 'co-responsible' entities, insuring the compatibility of actions falling within their constitutional competencies with other communitarian policies, and in general controlling implementation in these sectors.

In 2000–06, with the introduction of integrated Operational Programmes, the coordination between different authorities became

Table 5.2   Structural funds absorption level, by NUTS 2 region

Objective 1	Average absorption level (CSF evaluation)	Objective 2	Average absorption level (SPD evaluation)
Cantabria	75 %	Aragon	82 %
Castilla y León	75 %	Balearic Islands	70 %
Asturias	75 %	Catalonia	81 %
Castilla la Mancha	75 %	La Rioja	95 %
Canarias	62 %	Madrid	75 %
Galicia	62 %	Basque country	95 %
Andalucía	62 %	Navarra	95 %
Ceuta	62 %		
Comunidad Valenciana	62 %		
Melilla	62 %		
Murcia	52 %		
Extremadura	52 %		

Source: The authors, original data from Intermediate Evaluation documents 2000–06.

more complicated given that each OP was financed through different funds. Therefore, not only did each fund have a distinct MA at the national level, a government ministry in this case, but also at the regional level, where there was a specific council in charge of each fund and each line of intervention. Difficulties arose in the process of coordinating specific interventions with the more general, integrated vision of the OP. Moreover, horizontal coordination at the regional level between sectoral managers functioned better than vertical coordination between the central government and the ACs. The regions constantly had to ask the central government for more information regarding projects managed by ministries in their OP, in order improve their overall strategy of expenditure.

The administrative workload also increased compared to 1994–99, again due to the introduction of integrated OPs, and although the administrative staff was augmented this was not always enough. Thus, some regions performed better than others: for Objective 1, Asturias and Castilla y León had larger and better-trained administrative teams than Comunidad Valenciana or Extremadura, the latter proving to be less efficient in absorbing the funds.

All-in-all, the general trend in the administrative aspect of structural funds implementation in Spain is significant improvement from one programming period to another. In 2000–06, in spite of the increased complexity of the process, the administrative system was able to adapt and perform well, building upon accumulated experience, especially in regards to horizontal cooperation at both the regional and national levels (Ministerio de Economia y Hacienda, 2002, 2007).

For the 2007–13 programming period, however, the rules of the game have changed significantly. The CSF and SPD no longer exist; instead a new document exists to guide strategic planning: the Community Strategic Guidelines (CSG), elaborated by the Commission and upon which each country develops a National Strategic Reference Framework (NSRF). The latter is implemented through OPs, with each region preparing one programme for each fund, including the Cohesion Fund (see Table 5.3). Both the ERDF and ESF have also assigned funds to sectoral priorities that are implemented through SOPs. Within the European Territorial Cooperation (ETC) objective there are also several OPs financed through the ERDF.[6]

Implementation of the OPs is coordinated by the central authorities in charge of each Fund. For ERDF, the MA is the Ministry of Economy. For ESF, the responsible authority is the Ministry of Labour and Social Affairs. The participation of the regional governments consists in drafting the documents and implementing the funds assigned to them, according their competencies. Several forums and committees insure coordination between different levels, summoning representatives from national and regional level, plus other involved actors such as local authorities, chambers of commerce and municipal federations.[7]

In 2007–13 the government has made efforts to include a wider range of social partners. Especially in designing the OPs, regional authorities report having participated in various consultations with the central government and close collaboration with state authorities in elaborating programmes.

The loss of funds: different perspectives

In spite of the relatively 'happy ending' of the financial perspective negotiations for 2007–13, the fact is that Spain has lost a good deal of the financial support it is accustomed to receiving from the EU. The effects of this loss can only be estimated at this point in time. In doing so, we need to make reference to the importance of EU support for Spanish economic growth in the past and predict a logical slowing of growth, which will most likely be counterbalanced by macroeconomic measures adopted by national, regional and local authorities.

Table 5.3   OPs in Spain and financial allocations, 2007–13

Convergence regions

	ERDF	
Regional OPs		
Convergence		**Allocated amount** (in €)
Andalucía		6,843,929,341
Castilla la Mancha		1,439,393,894
Extremadura		1,580,187,909
Galicia		2,191,544,341
Phasing-out		
Asturias		395,215,192
Murcia		523,859,034
Ceuta		45,272,610
Melilla		43.788.494
SOP research, development and innovation (I+D+I)		1,686,342,363
SOP knowledge-based economy		1,238,138,404
SOP technical assistance		44,557,905
	ESF	
Regional OP		
Convergence		
Andalucía		1,155,756,489
Castilla la Mancha		180,400,219
Extremadura		250,085,797
Galicia		358,501,812
Phasing-out		
Asturias		100,787,496
Murcia		75,743,963
Ceuta		10,249,664
Melilla		7,193,432
SOP adaptability and employment		2,878,889,345
SOP fight against discrimination		208,068,774
SOP technical assistance		22,129,144
Total convergence		26,180,199,964
ERDF		17,389,180,821
ESF		5,247,806,135
Cohesion fund		3,543,213,008
Competitiveness and employment regions		
	ERDF	
Regional OP		
Phasing-in		
Castilla y León		818,194,437
Comunidad Valenciana		1,326,340,547
Canarias*		529,605,088

Continued

Table 5.3 Continued

Regional competitiveness and employment	
Cantabria	89,030,873
Aragon	163,101,304
Baleares	107,196,565
Catalonia	679,047,228
Madrid	336,953,127
Navarra	47,108,905
Basque Country	240,582,157
La Rioja	32,622,095
SOP I+D+I	562,114,121
SOP knowledge economy	227,054,517
SOP technical assistance	19,340,693
ESF	
Phasing-in	
Castilla y León	125,276,907
Comunidad Valenciana	198,374,973
Canarias	117,291,876
Regional competitiveness and employment	12,684,118
Cantabria	
Aragon	74,523,363
Baleares	38,732,058
Catalonia	284,711,549
Madrid	256,903,019
Navarra	19,214,969
Basque Country	61,104,788
La Rioja	13,933,419
SOP adaptability and employment	1.422.525.230
SOP fight against discrimination	172,810,109
SOP technical assistance	11,436,309
Total competitiveness and employment	8,477,534,017
ERDF	5,668,011,330
ESF	2,809,522,687

Note: *Canarias receives an additional allocation for peripheral regions of €488,692,672.

Source: Ministerio de Economía y Hacienda, modified by authors.

It is impossible to precisely gauge the situation of the Spanish economy today in the absence of EU support. However, there is no doubt that the economic situation of the country would be, to put it bluntly, worse off. For example, it is calculated that the structural funds alone have accounted for 7 per cent of the total growth of Spanish GNP up until 2006. Also, between 1989 and 2006 the structural funds helped boost average per capita income by €638. In terms of employment, the structural funds were responsible for 2.07 per cent of all new jobs created in this period, equivalent to 299,000 persons employed (Sosvilla and Herce, 2004). Considering the significant contribution of cohesion policy to the growth of the Spanish economy, it is not hard to imagine that even a gradual reduction of EU support will have an effect. In a *ceteris paribus* scenario, which does not take into account any possible counter-measures by the Spanish government, the loss of funds would produce negative effects for most macroeconomic indicators. Therefore, if the continuation of 2000–06 allocations would have encouraged an overall economic growth of 3 per cent, in the current situation we may expect 0.29 per cent less. If we look at per capita income, Spain would have reached 95.56 per cent of the EU average if the previous level of support had been maintained, compared with the prediction of 93.56 per cent based on 2007–13 allocations (Sosvilla and Herce, 2004).

These figures, although speculative, provide a general picture of the expected impact on the Spanish economy of reduced EU funding. However, the effects at regional level are not unitary, as some regions have been more efficient in taking advantage of EU assistance than others. As the intermediate evaluations for 2000–06 reveal (Table 5.2), in terms of absorption capacity Objective 2 regions have benefited the most from EU support; Objective 1 regions, by comparison, are less efficient than regions with a better economic situation and less funding when it comes to using EU support.

In evaluating the consequences of reduced funding for Spain, one should take into consideration several important aspects, going beyond the negotiating strategy of the Spanish government which legitimately emphasized the negative effects of an abrupt loss of funds. We must not forget that the balance for 2007–13 will be positive, with Spain continuing be a net recipient even after achieving convergence with the EU average for per capita income. Transition mechanisms will enable regions affected by reduced funding to continue the modern-ization begun in previous programming periods (Torreblanca, 2005b). Moreover, reduced funding does not come in a void, but will build upon an existing social capital: experience in managing EU sup-port, networks of cooperation and so on. Therefore, the concept of funding losses should be nuanced, bearing in mind what Spain has already achieved over the years with the help of the EU assistance. As Torreblanca puts it, to speak of sheer losses would be like '... saying that a person who no longer receives unemployment benefits after finding a job has lost money' (2005b, p. 5).

The strategy of the regions in the face of reduced levels of funding consists of a reorientation towards the Lisbon Agenda priorities. For example, regions qualifying for EU support under objectives with less allocated funding – Regional Competitiveness and Employment (RCE), and ETC – have emphasized the necessity of taking advantage of already-created interregional networks and enhancing the involvement of local actors in EU-funded projects (Generalitat de Catalunya, 2005).

This is a general trend in Spain: a clear turn towards the Lisbon Agenda reflected in the decision of the Zapatero government to turn the Lisbon Strategy into a governmental priority. A stable coalition has provided the Zapatero government with wide space of manoeuvre for dealing with European policy and the budgetary cuts imposed by reduced funding (Torreblanca and Sorroza, 2006). Furthermore, the support of the Spanish people for enlargement, despite its possible negative effects, enhanced the government's legitimacy in dealing with the new financial situation without major restrictions.

The renewed Lisbon agenda and cohesion policy in Spain

Responding to the alarm signal of the Kok report, the European Council agreed in 2005 to 'resuscitate' the Lisbon Agenda, through a new integrated policy approach towards achieving the main strategic goals agreed at the Lisbon and Gothenburg summits regarding sustainable growth and employment. As part of this effort, each member state was required to elaborate a National Reform Programme (NRP), detailing the macroeconomic and institutional measures needed to align domestic economies with the Lisbon Agenda goals. Member states were also encouraged to create the position of 'Mr/Mrs Lisbon', which would give more visibility to the NRP and act as an interlocutor for related matters. Spain was the first member state to take these steps and, generally speaking, it has made consistent efforts to comply with EU guidelines, with good results (Granados, 2006).

In October 2005, Spain presented its first draft of the NRP, which was revised and improved in 2006 following evaluation by the Commission. Based upon a thorough diagnosis of the Spanish economy, the NRP is structured around seven pillars of action: (1) reinforcing macroeconomic and budgetary stability; (2) improving strategic infrastructure and transport and water supply; (3) increasing and enhancing human capital; (4) R&D and innovation; (5) improved competence, better regulation and efficiency of public administration and increased competitiveness; (6) labour market and social dialogue;

and (7) entrepreneurship promotion. In the 2006 NRP, a chapter was inserted indicating the correlation between the Lisbon objectives dealt with in the Plan and structural funds programming in 2007–13 (Oficina Económica de la Presidencia, 2006).

The correspondence between the regional policy objectives of the NSRF and the Lisbon strategic directives of the NRP represents, at least in discursive terms, a clear reorientation of the structural funds towards the Lisbon goals, and Spanish authorities seem sincere in wanting to comply with the new directives. This reorientation is indicated by the fact that, out of the sums managed by the central government, 85 per cent are dedicated to meeting the Lisbon goals, exceeding the targets of 60 per cent (for the Convergence objective) and 72 per cent (for the RCE objective) established by the December 2005 European Council.

It is certainly premature to embark on a detailed evaluation of cohesion policy implementation in the current programming period and its correlation to the Lisbon objectives. As a general conclusion, all regions have stressed the importance of the Lisbon Strategy in their programmes. They have made significant efforts not only to follow EU recommendations by building their programmes around the Lisbon priorities, but it is also remarkable the emphasis they place on the transparency of their actions, clearly outlining those measures that support the goals of improving sustainable growth and better employment promoted by the Lisbon Agenda.

Conclusions

This chapter has examined cohesion policy implementation in Spain, including the 2007–13 programming period. The analysis followed a twofold approach. First, we analyzed the incomplete process of state devolution and empowerment of the regions, offering an overview of the domestic institutional factors that influence the implementation of cohesion policy. Nevertheless, we have seen that these conditions are not static; instead they evolve in concordance with external factors, such as the presence of EU incentives and constraints, thus making the difference between dependent and independent variables more blurred.

Next, we looked at the impact of the cohesion policy in terms of actor mobilization and the creation of partnership networks, followed by a discussion of the reaction of Spanish authorities to the 'Lisbonization' cohesion policy. The opportunity offered by cohesion policy was utilized by all Spanish regions, especially those with a pronounced historical identity, to mobilize their institutional capacities and exert pressure for a greater voice in those policy areas that directly affected them. Consequently, the emergence of new networks of cooperation involving an increased number of public and private actors, both inside and outside the borders of the state, shaped the framework for introducing innovative modes of governance which help ensure a more creative and efficient use of EU funding.

The Lisbonization of cohesion policy is taken seriously by Spanish authorities at all levels, who have endeavoured to redesign programming documents in the spirit of the Lisbon Agenda. Although not all expenditures are reoriented towards the Lisbon priorities, the elaboration of financing followed a principle of transparency, mentioning the proposed investments which contribute to the Lisbon strategy. Moreover, the elaboration of programming documents and the NRP respected, to a greater extent than before, the recommendations of the Commission regarding the consultation of a wider range of actors from both the public and private spheres.

This reorientation is a central preoccupation not only for the central and regional governments in Spain, but also for local and intermediate levels of territorial administration. Municipalities, *'diputaciones'*, and the multitude of associations they comprise have taken action in order to evaluate the current status of adaptation to the Lisbon priorities, and to design strategies for adapting to the new format of EU-financed projects in the future.[8] The importance of local and intermediate administrations in managing strategies for growth, innovation, education and encouraging entrepreneurship is undeniable, due to factors such as proximity, experience, or political and social interest. However, there are weaknesses at this level as well, for example: the relatively low level of involvement of these entities in regional policymaking; a lack of horizontal coordination in managing projects; a lack of information about the new strategies; and the persistence of old, hierarchical modes of governance that limit the capacity to efficiently adapt to new challenges. For 2007–13, these authorities are focusing on several key objectives: a clear new thematic orientation respecting the Lisbon priorities; identifying new indicators for evaluating the impact of projects and the performance of partners; increased efforts to disseminate results and good practices; strengthening existing networks of cooperation (interregional, cross-border, transnational) and creating new ones; greater emphasis on benchmarking and the transfer of information; and educating local administrations to achieve more cooperative modes of governance. In the final analysis, it is assumed that a clear reorientation of cohesion policy towards the Lisbon priorities cannot be attained without a stronger involvement of the local level, which implies a reform of the governance style within this particular sphere.[9]

It is still early for definitive conclusions on the implementation of cohesion policy after 2006 and its implications for governance and achievement of the Lisbon goals. Nevertheless, at this point there are enough signs that the experience accumulated by Spain in this field, manifested in the multitude of collaborative networks created at all levels, combined with the clear reorientation towards the Lisbon Agenda can help Spain to achieve more results with less funding. From 1998 to 2006, most Spanish regions were able to use EU funding to modernize socio-economic infrastructure and services. In coming years, they will have to compete to achieve more qualitative objectives, such as job-creation, improving economic and social governance, technology innovation, sustainable development and territorial cooperation.

Notes

1. Although in terms of population, Portugal, Greece and Ireland have benefited more from the structural funds than Spain.
2. Upon accession in 1986, Spain's per capita GDP was only about 72 per cent of the EU average, while in 2006 it had almost reached the EU average, standing at more than 98 per cent (Spain National Reform Programme – 2006 Progress Report, October 2006. p. 49). However, one has to consider the 'statistical effect' of the 2004 enlargement.
3. After wining the general elections in March 2004, the Socialist party was forced to negotiate parliamentary support with a number of small parties, especially the Catalan Independentist Republicans (ERC) and Izquierda Unida/Iniciativa per Catalunya-Verds. Both groups had, among their priorities, participation of the ACs in EU decisionmaking.
4. Some examples of cross-border cooperation in Spain would be: W*orking Community Galícia-Regiao Norte* – one of the most successful experiences in Spanish cross-border cooperation, created on the basis of traditional socio-cultural links between Galicia and Portugal; *Arco Latino* – created and led by the Diputació de Barcelona, it brings together more than 60 'second degree' administrations of the western Mediterranean; and *Euroregión Extremadura Alentejo-Algarve* – a cooperation between Spanish and Portuguese regions, created on the base of micro-projects within INTERREG.
5. Maluquer, cited in Morata (2004b), asserts that 'The Generalitat of Catalonia was only allowed to present proposals on general aspects of the regional programmes, which in some cases were not even considered by the central Administration'.
6. Cross-border Cooperation: OP Spain-Portugal (covering Andalucía, Castilla y León, Extremadura and Galicia); OP Spain-France (for Aragon, Catalonia and Basque Country); Transnational Cooperation (South-Eastern Europe,

Mediterranean; Madeira-Azores-Canary Islands and Atlantic Space); and Interregional Cooperation.
7. The coordination committees are: (1) The Forum for Cohesion Policy; (2) Coordination Committee for Communitarian Funds; (3) The Forum for the Social Fund; (4) Sectoral Networks; and (5) Monitoring Committee.
8. See, for instance, the project ALSO 'Achievement of the Lisbon and Gothenburg Strategy Objectives by INTERREG', with the participation of the Diputació de Barcelona.
9. Seminar 'L'estrategia de Lisboa i Goteborg a nivell local i la seva relació amb el nou objectiu de Cooperació Territorial', Barcelona, 10 May 2007.

6
Ireland

Irene McMaster

Introduction

Ireland is commonly viewed as a 'cohesion policy success story' and an exemplar of the use of EU cohesion policy funds. The exact extent to which Irish economic growth can be attributed to EU funding is debated. However, EU cohesion policy funding is generally considered to be at least a contributory factor in driving Ireland's economic success (Rees, Quinn and Connaughton, 2006). According to European Commission estimates, economic growth in Ireland between 1991 and 2002 was 2.8 per cent higher than it would have been without cohesion policy funding (CEC, 2004a).

Ireland is a relatively small state, with a weak tradition of regional policy and regional governance. However, over recent years, a highly integrated approach to domestic and EU regional economic development policy has emerged and levels of decentralization and regional participation in policy development and implementation have increased. To what extent these developments are attributable to EU cohesion policy practices or shaped by domestic conditions and to what extent they will be retained in the future is the subject of this chapter.

As previous chapters outline, approaches to the management and implementation of EU cohesion policy can vary considerably and the influence of the EU on governance structures and policy implementation practices is the subject of academic and policy debate. In the context of these debates, this chapter focuses on experience in Ireland. At the beginning of the 2007–13 structural funds programming period, as the country moves from being a net beneficiary of EU Funds to a net contributor to the EU budget, the Irish case is particularly interesting. Key questions are, as a long-time net beneficiary of EU funds, how has Ireland adapted to, or adopted, EU cohesion policy structures and practices? Has EU cohesion policy been instrumental in shaping regional policy implementation and governance structures in the country? Alternatively, have domestic institutions and structures determined policy and institutional approaches to regional economic development challenges? Finally, to what extent will the new round of structural funds programmes involve a change in approach to the management and implementation of cohesion policy in Ireland?

In order to set these questions in context, it is important to briefly review the main regional development challenges in Ireland, the amount and type of cohesion policy support that the country has received, and the administration of regional development policies. Drawing on the preceding sections, the chapter goes on to examine how cohesion policy programmes have been implemented in Ireland; the extent to which EU cohesion policy has been instrumental in shaping policy implementation and governance approaches in the country; and how this could change in the future. The chapter concludes by suggesting that much has been done in Ireland to adapt domestic policy approaches and structures to the demands of EU cohesion policy, in order to maximize the positive impacts of the funds. However, EU influence has involved a gradual process of adaptation over time and at various stages domestic policy structures have also exerted a strong influence. The 2007–13 programming period, poses new challenges for Ireland and systems for the management and implementation of EU and domestic funds have had to adapt. However, core elements of the Ireland's previous, distinctive approach to the management and implementation of EU funds have been retained.

Regional development and regional development policies in Ireland

Ireland is a small state with a highly centralized system of government. The country has a comparatively weak tradition of regional policy and regional governance. On joining the EU in 1973, economic development policy in Ireland, including EU programmes, focused on promoting and sustaining national economic growth, with a view to catching-up with and exceeding EU development averages. As Adshead (2005, p. 162) notes, unlike the situation in some other countries, the issue of EU membership did not lead to internal splits between the country's political parties, *Finna Fál* and *Fine Gael*. Both campaigned for EU membership and broadly supported the aim of promoting national economic growth and catch-up. By the mid-1990s, GDP per capita in Ireland was close to the EU average. Since then, GDP in the country has increased to become the second highest in the EU, 138 per cent in 2004 (CEC, 2004b). In 2005, GDP growth levels remained above the EU average at 4.8 per cent. In the same period, employment grew by 5 per cent and unemployment was recorded at 4.4 per cent (IDA-Ireland, 2006).

However, Ireland's overall growth masks a spatially imbalanced pattern of development. Regions in the more prosperous eastern and southern parts of the country, which started out on a relatively more developed basis, were prospering to a much greater extent than those in the west, north-west and midlands. In contrast, levels of development continue to lag in the Border, Midland and West regions. For instance, Gross Value Added (GVA) per person in the Dublin region and South-West was over 170 per cent of the EU average in 2002, whereas the Midland region had a level of 84.1 per cent (Central Statistical Office, 2004).

Associated with this varied pattern of economic development are differing regional development challenges. On the one hand, economic centralization, congestion, labour shortages, and urban sprawl are concerns in the Greater Dublin region. On the other hand, the Border, Midlands and West regions retain economic weaknesses relative to the rest of the country, including a limited industrial base with GVA across key sectors lower than the national average; an economy which contains a number of vulnerable sectors; a weak urban structure and deficiencies in infrastructure; poor graduate retention and consequent 'brain drain'; and low levels of clustering of economic activity (BMW Regional Assembly, 2006, p. 3).

As previously noted, the receipt of EU cohesion policy funds has been closely linked to Ireland's rapid economic growth. Between 1973, when Ireland joined the EU, and 2003, the country received over €17 billion in structural and Cohesion Funds support (Irish Regions Office, 2006). Support from the structural funds was available throughout Ireland, as all of the country was eligible for some level of Objective 1 support, although for the more prosperous regions this support was gradually reduced over the 2000–06 period.

Since the reform of the structural funds in the 1980s, EU cohesion policy support and Irish domestic policy have been managed as part of an integrated, coherent policy framework. National Development Plans (NDPs) have been used to form the basis of negotiations between Ireland and the European Commission, which resulted in the agreement of Community Support Frameworks (CSFs). For each programming round up to 2006, the NDP and the CSF were implemented as an integrated investment plan and strategy for economic and social development, drawing on domestic and EU resources.

As Table 6.1 illustrates, the NDPs have involved substantial resources. They also span a wide range of activities. For instance, during the 1994–99 period, the key issues were employment creation, training and economic growth. In the early programming periods, requests by regional development organizations to have the funds concentrated on more underdeveloped areas were not accepted (Hart, 1985, p. 225). However, the focus of the 2000–06 NDP is significantly different from that in the previous programming period. The 2000–06 NDP provides a national framework for the investment of over €57 billion over seven years in Irish infrastructure, education, training, industry, agriculture, forestry, fishing, tourism, social inclusion, and rural and regional development. It has operated in a set of circumstances where the economy has expanded considerably and unemployment has decreased markedly, to 4 per cent in spring 2001. Therefore, the main priority of the NDP is to address infrastructure bottlenecks and regional imbalances, in order to facilitate continued economic growth.

The development and implementation of long-term, integrated development plans has necessitated a high level of coordination and partnership across sectors, levels of government and social partners. As a result, the partnership process in the country has been widened and deepened and a more analytical, consultative approach to policy making has evolved. In terms of the formal management and implementation of the plans, to date, they have been largely centrally managed and nationally oriented. Overall responsibility for the implementation of the NDP and EU cohesion policy funds rests with the government's Department of Finance. Accompanying Operational Programmes (OPs) are administered by Managing Authorities (MAs), which are mainly government departments. The MAs, in turn, delegate the implementation

Table 6.1   EU cohesion funding in Ireland (€ mn)

	1989–93	1994–99	2000–06
National Development Plan (total)	12,275	16,800	57,111
(of which) co-financed investment	8,339	10,383	7,680
(of which) structural/cohesion funds	3,672	6,921	3,739

Source: Irish Regions Office, 2006.

of individual measures to an Implementing Body, again, in most cases, a government department or state agency.

More generally, no single government department has overall responsibility for a distinct 'regional policy'. Instead, a range of departments are involved in various regional development initiatives and strategies. At the national level, the Department for Enterprise, Trade and Employment is the main government department involved in the development and delivery of enterprise policy, which has a regional component. The department also has policy responsibility for the key agencies involved in the delivery of development policy, Industrial Development Agency (IDA)-Ireland and Enterprise Ireland. The Department for the Environment, Heritage and Local Government is responsible for the country's National Spatial Strategy (NSS), launched in 2002, and provides guidance in relation to how the spatial aspects of other policies, plans and programmes can support the spatial framework set out in the NSS. As previously mentioned, the Department of Finance has a coordination role for the NDP and EU structural funds. More broadly, the Department functions to promote and coordinate economic and social planning – including sectoral and regional planning – identify development policies, review the methods adopted by departments of state to implement such policies, and generally to advise the government on economic and social planning matters.

In contrast to the strong role of central government departments and agencies, subnational participation in the development and implementation of policy is traditionally weak. The county is the main subnational administrative unit. At county/city level there are 29 County Councils, five City Councils, five Borough Councils and 75 Town Councils. These local authorities are multi-purpose bodies that are responsible for a range of services, including housing, planning and roads. However, in terms of economic development functions, the County Councils have a relatively limited remit and resources.

The potential role of regional authorities has been the subject of some debate. In the past, a number of factors mitigated against the development of regional structures similar to those evident in many EU member states. First, the centralized nature of the Irish administrative system was firmly embedded. Second, strong local and national identity meant that regionally based political parties and allegiances have not been formed, although some areas have set up development organizations to advance their economic positions, for example the Western Development Commission (Hart, 1985; Laffan, 1996). Third, the small size of the country and the perceived need to boost overall national economic development led politicians and policymakers to focus on constituency or national issues, as opposed to regional concerns (Hart, 1985).

However, debate about regional government and decentralization gained momentum after reform of the structural funds in 1988 emphasized geographically based programmes drawn up in consultation with local and regional authorities. Additionally, the increasingly complicated array of agencies and authorities active in the regional policy field highlighted the need for better coordination at some level. Relatedly, as part of a comprehensive review of local government in 1990, it was recommended that eight new Regional Authorities (RAs) be established, in line with the principle of subsidiarity.

Following these recommendations, RAs were eventually established in 1994 (see Map 6.1). However, these institutions are primarily 'review bodies' (Adshead, 2005, p. 164). They are not directly elected and have only limited responsibilities. Members of the RAs are nominated representatives from each of the counties in the region. The primary role of the RAs is to promote the coordination of the provision of public services at regional level and to review development needs and the provision of public services in the region. In doing so, they fulfil an umbrella, coordination role, for example, by taking a lead role in the preparation of regional development strategies and providing a 'link' between central and local government and coordinating the activities of various, sectoral government agencies at regional level (Midland Regional Authority, 2006). However, they are not providers of infrastructural or mainstream services, as these are dealt with either at central or local government levels.

Despite these modest changes, until 2000, the role and profile of regions in Ireland was limited and the country was designated as a single NUTS 2 region for the purposes of EU cohesion policy. However, the inclusion of a broad commitment to pursuing 'balanced regional development' in the 2000–06 NDP and, crucially, the introduction of two Regional OPs (ROPs) signalled a shift in approach. Two new NUTS 2 regions were formed, each with their own OP, to replace the single NUTS 2 designation for the entire country. One region covered the Border, Midland and West (BMW) area of the country, with an allocation of €4,094 million, and the other the South and East (S&E), with a total investment of €5,380 million. Both programmes targeted local infrastructure, the local productive sector and the promotion of social inclusion; and offered favourable rates of enterprise support for regions lagging behind national levels of growth and living standards.

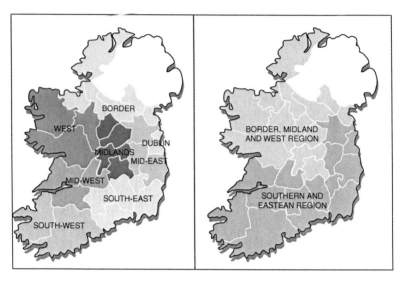

Map 6.1 Irish Regional Authority and Assembly areas
Source: Irish Regions Office, Brussels < http://www.iro.ie/>.

Linked to the adoption of the ROPs, two Regional Assemblies were established to take on the role of programme MAs (see Map 6.1). These institutions are based on the existing regional authority structure and cover: the RA areas of the Border, Midlands and West; and the RA areas of Dublin, the Mid-East, the Mid-West, the South-West and the South-East. The Assemblies are comprised of representatives of the relevant County Councils and meet twice a month. They are responsible for managing their respective OPs, monitoring the general impact of all EU programmes under the NDP/CSF in the region and promoting the coordination of the provision of public services in the region. This is still a relatively limited role, in comparison with the continuing role of central government in guiding and implementing development policy. However, in what had been an extremely centralized state, the decentralization of the management and implementation of the ROPs was a notable shift in approach.

Steps towards a greater regional involvement in the development and delivery of policy have been accompanied by broader measures to 'decentralize' government. The government's decentralization plan, which involves the relocation of government department headquarters from the capital city, Dublin, was announced on 3 December 2003. It is hoped that the programme will provide a significant boost to local economies and lessen development pressures in Dublin. A total of eight departments and the Office of Public Works are moving their headquarters from Dublin to provincial locations, leaving seven departments with their headquarters in Dublin. It is expected that this will involve over 10,000 civil and public service jobs and 58 locations throughout Ireland (Gilmartin, 2006). The process is being pursed in phases, with a target of 7,000 jobs decentralized by 2009. However, practical problems such as potential skills shortages, staff reluctance to move and infrastructural deficits in new locations mean that the proposals are still highly controversial (McMaster, 2004a). Yet, despite the controversy surrounding the government's decentralization plans, it is still apparent that the development and implementation of regional economic development policies in Ireland have a greater regional emphasis and involvement than in the past.

As the preceding analysis suggests, over the last ten to fifteen years, Ireland has received a considerable amount of EU cohesion policy funding, which has supported investment in a wide range of policy areas. The management and implementation of both EU funds and regional economic development policy have been characterized by the development of an integrated policy approach, involving partnership working and coordination and a gradual shift from centralization to an increasing level of decentralization and regional participation in policy development and delivery. However, the 2000–06 rounds of EU and domestic policy programmes are now entering their final stages. Related, future development strategies and structures are being developed, taking into account the reform of cohesion policy and a considerable reduction in Ireland's allocation of structural funds resources.

In a number of respects the relative role and position of the structural funds in Ireland will change considerably. Sustained growth in the country means that for the 2007–13 programming period no Irish region falls below the threshold used to determine eligibility for the new structural funds Convergence priority, which is 75 per cent of the EU average GDP. In terms of mainstream structural funds programmes, both of the country's NUTS 2 regions will only be eligible for the EU's Regional Competitiveness and Employment (RCE) funding, with less emphasis on investment in infrastructure investment and more focus on support for innovation, R&D and competitiveness policies (see Map 6.2).

Relatedly, Ireland faces a substantial reduction of cohesion policy funding and is no longer a net beneficiary but a net payer. It is expected that the country will receive approximately €800 million in structural funds for 2007–13, compared to €3.32 billion from the structural funds

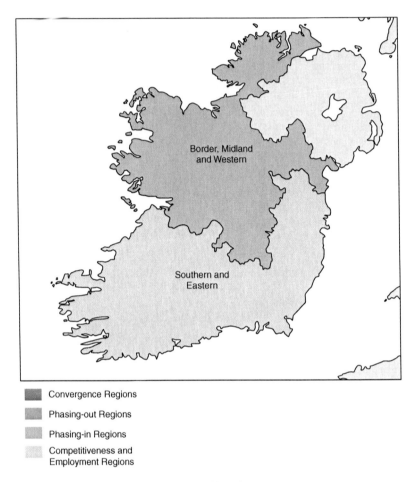

Convergence Regions

Phasing-out Regions

Phasing-in Regions

Competitiveness and
Employment Regions

Map 6.2   Structural funds eligibility, 2007–13
Source: European Commission, DG Regional Policy.

and €797 million from the Cohesion Fund for 2000–06 (at 2004 prices;
see Table 6.2).

In the lead up to the 2007–13 programming period, key questions
that policymakers had to address included: how can these more limited
resources best be managed and implemented; can current approaches
to policy governance be maintained; how can the requirements of the

Table 6.2 Cohesion policy allocations in Ireland, 2000–06 and 2007–13

Allocations 2000–06 (€ mn, 2004 prices)		Allocations 2007–13 (€ mn, 2004 prices)	
Cohesion Fund	797	Cohesion fund	NA
Objective 1	1,345	Convergence	NA
		Statistical phasing-out	NA
Phasing-out	1,813	Phasing-in	419
Objective 2	NA	Regional competitiveness and employment	260
Objective 3	NA		
Community initiatives	158	European territorial cooperation	134
Total	4,113	Total	813

Source: European Commission, (2006f).

new RCE support be addressed, such as the requirement to maintain a strong focus on Lisbon-oriented goals; and how can Ireland's own development needs best be addressed?

The remainder of this chapter examines current trends in cohesion policy management and implementation and the extent to which they have influenced wider governance trends in the country. However, taking into account changing economic conditions in Ireland, the amount and type of structural funds support and the recent reform of EU cohesion policy, it also considers how cohesion policy funding will be managed in the future and the extent to which current patterns of policy governance could change.

Cohesion policy and regional policy governance in Ireland

Rees, Quinn and Connaughton (2006) describe Ireland's response to EU cohesion policy as one of 'pragmatic adaptation'. As opposed to stressing the dominance of either the EU or domestic conditions, they propose that EU and domestic institutional and policy-making structures interplay, resulting in policy and institutional shifts in some areas and resistance to change in others. Taking each of the main, recent trends in the development and implementation of regional economic development policies in turn, it is possible to identify a number of examples of 'pragmatic adaptation' and the interaction between EU and domestic policies and institutions which have shaped, or are shaping, the development and implementation of regional economic development policies in Ireland.

Integrated policymaking

As previously noted, in recent years the central pillar of economic development policy in Ireland has been an integrated 'programming' approach to policy, through the development and implementation of NDPs. The promotion of multiannual, multi-sectoral programming is most closely associated with the EU structural funds; however, the programming approach has been implemented differently across the EU. Some member states, particularly those with strongly sectoral policy-making traditions, have struggled to adapt to this approach. Others have developed highly 'differentiated' and separated systems for the management and disbursal of EU and domestic policy funds, for example in the United Kingdom. In contrast, in Ireland there has been a very successful 'marriage' of EU and domestic policy (Adshead, 2005; Rees, Quinn and Connaughton, 2006). By choosing to programme EU and domestic policy resources together in NDP, cohesion policy was 'grafted' on to the business of various government departments (Laffan, 2000; Rees, Quinn and Connaughton, 2006) and assistance from the structural funds was integrated into a coherent national policy framework. The European Commission's Second Cohesion Report (2001, p. 130) goes as far as stating that Ireland is an example of 'good practice' of the first order, as it demonstrates what can be achieved if structural funds assistance is integrated into a coherent policy which, in particular, maintains healthy macroeconomic conditions and which is supported by social consensus.

In the Irish context, the scope to pursue such an integrated approach relied on both EU and domestic conditions. As a cohesion country until 2006, Ireland has received a considerable amount of cohesion policy funds. The scale of funding available made policy integration desirable from an economic and political point of view. Particularly during the early 1990s, structural funds payments provided a real, and a psychological, boost at a critical point in the country's economic transformation, by allowing investment to be sustained at a point where continued retrenchment might otherwise have been required (Irish Regions Office, 2006). The funds contributed by increasing the net capital inflow into the economy and, more importantly, co-financed structural measures for regional development, infrastructure and human resource development (Irish Regions Office, 2006). The scale of the resources available from the structural funds and the need for domestic co-financing of EU programmes made the integration of EU and domestic policy a logical choice, in order to make best use of the resources available and avoid any duplication of effort (Adshead, 2005). Consequently, multiannual budgeting, in line with the programming cycles of EU programmes, is now a firmly embedded part of government financial planning in Ireland.

As well as shaping formal policy structures, EU policy practices can shape institutional structures, procedures, codes and cultures (Bulmer and Burch, 1998). According to Adshead (2005), the Irish experience with the structural funds has been very positive from a policy process point of view. Just as the structural funds have contributed hugely to the financing of investment programmes since 1989, they have also helped to shape the priorities of these programmes and exposed policymakers and administrators to new and innovative approaches to development policy. For instance, the core requirements and regulations attached to the structural funds are considered to have had a very beneficial effect on governance and public administration, in areas such as monitoring and evaluation, and social and regional partnership.

A more analytical approach to policy has developed, linked to the development of long-term development programmes. For instance, research from the country's Economic and Social Research Institute (ESRI) is used to underpin decisions on the content of the NDP. Following the requirement to evaluate EU cohesion policy programmes, the Irish authorities implemented a number of measures to build evaluation capacity and mainstream the process across a wide range of policy fields. There are now units that specialize in structural fund evaluations and more integrated evaluation practice, and all government departments are required to set meaningful objectives, conduct three-year spending reviews, and organize publicity for evaluation studies (McMaster, 2006). Thus, in Ireland, the structural funds acted as a catalyst for what has now become the wide use of evaluation.

The multiannual, multi-sectoral programming approach has also necessitated a more coordinated policy approach across government departments, levels of government and partner organizations. Relatedly, the adoption of the 'partnership principle' facilitated partner input and involvement in programmes, broadening and deepening links between social partners, private enterprise, local and regional administrations and central government authorities. For instance, the requirement for public consultation on programmes has increased the opportunity for wider dialogue with a broad range of participants (Adshead, 2005). As a result, partnership working is seen as strengthening the content, awareness of and ownership of the final strategy. Partnership working and long-term development planning has also helped to maintain more consistent policy approaches overtime, as agreed plans have been less open to short-term revisions by political leaders.

EU structural funds have been central to embedding and reinforcing an integrated, programming policy approach. However, it is also important to consider the influence of domestic conditions on approaches to the management and implementation of the funds for a number of reasons. First, existing, domestic policy approaches offered a base for integrated EU programmes to build upon and opportunities to develop an integrated, multiannual, multi-sectoral policy approach. In seeking to reform the economy the Irish government introduced a number of large-scale, national 'Programmes' aimed at promoting consensus regarding levels of growth and the measures required to achieve them, for example the *National Understandings* (1979 and 1980), *Programme for National Recovery* (1987–90) and the *Programme for Economic and Social Progress* (1991–93). Experience of these programmes and the commitment to long-term and consultative policy that they signified meant that the EU programming approach was able to build on and develop existing domestic policy structures and trends.

Second, it is also important to note that a strong basis for consultative policy was already in place in the country. Therefore, the structural funds' partnership principle also built upon pre-existing social partnership arrangements in Ireland (e.g., employer/business, trade union, farming, community and voluntary interests). Experience of partnership working is based around civil society groups, as opposed to regional representatives. Since 1987, social partnership has been an important basis for government planning and policy making in Ireland. According to the Ireland's NDP, 'Ireland's experience of social partnership has been very positive ... [and] has been a significant contributory factor to Ireland's economic success' (Government of Ireland, 1999, p. 261). In advancing the 2000–06 NDP, the 2003 national agreement *Sustaining Progress*, which sets out commitments in relation to economic inclusion based on full employment, consistent economic development that is socially and environmentally sustainable, social inclusion and social justice, and continuing adaptation to change, was taken into account. Further, in 2006, the government embarked upon the process of negotiating a seventh national agreement, *Towards 2016*, which will have implications for the funding and policy priorities in the new round of programming documents.

Third, in contrast to developments in the new member states, the programming approach has developed over time in Ireland. During successive rounds of programming, it has been possible to refine and enhance policy coordination mechanisms and reinforce partnerships, with a view to maximizing the benefits of the funds. According to McAleese, the Irish forte 'has been the management and adaptation of policy' (2000, p. 103). In part, this apparent flexibility can be attributed to creative administrative responses based on much less formal ways of doing business in Ireland, which have allowed for significant policy innovations (Adshead, 2005, p. 167). The scope to maintain these relatively flexible forms of governance is linked to the relatively small size of the Irish polity, with 'everyone knowing one another'. As a result the Irish system of policy formation is much less institutionalized than in other member states, possibly leading to more openness to change and adaptability (Adshead, 2002, 2005).

Finally, the new, 2007–13, programming period for structural funds raises some interesting questions in relation to future governance and policy implementation approaches in Ireland and the 'durability' of the integrated policy programming approach. For 2007–13, change in the scale and type of EU funding has prompted a change in approach to the overall management and implementation of the funds. In a substantial shift from the integrated EU/domestic policy-making approach that has been pursued in recent years, EU structural funds will be programmed separately from domestic policy.

The country's plans for the structural funds in 2007–13 are set out in a separate National Strategic Reference Framework (NSRF). The NSRF was developed in line with key domestic policy documents, but is not directly integrated with an NDP. Interventions have a strong focus on themes which are in line with the EU's Lisbon Agenda, including innovation and the development of education, training and the knowledge economy, access to economic and technical infrastructure, environmental sustainability and sustainable urban development. In comparison with past programmes, this is a much more narrow policy focus, which aims to maximize the impact of reduced funding, by focusing on a more limited range of interventions and rationalizing the administrative burden of working with the funds over a wide range of activities.

In terms of domestic policy planning, a strong commitment to integrated multiannual programming of domestic policy resources remains. In August 2005, the government announced that a new NDP would be developed for the 2007–13 period. The 2007–13 NDP is mainly nationally funded and closely linked to rolling five-year 'envelopes' for investment that are set out under the government's Public Capital Programme, which sets out the broad amounts available for each government department over most of the next investment period.

Although EU structural funds will be programmed separately, the new NDP remains a high-level, strategic framework and will involve the investment of €184 billion. The programme was developed with in line with social partnership negotiations and existing strategies, such as the NSS. The resulting plan is based around the following broad range of objectives:

- tackling infrastructure deficits;
- enhancing enterprise development, Science, Technology and Innovation, working age training and skills provision to improve economic performance, competitiveness and capacity;
- integrating regional development within the NSS framework of Gateway cities and Hub towns;
- investing in long-term environmental sustainability;
- realizing the opportunities of strengthened all-island collaboration in areas of mutual interest;
- delivering a multi-faceted programme for social inclusion; and
- providing Value for Taxpayers' Money through robust and transparent appraisal, management and monitoring systems for NDP investment (Government of Ireland 2007, pp. 13–14).

The NDP reflects a number of objectives that are closely in line with those of EU cohesion policy, such as promoting regional competitiveness and supporting innovation and R&D. However, many of the planned interventions, such as investment in infrastructure, would not be eligible for funding under the RCE objective, or would be too costly for comparatively small structural funds programmes to support. In contrast, domestic policy programmes have the scope to be more flexible. In this context, it is also worth taking into account the fact that aspects of the integration of national and EU policy programmes can be extremely complex, and not necessarily involve 'benefits' and 'improvements' to existing systems. EU structures are commonly criticized as extremely bureaucratic and cumbersome. In some fields of development activity, development actors in Ireland have struggled to commit EU resources, as potential beneficiaries are reluctant to participate in the demanding process of managing and implementing an EU-funded project. Therefore, by programming domestic resources separately it may be possible to allow greater flexibility in the management and implementation of the programme.

In terms of the delivery of future development programmes, increasingly, effective coordination and partnership is seen not just as a key element of EU programmes but also as a requirement for future economic growth as greater emphasis is placed on networking activities and knowledge-exchange. From a practical policy implementation point of view, emphasis on cooperative working and partnership is also a pragmatic response to the need to pool resources based on the fact that development agencies are likely to have fewer financial resources to award independently. Consequently, in terms of policy administration, a key theme in recent years and for the future is building opportunities to improve synergies and cooperation between agencies, for example between Enterprise Ireland, IDA-Ireland and partners such as the Science Foundation Ireland and FÁS (National Training and Employment Authority). IDA-Ireland states that 'nationally and regionally, every investment is won by the combined efforts' of many partners and success in meeting future targets will be attained 'not by any one agency alone but by the combined efforts of many' (IDA, 2006, p. 8). Similarly, Enterprise Ireland's strategic plan for Irish industry stresses the need for partnership with government departments, industry representatives and state agencies and views it as central to increasing the effectiveness of the agency's interventions. Examples of how cooperation and coordination between development actors have been addressed in Ireland are enterprise support networks. Within these networks, Enterprise Ireland works with organizations to drive enterprise development at the local level. These organizations include: business innovation centres; county and city enterprise boards; Regional Assemblies; business incubation centres; Regional Authorities; local authorities; universities and colleges; chambers of commerce (Enterprise Ireland, 2006, pp. 8–9).

EU cohesion policy has exercised considerable influence over elements of Irish policy practice. However, it also has to be recognized that elements of the EU cohesion policy approach have 'suited' the Irish context. In terms of integrated policy making and partnership working, existing, domestic policy approaches and requirements could be adapted to the requirements of EU programmes and were a good 'fit' with EU practices and structures, which allowed these aspects of cohesion policy programmes to become well-established parts of policy and governance structures. In 2007–13, another example of 'pragmatic adaptation' is apparent. Structural funds programmes, with a narrower focus and fewer resources, are separated from large-scale domestic policy plans. This allows these programmes to take a focused, more targeted approach, in order to maximize the impact of the funds and meet

EU targets. Meanwhile, domestic policy programmes are freed from the administrative burden of cohesion policy regulations, while retaining the more 'beneficial' elements of the cohesion policy programming approach, such as partnership and multiannual programming.

Decentralization and regionalization

As previously noted, there is a perceptible trend towards greater regionalization and decentralization in Ireland. This appears to be in line with developments across the EU and EU cohesion policy, although as noted in Chapter 1 the degree to which the EU has influenced regional institutional developments in the member states and contributed to regional 'empowerment' is debated. In the case of Ireland, the apparent trends towards regionalization and decentralization have to be interpreted carefully, taking into account the small size of the country and the previously high levels of centralization of resources and responsibilities. Whilst the influence of EU cohesion policy on integrated policy approaches could be viewed as comparatively strong and reinforcing domestic policy trends, its influence on formal processes of regionalization in Ireland is more mixed.

For the 2000–06 programming period, the adoption of two ROPs and the establishment of two group Regional Assemblies can be interpreted as a step towards greater regional participation in the content, management and implementation of development funds in Ireland. For the first time the NDP, including the structural funds and related national co-finance, was allocated in accordance with a regionalized NUTS 2 structure, regional programmes were introduced and new regional administrative and management arrangements were put in place. These are also developments that are broadly in line with structural fund requirements, namely the regulatory requirement of subsidiarity. Additionally, structural funds have enhanced the financial resources available to regional and local authorities. As a result, they have given a wide range of local and regional institutions the impetus to develop territorially based partnerships and mobilize projects from the 'bottom-up', as opposed to relying on central government intervention.

In 2007–13, a greater proportion of structural funds expenditure will be disbursed through ROPs (see Table 6.3). The broad goals set out in the NSRF will be pursued through three OPs, only one of which will be a national OP, Human Capital Investment. The ROPs are developed in line with common EU and national development goals, but also aim to take into account existing economic, social and territorial disparities.

Table 6.3 NSRF indicative annual allocation by fund and OP

Operational Programme	Fund	Total € mn (2007 prices)
Southern & Eastern Regional OP	ERDF	146,603,534
Border, Midlands & Western Regional OP	ERDF	228,758,838
Human Capital Investment	ESF	375,362,370
Total all funds NSRF 2007–13		750,724,742

Source: Department of Finance of Ireland (2007, p. 66).

For both of the ROPs, a key challenge is 'whether the very limited funding available ought to be concentrated on a highly restricted number of actions...or whether..., the available funding ought to be used to support a wider range of activities' (Southern and Eastern Regional Assembly, 2007, p. 34). It is anticipated that a number of 'niche' investments will be selected under key priorities. The S&E ROP for 2007–13 aims to focus investment on building research capacity in the region, tackling selected environmental risks and investing in designated development gateways and hubs. Similarly, the BMW ROP has three proposed funding priorities targeting the following issues: support for research, innovation, Information & Communications Technology (ICT) infrastructure and improving capacity to promote entrepreneurship, collaboration and technology transfer; environmental risk prevention and energy efficiency; and investment in urban growth centres (BMW Regional Assembly, 2007; Southern and Eastern Regional Assembly, 2007).

The country's two Regional Assemblies have responsibility for developing the new ROPs and they will continue to be the programme MAs. This suggests that, in terms of policy governance, more administrative power and experience is lying with the Regional Assemblies than in the past. Additionally, the new regional structures introduced in the 1990s have increasingly become more experienced, well-connected and 'recognized' parts of the policy-making process. Consequently, the influence of the Regional Assemblies and NUTS 3 regional authorities in the development of key policy documents, such as the new structural funds programmes, has increased.

Regional development issues and regional involvement in policy delivery are also addressed in the new NDP. The Plan places particular emphasis on the development of strong urban centres, or 'gateways', across the country, which will be supported by 'hub' towns and a diversified rural economy and act as motors of development for the regional and national economy. The NDP sets out detailed priorities for each gateway and anticipates that national, regional and local authorities will all be involved in delivering the country's regional development objectives. Additionally, results and impacts will be more closely monitored at the level of the eight RAs. However, strategic management and control responsibilities still lie with central government. Relatedly, the Regional Assemblies are pushing for an even greater say in decision-making. For instance, the BMW region has pressed for a higher profile to be given to regional policies and views, for example by providing a forum whereby regional issues can be included in the social partnership process (BMW Region, 2005).

More generally, an increasingly strong network of institutions and actors are involved at regional level. At the same time as boosting the representation of regions in policy governance, central government and state agencies have also sought to decentralize their own activities, particularly those linked to regional economic development. As previously noted, it is hoped that the government's decentralization plan will provide a significant boost to local economies and lessen development pressures in Dublin. Related to development needs and regional reform, the country's two main development agencies have adopted more regionalized structures, boosting their representation in the regions. For instance, IDA-Ireland has upgraded its regional offices, which have more resources and responsibilities and moved key divisions of the Agency to regional locations. The movement of resources and staff to the North-West, Midlands and South-East is designed to stimulate and support new growth from *within* these regions and improve coordination with local and regional actors. Enterprise Ireland has also recently (2001–02) reorganized its regional structure in line with the new regional administrative boundaries. There are now over 100 regional staff, with specific expertise provided in each office relating to business development, finance, human resources, marketing and other specialist skills.

However, the extent to which these developments are directly attributable to EU influence and pressure and the extent to which domestic structures and institutions have allowed substantial regionalization can be questioned for a number of reasons. First, the EU's position on regional participation and capacity to influence regional reform in Ireland has changed over time. In contrast to the current focus on subsidiarity in the development and delivery of structural funds programmes, the initial designation of Ireland as a single NUTS 2 region for the structural funds programming periods up to 2000 and the resulting central administration of the funds did little to encourage any form of regional reform (Keogh, 1994; O'Donnell and Walsh, 1995; Rees, Quinn and Connaughton, 2006). Instead, an uncoordinated web of agencies, boards and authorities emerged, each with some direct or indirect involvement in policy delivery and many operating at different levels with differing regional or local divisions (Chubb, 1992; Adshead, 2005).

Second, to date, EU-supported programmes in Ireland have retained a strong focus on promoting national-level development. For instance, the strategic priority of the 1989–93 and 1994–99 NDP/CSFs were to promote development at national level and convergence of living standards between Ireland and the rest of the EU. The regional input during the 1989–93 programming period was limited to the single function Sub-Regional Review Committees, which had no statutory basis and very limited resources (Irish Regions Office, 2006). For the 1994–99 programmes, the eight RAs were in a position to provide a review of the implementation of programmes and could 'advise on the deployment of EU Structural and Cohesion Funds in their regions' (Adshead, 2005, p. 164), but they were not actively involved in programme implementation.

Third, Ireland's strong tradition of social partnership and local representation has limited pressure for regional reform. The partnership requirements of EU funding have, according to some commentators, also led to a strengthening of these networks at the expense of links with local and regional government (Marshall, 2002). RAs are even dismissed by some as 'window dressing designed to cut off Commission complaints about a lack of devolution and subsidiarity in Ireland' (Marshall, 2002). For instance, as O'Hara and Commins (2002) note, regional interests were not directly represented in the country's partnership negotiations. Therefore, in practice, it is possible to question the overall influence of the Regional Assemblies and Authorities, as they do not have extensive powers in the development and delivery of policies beyond their involvement in structural funds.

Fourth, as opposed to viewing regionalization in Ireland as a response to EU regulatory pressures, the decision to establish two NUTS 2 regions and introduce ROPs can also been seen as a pragmatic, centrally driven response to changed economic development conditions in the country. Through the designation of two separate NUTS 2 regions the NDP for 2000–06 could more directly address the aim of balanced regional development, which had become more of a problem with the sustained but imbalanced growth of the 1990s. Crucially, the country could also maximize its structural funds receipts: the newly formed BMW region had a GDP level below the eligibility threshold; the S&E region would continue to qualify for Objective 1 transitional support, which offers assistance on a decreasing scale; and the country as a whole could continue to draw support from the Cohesion Fund.

Relatedly, in the Irish context, it is also important to note that the 'establishment of regional-level public institutions has been by way of executive discretion rather than bottom-up mobilization or lobbying' (Hayward, 2006, p. 4). Key debates on the structure and role of the new regions primarily took place between development agencies and interests and the government and the European Commission, as opposed to between regionally based political interests. This reflects the lack of any 'popular use of regionalism as a political or social reference' (Hayward, 2006, p. 4). During debates on the issue, as Boyle (2000, p. 750) notes, there were no serious calls for the establishment of new, elected regional authorities with wide-ranging powers. Instead, calls for devolution amounted to little more than the introduction of spatial as opposed to national or sectoral planning and an enhanced role for the regions in the preparation of regional plans. Ultimately, the final decision was more closely linked to the government's commitment to securing the optimum level of funding for the country.

Finally, looking to the future, the orientation of policy could demand new delivery structures and mechanisms. Regional economic development policies are increasingly oriented towards boosting innovation, R&D and the knowledge economy. Relatedly, questions are raised about the need to focus on overall national competitiveness, the development of new, flexible, cooperative responses to policy development, and the need for a less 'regionalized' view of development. Thus, the need for cooperation between regions and potentially a less 'regionalized' or 'localized' view of the country is suggested by some authorities. For instance, according to IDA-Ireland, every location in Ireland has to think beyond its boundaries if it wishes to succeed, particularly when competing for large-scale foreign direct investment. Within a small country there is perceived to be little scope for competition between regions and locations. With this in mind, one suggestion is that an important element of the two new ROPs is their provisions for cooperation between the regions.

Yet, as government and EU cohesion policy increasingly focuses on the promotion of innovation and R&D activities and EU funding is cut, strong arguments have emerged to suggest that the BMW region and more rural regions will 'lose out' relative to the S&E region, which has greater capacity to absorb this type of support. Already in terms of regional development, some of the 2000–06 NDP's achievements have been criticized. According to the findings of a study commissioned by the BMW Regional Assembly, expenditure rates show stark regional disparities in key areas such as national roads, public transport and Research and Technological Development and Innovation (RTDI) (BMW Regional Assembly, 2006). This issue has been a particular point of contention between the government and the current opposition party (*Fine Gael*), which proposed more concrete support for the regions in the future, for example by ring-fencing resources for the regions, and setting targets for the delivery of key projects in the region (*Fine Gael*, 2006).

With these challenges in mind, new, more inclusive forms of regional participation and policy governance may be necessary in the future. Relatedly, independently from structural funds programming arrangements, efforts to involve and engage regional authorities in 2007–13 have increased. Currently, overall coordination of NDP implementation is the responsibility of the Sectoral Policy Division in the Department of Finance. Implementation of NDP investments at the programme and project level is carried out at the level of government department or agency. However, representatives of the two Regional Assemblies and eight RAs are involved in the NDP's Central Monitoring Committee, representing the integration of regional representatives into high-level domestic, as well as EU, policy management activities. If successful, the inclusion of regional involvement at a strategic level and in monitoring the impact of the NDP at regional level will be an important way to increase regional involvement in policy governance, while at the same time retaining an integrated national plan.

Conclusion

This chapter began by noting that Ireland's rapid economic growth is commonly linked to the country's use of EU cohesion policy funds. What is less widely discussed is whether key developments in the implementation and governance of regional economic development policy are also related to the influence of the structural funds and how domestic structures have shaped the management and implementation of the funds.

In Ireland core aspects of the management and implementation of cohesion and domestic policies are a highly integrated policy approach, involving extended partnership arrangements, and an increased level of decentralization and regional participation in policy management and implementation. Both of these developments have strong parallels in EU cohesion policy approaches, which emphasize multiannual, integrated programmes, partnership working and subsidiarity.

The practice of programming EU cohesion policy funds and national policy together means that EU policy practices have been grafted onto domestic structures and exerted considerable influence across the whole policy spectrum. For instance, the requirement to monitor and evaluate EU funds has led, first, to considerable investment and training in evaluation and monitoring capacity and, second, to the widespread adoption of monitoring and evaluation across a wide range of policy fields. Similarly, the 'partnership principle' of structural funds programmes has facilitated and embedded partner involvement in policy development and implementation across current and future programmes.

In terms of regionalization, the EU's emphasis on subsidiarity and focus on geographically based programmes stimulated debate on regional reform, although regionally based politics and identities in the country were weak. The aim of maximizing receipts in 2000–06 led to the establishment of two Regional Authorities and an increased role for regional administrations in the management and implementation of the structural funds. Subsequent efforts at government and institutional decentralization suggest an ongoing commitment to greater regional participation in the policy process, which has its origins in pressures exerted by EU cohesion policy.

However, as the preceding sections have illustrated, it is also possible to question the extent to which these two key developments can be directly attributed to the influence of cohesion policy and the extent to which future programmes will retain these elements. Existing political and social structures and practices have exerted an influence, as have the country's size and levels of economic development. In the case of integrated policy making, experience of national 'programmes' aimed at promoting social consensus and economic reform provided solid foundations for new EU programmes to be built upon. Relatedly, a strong basis for consultative policy making already existed, through the country's experience of social partnership. Even then, there was no sudden, successful, wholesale transfer of the EU policy approach. During successive rounds of programming, policy coordination had to be worked on and modified in order to maximize the benefits.

In terms of regionalization and decentralization in Ireland, the extent to which development in the country can be directly attributable to EU influences and pressures can be questioned for a number of reasons. First, the country's small size and early designation as a single NUTS 2 region for the purposes of cohesion policy did little to encourage any regional reform. Second, to date, EU-supported programmes have retained a strong focus on boosting national economic development, as opposed to being geographically targeted. Third, Ireland's own centralist tradition and emphasis on social partnership have meant that links with regional institutions have been slower to build up. Fourth, as opposed to viewing regionalization as a response to EU regulatory pressures, many of the decisions to pursue regionalization can be viewed as pragmatic responses to changing economic conditions in the country.

Looking to the future, new questions arise regarding the ongoing influence of EU policy on governance structures and changes in the management and implementation of the structural funds. On the one hand, the reduction of EU funding for the country in 2007–13 and the separation of domestic and EU policy programming appears to signal a reduction in the 'importance' of EU cohesion policy in Ireland. Many of the activities now planned under domestic policy fall outside the remit of RCE funding that the Irish regions are entitled to. On the other, a strong emphasis on integrated policy making in the new NDP, the emphasis on consultation and coordination in the programming process, and an element of regional participation in policy development and implementation are carried forward and have strong echoes of structural funds programming approaches. Finally, as both EU cohesion policy and domestic policymakers focus on new development challenges, new approaches aimed at building economic competitiveness are sought for both EU and domestic regional economic development programmes, drawing lessons from cohesion policy but also looking for new approaches to meeting contemporary development challenges.

In conclusion, the influence of EU cohesion policy on domestic institutions is difficult to measure precisely. In some cases, cohesion policy requirements have 'necessitated' change and the national authorities were 'forced' to accept change. In others, new policy approaches, with their origins in cohesion policy, were enthusiastically embraced and shaped mainstream structures of policy and institutional governance. In other cases, although substantial changes have taken place, domestic conditions meant that cohesion policy approaches simply complemented or supported an existing policy or institutional trend. As a long-time net beneficiary of EU funds, Ireland has adapted to, or adopted, core elements of cohesion policy structures and practices. Successive rounds of cohesion policy funding have been managed in an increasingly integrated and regionalized way, which has informed and influenced wider approaches to regional policy implementation and governance structures in the country. However, through a process of adaptation EU policy approaches and structures have also been adapted to the national context and domestic institutions and practices have shaped and informed the management and implementation of the funds. The 2007–13 round of cohesion policy funding poses new challenges for Ireland, for example reduced levels of funding and a reorientation of the type of support offered towards the Lisbon Agenda and building regional competitiveness. Systems for the management and implementation of EU and domestic funds have had to adapt. However, core elements of Ireland's previous, distinctive approach to the management and implementation of EU funds have been retained.

7
Greece

Christos J. Paraskevopoulos

Introduction: cohesion policy in Greece – the national and EU context

Greece's accession to the EU in 1981 marked the beginning of a long and complex transformation process. Cohesion policy is the policy area most affected by and exposed to the Europeanization process since the pre-accession period. This has had serious consequences for the country's institutional and policy-making structures, particularly challenging Greece's traditional centralized administrative structure. Indeed, prior to accession, the highly centralized and hierarchical structure of the Greek state was based on decentralized administrative units at the level of prefecture, headed by Prefects, central government appointees who played a considerable role in local affairs as local self-government at the municipal and commune level remained fragmented and weakened by limited power, responsibilities and financial resources (Spanou, 2001). On the other hand, traditionally centralized and party-dominated, the Greek administrative system prevented the decentralized administrative units from developing the necessary management and decision-making capacity, thus leading to functional interference by the central state in almost all policy areas (Sotiropoulos, 1993). With regard to regional policy, in the pre-accession period it was primarily based on central planning initiatives that focused on the serious problem of regional disparities, the main feature of which is the concentration of population and economic, social and cultural activities primarily in the greater Athens area and secondarily in Thessaloniki. In that respect, national regional policy in the postwar period has evolved through several phases characterized by fiscal or monetary incentive packages for attracting private investments to the periphery, the provision of basic infrastructure through the creation of an extensive Industrial Areas Network across the country, and experimentation (especially during the post-authoritarian period after 1974) with the nodal or 'growth-poles' model of spatial planning focusing on the reduction of regional disparities through the development of a rival network of cities to Athens and Thessaloniki.

Thus, EU accession in general, and the gradual Europeanization of public and cohesion policies in particular, with the introduction of the Integrated Mediterranean Programmes (IMPs) (1986–89) and the three Community Support Frameworks (CSFs) (1989–06), has substantially contributed to the transformation of Greece's administrative and policy-making structures. In terms of administrative structure, the country is now divided into 13 administrative-planning regions, each headed by a government-appointed General Secretary who represents the central government and has responsibility primarily for planning and implementing EU cohesion policy at the regional level; 54 prefectures headed by a prefectural council and a directly elected (since 1994) Prefect; and local governments at the municipal and commune levels headed by mayors enjoying a public mandate. In terms of cohesion policy structures, Europeanization brought about the establishment of democratic planning procedures at each spatial level, facilitated by institutional changes in intergovernmental relations, and simultaneously, the maintenance of a hierarchical, top-down structure, within which the coherence and complementarity of projects would be achieved, thus leading to a planning system combining 'top-down' control with the 'bottom-up' definition of priorities (Paraskevopoulos, 2001a).

It is in this respect that, in public policy in general and regional policy in particular – and especially in the cases of Greece and other cohesion countries – Europeanization is viewed as an independent variable that crucially affects and challenges well-established structures within domestic systems of governance and plays an important role in the administrative restructuring and devolution processes within member states by enhancing institutional capacity at the subnational level. In particular, its impact on the regional and local policy-making arenas is supposed to be twofold: a direct impact, by providing increased resources through redistribution and a new set of rules and procedures for the formulation and implementation of cohesion policies; and an indirect impact, by shaping intraregional interactions and thus promoting local institutional capacity through the creation of intra-, inter- and transregional networks that support local development initiatives.

Given the complexity of multilevel governance structures within which the adaptation process takes place and the distinctive character of policy-making structures at the EU level,[1] however, the degree of 'adaptational pressures' facing domestic institutions and policy-making structures in order to comply with European rules and regulations in public policy in general, and cohesion policy in particular, is especially high in unitary and centralized states like Greece. Yet, the presence of a high degree of adaptational pressure constitutes a necessary but not sufficient condition for domestic institutional and policy change. Indeed, there is evidence to suggest that the latter is crucially conditioned by the presence of specific institutional structures at the domestic level of governance that may facilitate or inhibit the adaptation process (Paraskevopoulos, 1998, 2001a, 2001b; Börzel and Risse, 2000). In other words, although the Europeanization process plays a key role in the transformation of domestic systems of governance in general, and public and cohesion policy-making structures in particular, domestic institutions, and especially specific features of the pre-existing institutional infrastructure at the national and subnational levels of government, matter for adaptation (Garmise, 1995; Lenschow, 1997; Jeffery, 2000; Paraskevopoulos, 1998, 2001a, 2001b; Börzel, 2001; Risse, Cowles, and Caporaso, 2001; Keating, Loughlin, and Deschouwer, 2003). Therefore, as discussed in Chapter 1, specific features of the domestic institutional infrastructure constitute a crucial intervening variable between Europeanization and domestic policy and institutional change that can account for the pace of the Europeanization process.

Within this theoretical framework, this chapter examines the evolution of institutional and policy-making structures for cohesion policy in Greece as the outcome of the process of Europeanization-induced domestic change and points to some aspects of the learning process that may help account for it. Thus, the first section critically examines the changes that occurred in cohesion policy structures from the first (1989–93) to the second (1994–99) and third (2000–06) programming periods for EU cohesion policy, throughout which the entire country was an Objective 1 region. The second section focuses on the impact of the so-called Lisbonization of cohesion policy on the programming procedures for drafting the National Strategic Reference Framework (NSRF) for 2007–13 and critically examines the changes in policy design and orientation reflected in the sectoral and regional Operational Programmes (OPs). The third section attempts a very brief assessment of key qualitative features of the learning process, such as the role of pre-existing institutional structures and the involvement of non-state actors in the policy process that may account for the specificities of change. Finally, the chapter draws its main conclusions and discusses the way in which cohesion policy in Greece over the last decades may be viewed as a lesson-drawing exercise with regard to the impact of the Europeanization process on domestic policy-making structures at large.

Changing tune: from the first to the second and third CSFs[2]

This section examines the way in which a major shift in the main goals and priorities of cohesion policy, namely from extensive experimentation with democratic participation in the policy planning and implementation processes, especially at the subnational level of government, towards greater efficiency and perhaps transparency in the use of EU funds by exploiting economies of scale and developing the country's infrastructure through large, national-scale projects, was brought about after completion of the first CSF in 1993–94. Additionally, it analyzes implementation of the third CSF (2000–06).

From democratic participation towards efficiency in the use of EU funds

Greece's entry into the EU in 1981 coincided with a major change in Greek politics: the coming to power of the first PASOK (Pan-Hellenic Socialist Movement, Πανελλήνιο Σοσιαλιστικό Κίνημα) government. Thus, Greece's initial response to the challenge of adjusting to the new European environment in the 1980s was marked by the presence of a new socialist government, which came to power with a strong commitment to a widely publicized programme of decentralization, devolution of power and encouragement of civic participation in the policy-making process. Thus, the EU's initiation of the IMPs[3] in the mid-1980s – which marked the departure from a sectoral and project-oriented towards an integrated and programme-oriented approach to development, thus beginning the formulation of a coherent EU regional policy – coincided with and gave impetus to reform of the system of centre-periphery relations, involving, formally at least, decentralization of power, extensive institution building and experimentation with new, for Greece, forms of civic participation in the policy process (see Mitsos, 2001; Paraskevopoulos, 1998, 2001b).[4] With the introduction of the first CSF in 1989, these features of coherence in regional policy were further strengthened through the adoption of a multiannual programming approach and introduction of the concepts of partnership, additionality, proportionality and subsidiarity as dominant policy principles (see Paraskevopoulos, 2001b).

In Greece, despite the experience with the IMPs, the initiation of the CSFs brought about an almost completely new policy environment, especially in the areas of policy planning and implementation, which actors had to cope with. This new environment was characterized by a system of multilevel planning, involving sectoral programmes of national scale (the national component) and Regional Operational Programmes (ROPs) for each of the 13 regions, as well as by innovative, for Greece, institutions for the participation of nongovernmental actors in policymaking at each level of government, such as the Monitoring Committees (MCs) of the OPs. However, although both the IMPs and the first CSF functioned as catalysts for the creation of a plethora of new institutions at the subnational level, such as the Regional Development Agencies (RDAs), and the upgrading of old ones, the weakness of the institutional infrastructure at large, marked by the role of clientelism in the policy-making process, led to overall poor policy outcomes (see Paraskevopoulos, 2001b).

Amidst the unfavourable domestic political climate of the early 1990s, accompanied by deterioration of the macroeconomic situation of the country and intense pressure to meet the Maastricht criteria in order to qualify for joining Economic and Monetary Union (EMU), there was increased emphasis in the domestic political discourse on the importance of accelerating the pace of development as a way of catching up with other member states. This trend was underpinned by arguments about the generally bad condition of almost all sectors of the country's physical infrastructure, as well as by references to what other comparable (cohesion) countries, notably Portugal and Ireland, had already done or were doing. In fact, there was a widespread feeling that funds from the first CSF, having been dispersed on small-scale, regional projects across the country, had much less of an impact than they would have had they been concentrated on large-scale infrastructure projects. Yet, it has to be stressed that this was a rather tacit, knowledge-based and not expertise-informed debate. Nonetheless, over the period of the 1980s and early 1990s cohesion policy was an important issue in the domestic political arena and party politics at large. At the heart of the political discourse on cohesion policy was the issue of democratic planning and participation initiated by the PASOK government *vis-à-vis* effectiveness, efficiency and transparency in the use of EU funds. More specifically, the main opposition centre-right party, New Democracy (ND), argued that what the democratic planning procedures were substantially about was the dispersion of EU money on small-scale projects to satisfy PASOK's clienteles at the local level, at the expense of effectiveness, efficiency and transparency in the use of EU funds. Ironically, it is in this way that the issue of developing physical infrastructure as a prerequisite for facilitating the development of other sectors of the economy, and society as a whole, came to the fore and influenced the planning and implementation processes of both the second and third CSFs under subsequent PASOK governments of the 1990s. The same considerations also led to the increased involvement of technocrats in the policy process in the 1990s (see below).

Indeed, although the development of basic infrastructure, along with human resources and the productive environment, constitute common features of the sectoral or national programmes of all three CSFs, it represents by-far the greatest share of total expenditure in both the second (1994–99) and third (2000–06) programming periods (46 and 43.2 per cent respectively) (CEC, 2001, p. 56), compared to 23.8 per cent in the first CSF (CEC, 1989). Additionally, given that the increase in infrastructure expenditure is financed through the sectoral component of the programmes, this has led to a significant increase in the share of the national component (Sectoral Operational Programmes, SOPs) *vis-à-vis* the regional one (ROPs) – although the latter still remains substantial – in the second and third CSFs, as indicated in Table 7.1 below.

This shift in the policy process from emphasis on participation to taking economies of scale seriously, and therefore towards large-scale infrastructure projects, has undoubtedly led to a significant improvement of infrastructure in crucial areas where the country was lagging behind. It seems, however, that a recentralization of policymaking has accompanied this shift.

Strengthening central administration capacity

In particular, the emphasis on large-scale projects was accompanied by significant institutional creation, in order to strengthen the capacity

Table 7.1   National and regional components of CSFs (€ mn, current prices)

	National component	%	Regional component	%
CSF I	7,142	59.6	4,845	40.4
CSF II	22,206	74.9	7,427	25.1
CSF III	31,093	74.2	10,825	25.8

Source: Kafkalas and Andrikopoulou (2003).

of central state administrative structures and especially the Ministry of the Economy. Moreover, this trend towards improving the central state administrative capacity also reflected increased concerns of the European Commission about the role of the central state bureaucracy in managing EU funds, as became clear with the 1999 Regulation of the structural funds. Thus, the need to allocate responsibilities for planning, management, payment and evaluation led to an enhanced role for the relevant administrative institutions (the central administration of the Ministry of Economy, General Secretary, Minister), as well as the creation of new institutions, such as the Managing Organization Unit (MOU), the Managing Authorities (MAs) for implementing the OPs, the Paying Authority (PA) and the Committee of Fiscal Control (Getimis and Demetropoulou, 2004). This trend seems to have led to the reluctant involvement of technocrats (independent consultants, experts) in policymaking and implementation at both the national and subnational levels of administration. The creation of new municipalities through the compulsory merger of the communes (the so-called Kapodistrias Plan) in 1997 should be viewed as another step in the same direction, namely improving the level of efficiency.

Additionally, emphasis on large-scale infrastructure projects and the increased share of the sectoral or national component in the second and third CSFs have also led to an overall increase in the share of private sector involvement in and contribution to projects, especially at the national level (Kafkalas and Andrikopoulou, 2003). This involvement, undoubtedly constituting a major innovation in terms of public policymaking in Greece, has taken the form of either Public-Private Partnerships (PPPs) or concession agreements and is mostly concentrated on projects of large scale and European magnitude.

The creation of the MOU and Joint Steering Committee (JSC) constitute the main institutional innovations related to the involvement of expertise in the policy process. The MOU is a support mechanism, operating under the guidance and control of the Ministry of Economy, but external to its civil service structure. The MOU's role is to support public administration by covering specific needs in highly specialized human resources and know-how for the successful implementation of CSF OPs that exceed the technical and administrative capacity of the implementing authorities (e.g., the organization of MAs, selection and training of personnel, transfer of know-how and provision of organization tools) (see Paraskevopoulos, 2005).

The JSC was established in January 1995 within the Ministry of Economy as a subcommittee to the CSF MC, with the aim of improving the system for the production of public works. Both Greek authorities and the Commission saw such an improvement as a prerequisite for the efficient realization of the infrastructure projects of the second CSF and the Cohesion Fund (CF). The JSC was focused on three broad areas related to the production of public works: studies for public projects and planning; the contracting system, including Calls for Tenders; and the construction of public works. In that respect, a wide range of experts related to these issues were directly or indirectly involved in the workings of the JSC. There have been two major problems particularly related to the production system of public works in Greece that the JSC tried to deal with: the problem of the so-called unusually low/abnormal prices of public works; and quality control. With regard to the former, a major comparative study involving France, Germany, Spain, Belgium and the United Kingdom was carried out in an attempt to draw lessons from the experiences of other member states. A great part of this investigation was concentrated on the pros and cons of the 'mathematical method' (the so-called *mathimatikos typos*) for dealing with the issue of abnormal prices. As for the problem of quality control, the JSC concentrated on making recommendations for improving the function of the External Consultant for Quality Control of Infrastructure Projects (ESPEL), which was established in 1996. Otherwise, the JSC was particularly active in the areas of concession agreements and the Private Finance Initiative (PFI) and PPP contracts (see Paraskevopoulos, 2005).

In sum, there have been some positive developments with regard to the involvement of non-state actors in the policy process and the learning capacity of the domestic policy environment at large, especially since the mid-1990s. However, given that there is no evidence of extended private sector involvement elsewhere in the policy process, for example, in the ROPs (see Paraskevopoulos and Leonardi, 2004), this may be sporadic and limited only to large-scale infrastructure projects. On the other hand, the involvement of experts, although significant, is not in the form of independent think tanks, but rather recruitment within or under the guidance of specific ministries. Additionally, Greece's institutional infrastructure is characterized by a low level of social capital and the weakness of civil society, which is particularly evident in the low levels of social trust and trust in public institutions (see Paraskevopoulos, 2007). This is accompanied by limited and problematic (not fully institutionalized) forums for dialogue and negotiation; the low presence of PPPs; the predominance of political parties (the so-called partitocracy) and clientelism in the policy process; and a relatively strong resistance to change closely linked to the patterns of interest intermediation. In that respect, statism, namely a centralized and simultaneously weak administrative structure, has been the main feature of the formal institutional infrastructure in public policy in general, and in cohesion policy in particular, with serious implications for the learning capacity of the domestic institutional infrastructure. Nonetheless, some of the above developments, especially the increased involvement of experts in policymaking, have strengthened the primarily technocratic character of the planning and implementation processes of cohesion policy, a feature already evident in the early 1990s when policymaking in cohesion policy gradually began to be removed from the realm of party competition and politics.

Implementing the 2000–06 CSF

Implementation of the 2000–06 CSF was strongly influenced by the improvements in central administration capacity described above, as well as by the legal requirements set out by the 1999 structural funds Regulation, which strengthened the progress already achieved in the 1994–99 CSF in improving the efficiency and transparency of implementing bodies and ensuring sound financial management at every level of government. Compared to the 1994–99 CSF, the new implementing system incorporated more detailed and systematic procedures. Significant progress has been achieved especially with regard to project selection and approval procedures and the streamlining of procedures for monitoring and control. In that respect, the compliance of structural fund interventions with EU law is a condition for granting payments. The CSF Managing Authority (MA) systematically informs the OP MAs on the state of transposition of EU directives into national law, and supports them in order to ensure compliance with the EU legal requirements. Special attention is paid to compliance with EU legislation on public procurement, environmental protection and state aid, rules on the equal treatment of men and women and rural development policy. The responsibility for project selection lies with the respective OP MAs. While over the previous programming periods the principle that only technically mature projects may be funded had been established, in 2000–06 a procedure for evaluating economic and social viability was introduced for both public and private sector projects. A system of open calls for project proposals was developed enabling a more effective choice to be made between alternative proposals. Thus the capacity, especially at the regional level, for ensuring professionally sound assessments of projects was strengthened and rules governing the selection of projects were clarified. In that respect, expenditure due to cost or time overruns is negligible, unless the projects are resubmitted to a second approval procedure and adopted with the new planning proposed.

The PA is responsible for monitoring the financial flows, for drawing up payment applications and for receiving payments from the Commission. It also ensures payments to the final beneficiaries in the least amount of time and in full. It is subject to external controls and, in case of irregularities, subject to financial corrections. Financial corrections can take place only after a hearing of the interested parties and in compliance with the principle of proportionality. In addition, they are subject to administrative and judicial appeal. The PA is the single entity authorized to access accounts kept in the Bank of Greece (one account for each structural fund, one for each Community Initiative and one for the CF). Commitments and payment provisions are registered in the Public Investment Programme. This budget contains data enabling the identification of the operation, the final beneficiary and the financial assistance. Payment information is controlled and registered in the CSF Management Information System by the each respective OP MA. The PA checks and verifies this information before the submission of payment applications to the Commission.

Control is organized on three levels: Internal (first level) control lies with the OP and CSF MAs. It concerns the material, financial and accounting aspects of the project. It takes place *in situ* and, when appropriate, in the headquarters of the entities keeping original documents related to the project in question. External (second level) control, carried out by the PA, consists of the audit and assessment of first level controls. Coordination and assessment of the whole system of control (third level), carried out by a special unit of the Ministry of Economy, comprises specific inspections and control of a sample of 5 per cent of all projects. The control unit is also responsible for drawing up the assessment declaration provided for in Article 38f of the structural funds Regulation (OJEC, 1999, p. 31). By virtue of its own tasks related to management of the EU budget, the Commission verifies that the control system ensures the correct and efficient use of the structural funds. On its own initiative it can perform monitoring inspections with the assistance, if necessary, of national authorities.

In terms of performance, there are no huge differences among the 2000–06 OPs. With the exception of OP Environment, which had an expenditure rate of approximately 63 per cent, all of the OPs had expenditure rates of 65–81 per cent as of December 2007 (CSF III for Greece). In terms of the 13 ROPs, the crucial variables affecting performance are the capacity of local institutional infrastructure and, most importantly, administrative capacity at the regional level of government. Given that there is no evidence of huge differences among the Greek regions in terms of the former, what really matters in the Greek context is administrative capacity at the regional government level, namely the Regional Secretariats. In that respect, an indicative case is the Secretariat of the Central Macedonia region whose increased capacity has actually counterbalanced weaknesses of the region's general institutional infrastructure. This is reflected in the level of performance of its ROP, with an expenditure rate above 80 per cent of public commitments, and further vindicated by the fact that the Central Macedonia region – a 'Phasing-out' region in 2007–13 – was named 'Southern European Region of the Future for 2006–07' by the Foreign Direct Investment (FDI) magazine of the *Financial Times* group.

Overall, contradictory trends in centre-periphery relations and institutional innovation are the main features of the incremental impact of Europeanization on domestic policy and institutional change in Greece: on the one hand, structural funds regulations and norms have initiated the process of institutional restructuring at the regional level; on the other, the tendency of pre-existing institutional infrastructure towards centralization continues to play a key role in the planning and implementation processes of regional policy. Thus, despite the fact that institution building is widely considered the main outcome of the learning process, the strengthening and stability of institutions still remains a key challenge for Greece's public policy arena within the EU's multilevel governance structure. Indeed, institution building was significantly absent from the democratization and Europeanization agenda during both the first post-authoritarian period (1974–81) and, most importantly, the first post-accession (1981–86) period. Changes were introduced in 1986 to Greece's statist structure through creation of the 13 administrative regions, and in 1994 with creation of the directly elected prefecture councils. Subsequent changes were also made through the 1997 reorganization of local governments. With regard to management of the structural funds, Greece has experimented with the introduction of expertise from outside of the administrative structure and new approaches to the implementation of cohesion policy (see Paraskevopoulos and Leonardi, 2004).

Impact of the 'Lisbonization' of cohesion policy

Drafting the 2007–13 national strategic development plan

The 'Lisbonization' of cohesion policy, with the reorientation of main policy goals towards economic growth through competitiveness and environmental sustainability, thus encouraging innovation, entrepreneurship and growth of the knowledge economy, which was reflected in the Community Strategic Guidelines on Cohesion (CSG), brought about changes in the programming procedures for drafting the National Strategic Development Plan (NSDP), as well as in the policy priorities and structure of the National Strategic Reference Framework (NSRF) for Greece for 2007–13. In that respect, the reduced level of funding due to enlargement (€18.2 billion, at 2004 prices, about a 26 per cent reduction from the €24.7 billion Greece received in 2000–06 – see Table 7.2) has not been the main issue of the fourth programming period, given that policy orientation and use of the funds has long been a crucial aspect of cohesion policy implementation in Greece.

The process of drafting the NSDP was initiated in June 2004, when a Circular was issued defining the various bodies and levels to be involved. Overall responsibility for drafting the NSDP lay with the Ministry of Economy, which worked in association with the other ministries involved as well as regional and local authorities. The whole planning process involved horizontal and vertical consultation with the appropriate agencies and economic and social partners at three levels. On preparation level 1, the Coordination and Policy Formulation Committee functioned as a central coordinating mechanism; it established the basic framework within which the NSDP was developed and determined the general and more specific issues to be discussed in the context of social dialogue.On preparation level 2, the key body was the Drafting Group, which supported the Coordination and Policy Formulation Committee

Table 7.2   Cohesion policy allocations in Greece, 2000–06 and 2007–13

Allocations 2000–06 (€ mn, 2004 prices)		Allocations (2007–13 € mn, 2004 prices)	
Cohesion fund	3,388	Cohesion fund	3,280
Objective 1	20,458	Convergence	8,358
		Statistical phasing-out	5,765
Phasing-out	NA	Phasing-in	582
Objective 2	NA	Regional competitiveness	
		and employment	NA
Objective 3	NA		
Community initiatives	857	European territorial cooperation	186
Total	24,703	Total	18,172

Source: European Commission (2006g).

on a day-to-day basis. On preparation level 3, the Ministry and Regional Authority Planning Groups acted as the liaison between the ministry or regional authorities and the Drafting Group.

A second Circular was later issued providing more detailed guidance for preparation of the NSDP, and describing the methodology and procedures to be used for planning sectoral and regional development priorities. It also described the principles to be followed in organizing Regional Development Conferences, which have made a crucial contribution to the planning of regional priorities.

Development planning for 2007–13 was based on specific Strategic Objectives or Development Axes (see below) that were consistent with overall EU strategy. Each sectoral policy agency (e.g., ministries) and each regional policy agency (Regional General Secretariats) drew up their own Development Programmes that would form the basis for OPs. In the OPs, the attainment of objectives would be monitored using quantified indicators wherever possible. It was envisaged that Development Programmes would receive funding not only from EU and national resources, but also from the private sector through joint PPPs.

The reorientation of development goals and objectives was strongly influenced by the new development phase of the Greek economy, particularly its progress towards greater competitiveness in the global economy. Thus, the cornerstones of the reorientation of development and cohesion policy in Greece are the continuation of structural change in the framework of the Single Market, economic integration, and the restructuring and modernization of public administration at all levels of government. In that respect, the Commission's guideline texts, and particularly the Third Report on Cohesion (CEC, 2004a), were viewed as creating the framework for the new Development Axes to be followed in drawing up the NSDP. These Development Axes are: strengthening competitiveness; improving accessibility and services of general economic interest; upgrading and protecting the environment and averting environmental dangers; developing human resources and promoting employment; improving the managerial competence of public administration; and strengthening cross-border, transnational and transregional cooperation.

Within this analytical framework, the prompt formulation of the NSDP came to be viewed as the most important phase of the programming process, given that the document would constitute the basis for negotiations with the Commission, while also providing the framework for drafting the new OPs. Yet, this formulation involved the increased participation and consultation of a wide variety of actors, including the government ministries responsible for the SOPs, Regional General Secretariats responsible for the ROPs, as well as local authorities and socioeconomic actors.

The NSRF for 2007–13

On the basis of the CSG, and taking into account domestic specificities, particularly Greece's weakness in relation to specific indicators of the Lisbon Agenda such as those for the 'knowledge economy',[5] the main

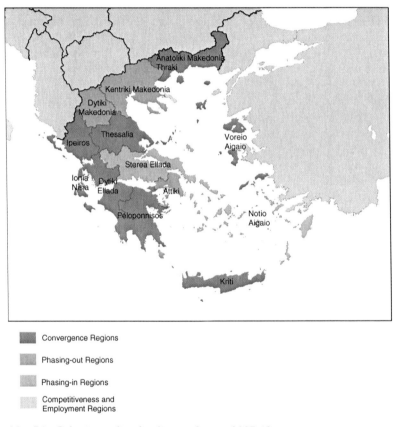

Convergence Regions

Phasing-out Regions

Phasing-in Regions

Competitiveness and
Employment Regions

Map 7.1   Cohesion policy funding in Greece, 2007–13

Source: European Commission, DG Regional Policy.

features of the NSRF are the reorientation of policy priorities, reflected primarily in the SOPs, and a major restructuring of the regional component (ROPs). The latter involves a new categorization of regions – eight Convergence (Eastern Macedonia and Thrace, Epirus, Thessaly, Western Greece, Ionian Islands, Peloponnesus, Crete and Northern Aegean), three 'Phasing-out' (Attica, Central Macedonia and Western Macedonia) and two 'Phasing-in' (Sterea Ellada and Southern Aegean) regions (see Map 7.1 below) – and the creation of new major spatial units incorporating several regions along the main axes of the country (e.g., Northern Greece, Western Greece, Island regions), which has led to five, instead of 13, ROPs. This decision was informed by size and geography considerations. Yet, given the 'creeping centralization' that seems to be entrenched by the new implementation system and the divergence of regions that have been put together within the same new spatial units, the gains in terms of effectiveness and efficiency remain to be seen.

The main policy priorities of the NSRF include the following:

- A shift in focus from infrastructure to entrepreneurship and competitiveness. More support will be given for entrepreneurship and innovation infrastructure ('soft' actions and support systems) and less for technical infrastructure, apart from cases of severe local problems and the completion of nationwide networks.
- The linkage of all national and regional interventions (in both Convergence and Competitiveness regions) to the goal of enhanced competitiveness.
- An emphasis on more balanced regional competitiveness. Despite the fact that development disparities among Greek regions are smaller than in many other countries, many regions are facing significant problems, especially with regard to productivity and competitiveness indicators: the per capita Gross Value Added (GVA) is significantly lower than the national average in six of the 13 regions, the GDP re-investment rate is extremely disproportionate in three regions, unemployment rates are particularly high in five of the 13 regions, and 60 per cent of all new businesses are established in Attica and 75 per cent in only two of the 13 regions.
- A clear analysis of the role of all interventions in addressing crucial challenges, such as the recent and future EU enlargements, international competition, interregional competition and the reform of EU policies (e.g., the CAP).
- A particular emphasis on policy areas showing a 'deficit' in previous programming periods, such as macroeconomic actions (e.g.,

deregulation of the energy market, privatization of state enterprises and mergers, the development of leading enterprises that have the potential to enter the international market) and 'targeted' interventions (support for Small and Medium-Sized Enterprise (SMEs), creation of internationally competitive 'development poles' in the regions, the emergence of 'areas of excellence' in the industry and tourism sectors, and the recapturing of domestic markets by SMEs).

- The shaping of a long-term development strategy, which includes all sectoral policies and which will be linked to macroeconomic policies;
- An emphasis in the OPs on cooperation between different sectors, OPs and ministries, and on networking among the regions.

The NSRF for 2007–13 incorporates 13 OPs (compared to 25 in 2000–06) – ten funded by the European Regional Development Fund (ERDF) and the CF, and three by the European Social Fund (ESF) – together providing €20.4 billion of EU funding (at 2006 prices). The ten OPs supported by the ERDF and the CF include four thematic or sectoral programmes, five regional programmes and one technical assistance programme, together representing €15.8 billion of EU investment. The three OPs supported by the ESF (Human Resources Development, Education and Lifelong learning, Improvement of Public Administration Efficiency) will receive €4.5 billion in EU funding. These programmes aim to promote a knowledge-based economy, improve the flexibility of the country's workforce and develop a more effective public administration. Special efforts will be made to tackle the problem of undeclared work and to fight discrimination against vulnerable groups. Table 7.3 below presents a summary of the SOPs and ROPs for 2007–13.

Domestic institutional capacity, policy learning and policy change in cohesion policy

Policy learning refers to the processes of 'learning from abroad' and 'learning through past successes and failures'. This section briefly examines aspects of institutional infrastructure, broadly conceived to include social norms (social capital) and cooperative culture, that are crucial for the learning process. It does so in a comparative way, by assessing Greece *vis-à-vis* other comparable cohesion countries, notably Ireland and Portugal.

The issue of policy learning, and particularly 'learning from abroad', has been raised relatively recently in the public debate on cohesion policy in Greece in relation to the much admired 'Irish model', which is often

Table 7.3 2007–13 Operational Programmes in Greece (financial allocations in €)

Programme	Fund	Total
1 OP Environment and Sustainable Development	ERDF	220,000,000
1 OP Environment and Sustainable Development	CF	1,580,000,000
1 OP Environment and Sustainable Development	TOTAL	1,800,000,000
2 OP Accessibility Improvement	ERDF	1,583,000,000
2 OP Accessibility Improvement	CF	2,117,160,864
2 OP Accessibility Improvement	TOTAL	3,700,160,864
3 OP Competitiveness and Entrepreneurship	ERDF	1,291,000,000
4 OP Digital Convergence	ERDF	860,000,000
5 OP Human Resources Development	ESF	2,260,000,000
6 OP Education and Lifelong Learning	ESF	1,440,000,000
7 OP Reinforcement of Public Administration Efficiency	ESF	505,000,000
8 OP Technical Assistance	ERDF	192,000,000
9 ROP Makedonia-Thraki	ERDF	2,675,000,000
10 ROP Dytiki Ellada-Peloponnisos-Ionia Nisia	ERDF	914,000,000
11 ROP Kriti & Nisia Aigaiou	ERDF	871,300,178
12 ROP Thessalia-Sterea Ellada-Ipeiros	ERDF	1,105,000,000
13 ROP Attiki	ERDF	2,438,000,000
14 OP Territorial Cooperation	ERDF	209,515,579
15 National Contingency Reserve	ERDF	158,800,403
Total NSRF 2007–13		20,419,777,000

Source: NSRF 2007–13 for Greece.

used in the domestic public policy discourse as a success story and paradigmatic case to be followed, but also to the Portuguese model, especially in relation to the use of EU funds and the development process at large. In particular, the shift in emphasis from small-scale to rather major infrastructure projects since the mid-1990s in Greece came to be viewed as an outcome of the 'learning from abroad' process with particular reference to the Irish and Portuguese cases. Yet, the weakness of domestic institutional infrastructure is widely considered a crucial impediment to the country's learning capacity, thus contributing to a rather slow pace of the learning process in Greece. Indeed, beyond the obvious factors, namely a well-trained, English-speaking workforce and close proximity to the main European markets (European core), which make the country attractive for FDI, the 'Irish model' of public policy and administration is based on a relatively strong institutional infrastructure, especially at the central state level, involving an effective and efficient central state bureaucracy that draws significantly on the UK Westminster model (see Paraskevopoulos and Leonardi, 2004; Rees, Quinn, and Connaughton, 2004). Although far from ideal, this institutional infrastructure is preferable to the ineffective and inefficient Greek state bureaucracy (Sotiropoulos, 2004). Additionally, and most importantly, Ireland demonstrates much higher levels of social capital and hence cooperative culture than Greece. In particular, Ireland appears to be well above Greece in all aspects of social capital measurement, namely social trust, trust in political institutions, especially in public service, and membership in and role of civil society organizations (e.g., NGOs) in the public policy process (Lyberaki and Paraskevopoulos, 2002; Paraskevopoulos and Leonardi, 2004). These features of the domestic institutional infrastructure, conducive to the building up of cooperative culture and probably related to the fact that Ireland has not had any experience of authoritarianism, facilitated social dialogue and allowed social partners to agree on a social pact in the mid-1980s that led to the stabilization and substantial improvement of the national macroeconomy and to an accelerated pace of development during the 1990s (Rees, Quinn, and Connaughton, 2004).

A similar picture emerges from comparison with Portugal, although the countries appear to be closer in several respects. In particular, public policymaking in Portugal is based on a French-educated/style central administration bureaucracy, which has been relatively more effective and efficient in the management of EU funds than the Greek public administration (see Nanetti, Rato, and Rodrigues, 2004). Additionally, Portugal does better than Greece on all social capital measurement indicators, especially the levels of social trust and trust in political institutions (Paraskevopoulos and Leonardi, 2004).

Overall, there is evidence to suggest that, while the development of physical infrastructure can undoubtedly be characterized as a major success of the modernization process in Greece, the process of institution building and the reform of public policy structures have proven to be much more difficult. Indeed, despite the serious efforts to combat clientelistic practices and create trust in public institutions, such as the establishment of the Higher Council for Personnel Recruitment (Ανατο Συ ο λιο Επιλο ής Προσωπ κο , ASEP),[6] statism, or more specifically a centralized and simultaneously weak administrative structure accompanied by the predominance of political clientelism in the policy process, still remains the main feature of the institutional infrastructure of public policymaking in Greece. This is not to deny important achievements of the modernization process, especially when it comes to separating the functions of the state and political parties, facilitated to a significant extent by the almost global trend towards a diminishing role for political parties, at least in the everyday implementation of public policy. Yet, in the Greek case this seems to have led to a sort of cross-party clientelism, the so-called clientelism at the bottom (see Sotiropoulos, 2004), accompanied by increased levels of *petit corruption*, especially at the subnational level of government. What has to be stressed, however, is that the limited success in institution building and the reform of public policymaking structures may arguably be accounted for by the 'burden' of deeply rooted patterns of behaviour and practices, inherited from past decades of statism, political clientelism and populism – especially from the 1980s – that the modernization process has had to confront.

Conclusions

The evolution of cohesion policy in Greece over the last decades is characterized by a shift in emphasis from the participation of actors and relatively small-scale interventions to rather large-scale infrastructure projects, especially in the area of transport. Although this trend was facilitated by the availability of increased financial resources due to the doubling of EU funds for both the second (CSF, 1994–99) and third (CSF, 2000–06) programming periods, it was fundamentally influenced by Europeanization and modernization processes and pushed forward by processes of 'learning from past successes and failures' and 'learning from abroad'. Particularly in the early 1990s, an era of high adaptational pressures for Greece, the importance of infrastructure for development came to the fore through lessons drawn from the past – the poor results of the first CSF – as well as from abroad, namely by reference to what other comparable countries, notably Portugal and Ireland, were doing. This policy learning, however, is characterized by a rather slow pace because of Greece's weakness in crucial variables for the learning process, such as the weakness of domestic institutional and policy-making structures. This is particularly evident in the case of social norms conducive to a cooperative culture, notably social capital, and the involvement of non-state actors in the policy process. Moreover, this seems to be, in relative terms, a key variable differentiating Greece from other cohesion countries, such as Ireland and Portugal. With regard to 2007–13, the 'Lisbonization' of cohesion policy has brought about changes in programming procedures for drafting the NSDP and NSRF for Greece. Additionally, a major reorientation of policy priorities towards the development of a 'knowledge economy', reflected primarily in the SOPs as well as major restructuring of the ROPs, has taken place. In that respect, reduced funding due to enlargement is not considered the key issue. Instead, the process of institution building, a crucial parameter for cohesion policy planning and implementation processes over the previous programming periods for Greece, is expected to be a crucial challenge for the current programming period as well.

Notes

1. Although significant variation from one policy area to another is considered the main feature of EU policy-making structures and practices, it has been argued that the EU institutional structure is more federal than unitary and its policy-making processes more pluralist than statist (Schmidt, 1997). In that respect, it has been predicted that the more centralized and unitary member states are likely to face stronger adaptational pressures than decentralized and federal ones (Ibid.).
2. Part of this section draws on Paraskevopoulos (2005).
3. It should be remembered that the 'memorandum' submitted by the PASOK government, which focused on improving aspects of Greece's EU accession, played a key role in the initiation of the IMPs. The memorandum was prepared by the Greek Commissioner, Grigorios Varfis, and his *chef-de-cabinet*, Dr. Achilles Mitsos. The latter would later play an important role in formulating EU cohesion policy in DG XXII, the Commission department responsible for coordination of the structural funds.
4. Institution building involved creation of the 13 administrative regions in 1986 and the elected second tier of subnational government at the prefectural level in 1994.
5. Greece lags far behind in relation to most Lisbon targets, such as the job creation and employment rate, particularly for women and older workers, risk-of-poverty rate after social transfers, long-term unemployment rate, greenhouse gas emissions and energy intensity of the economy. Yet, the most striking discrepancy, closely linked to the main goal of achieving a 'knowledge economy', is the case of gross domestic expenditure on R&D; Greece spent 0.57 per cent of GDP on R&D in 2006, compared to an EU27 rate of 1.84 per cent and the EU target rate of 3 per cent for 2010. It is indicative of Greece's position that the R&D expenditure target of 1.5 per cent of GDP has been postponed from 2010 to 2015 (see CEC, 2006b).
6. The ASEP is a special public sector body for civil service personnel recruitment through competitive examinations. It should be stressed, however, that such efforts towards enhancing trust in political institutions and thus building social capital constitute themselves byproducts of the lack of social capital and may have serious implications for the efficiency of public policy-making in the short to medium-term, namely by increasing transaction costs within the policy process.

8
Poland

Grzegorz Gorzelak and Marek W. Kozak

For Poland EU accession has been a great success, economically as well as in terms of the opportunities that have opened up for Polish citizens, firms and organizations for active participation in the social and economic life of Europe. Accession is fully accepted in Poland, with opinion polls showing that more than 80 per cent of Poles are satisfied with membership. This differs from the situation before accession, when there was a substantial minority against joining the EU; especially among farmers and rural residents there was a widespread belief that accession would be harmful to Polish enterprises and farms. However, as it became obvious that the economy was receiving a strong boost from accession, and that farmers were benefiting significantly from EU support (through the Common Agricultural Policy [CAP] and structural programmes), even the most sceptical politicians began to refrain from criticizing the economic impact of EU membership.

EU cohesion policy has had a significant and complex impact on Polish regional policy in at least three areas: planning, implementation and financing. It is important to remember that in 1999 Poland finally concluded the decentralization and reform of its territorial organization: 16 new regions (*Województwo*) were created and given substantial competencies in the field of development policy (although this was not necessarily matched by a proportionate share of public finances), something which gave new impetus to regional policy reform. From the very beginning, regionalization in Poland was done with EU cohesion policy in mind.

This chapter examines the implementation of EU cohesion policy in Poland. It begins with a brief look at historically influenced regional development patterns in Poland. The subsequent sections discuss the development of regional policy in Poland and the relationship between

141

Polish regional policy and state spatial policy. The chapter then examines the implementation of EU cohesion policy in the two programming periods (2004–06 and 2007–13) after accession and the implications of cohesion policy for Poland's economic development.

The regional patterns of Poland

Poland's basic spatial structure – the settlement system and major transportation corridors – began taking shape in the late Middle Ages. The main Polish river, the Vistula, acted as a barrier to modernization processes moving from the West, and 'filtered' the spread of innovation (the location of cities, for example) and material investment, thus leaving the eastern part of the country relatively less developed. The East-West divide is a stable spatial pattern in Poland that has persisted despite historical upheavals and frequent changes of state boundaries. It was not even overcome by the communist system, which was so strongly devoted to equalizing interregional differences through intensive industrialization.

Level and structure of development

Poland is a country with tremendous regional differences. The ratio of differences in per capita GDP is approximately 5: 1 between the wealthiest of the 45 Nomenclature of Statistical Territorial Units (NUTS) 3 sub-regions, Warsaw, and the poorest, Chełm-Zamo in southeastern Poland. Considerable differences can also be observed within individual regions, especially those with large cities. In the Mazowieckie *Województwo* (NUTS 2 region), for instance, in 2004 the per capita GDP ratio between Warsaw and the Ostrołęka-Siedlce sub-region (east of Warsaw) was 4.4: 1, while in the Małopolskie *Województwo* (mid-south, with Kraków the regional capital), it was 2.5: 1, and in Wielkopolskie (midwest, with Poznań as a main city) 2.6: 1.[1]

And yet, interregional differences in Poland are not greater than in other European countries. The ratio of highest to lowest GDP per capita in Poland's NUTS 2 regions is 2.2: 1, while in France and Spain it is 2: 1 and in Italy 2.4: 1.

Obviously, the differences between regions reflect differences in regional socioeconomic structures. The productivity ratio of a person employed in agriculture, hunting, fisheries and forestry and someone employed in non-market services is 1: 10, and it is 1: 8 compared to someone employed in industry. At the same time, the share of employment accounted for by the primary sector varies considerably, from slightly more than 10 per cent in the industrialized region of Śląskie to over 40 per cent in some eastern regions. Unsurprisingly, therefore, the latter display lower levels of per capita income than industrialized regions, and the highest per capita GDP levels can be found in metropolitan regions with the country's greatest share of employment in market services.

A more detailed picture of the discrepancies in the Polish economy can be obtained if we look at municipalities (*gminas*), which are the lowest tier of the territorial administrative system. It is definitely striking that nearly all the poorest municipalities are situated in regions that were under Russian and Austrian rule during the partition period (between 1815, after the Congress of Vienna, and the end of World War I in 1918). An arch runs along the former boundary dividing the two parts of Poland – Russian and Prussian – that concentrates poor municipalities that for 80 years have failed to overcome the negative legacy of their peripheral location in the former Russian empire, despite the two wars and three systemic transformations which have taken place in Poland during this period.

The historical heritage of the Polish socioeconomic space can also be illustrated by differences in education level. The belt with higher levels of education of the rural population has the same shape as the urbanization pattern, and corresponds to the part of Poland that for centuries boasted higher development levels and in the nineteenth century was under Prussian rule. The northern and western territories were regained from Germany by the postwar decision of the Allies, after several centuries of being a part of different German, Czech and Austrian states, and were settled by newcomers from the central and eastern parts of Poland (including areas lost to the former Soviet Union) after World War II. There is also a relatively higher level of education in the former Austrian part of Poland, in the southeast, which was due to the efficiency of the Austrian schooling system in the nineteenth century.

Thus, it is clear that the historical legacy has had an important bearing on the current regional structure of Poland. Moreover, this structure has been reinforced by developments since the collapse of communism in 1990. For example, the spatial pattern of Foreign Direct Investment (FDI) in Poland largely follows the pre-existing territorial distribution of wealth: foreign firms have located in the western part of the country, in big cities and their suburbs, and avoided localities with low income levels and poor tax bases.

A similar spatial pattern, also with clear historical roots, can be found in the territorial distribution of political preferences. It should be noted that the political preferences of Polish citizens are relatively stable, in some cases tracing back to the 1930s; western regions have always displayed more liberal (even leftist) profiles, and eastern, especially southeastern, regions more conservative preferences.

Earlier research (Gorzelak *et al.*, 1999) indicated that similar regional differences could be observed in the efficiency of local governments. In the initial years of the post-communist transition, the greatest use of innovative management tools was observed among local governments in the western regions; the lowest use of such tools, and the most traditional management approaches, were found in the eastern regions.

In conclusion, more developed regions that have enjoyed greater inflows of foreign capital display more progressive, liberal-oriented and pro-European values and preferences. Also, these regions are better managed on the local level, and – as other more recent research proves – on the regional level (Gorzelak, 2007). No doubt, these four dimensions: historically accumulated material endowment, transition processes, social values and political preferences, and managerial capabilities are mutually functionally interrelated, and all of them reinforce each other.

General differentiation dimensions

Generally speaking, when we combine the initial development level of Polish regions at the outset of the post-communist transition and take into account its progress in individual regions, we can see that there are two dimensions which are the strongest factors differentiating Polish space and affecting regional development; and also that developments are progressing in a way that is producing even wider interregional differences:

1. Large cities – rest of the country. This is a new expression of the traditional urban-rural division. Currently, however, city status and the dominance of the non-agricultural sectors of the economy alone are no longer indicators of development potential because only huge cities (mainly Warsaw, as well as Poznań, Kraków, Wrocław and 'Tricity' – Gdansk, Gdynia and Sopot) – with diverse economic structures, connected with Europe via relatively well-developed transport and telecommunications infrastructures, furnished with various institutions including R&D centres, and with a relatively well-educated population – are able to establish links with the competitive global economy. The diffusion of development from a large city around its vicinity does not exceed a 30-kilometre radius (in the case

of Warsaw, and probably even less in the case of other large cities), whereas a larger area (50–100 kilometre radius) is characterized by the 'draining' of resources from the metropolitan region to its metropolitan centre (Gorzelak and Smętkowski, 2005).

2. East-west. This dimension is one of 'long duration', strongly determined by historical factors. Since the Middle Ages, the western part of what is now Poland has demonstrated a higher level of development than the eastern part (for instance, the Romanesque style did not reach beyond the Vistula river). This division was further reinforced by the partitions, the boundaries of which are still visible in the country's social and economic space today. After 1990, eastern Poland, with a largely pre-industrial economy, suffered lower costs of structural change (in the years 1990–92), but after 1992 also demonstrated considerably less ability to meet the challenges of an open, competitive and knowledge-based economy. The current regression of some of Poland's eastern regions is largely due to this structural backwardness and the inability of these regions and non-metropolitan central regions to satisfy the requirements of the contemporary open economy.

Polish polarization is akin to processes taking place in other post-communist countries and most of Western Europe (although on a smaller scale). Regional divergence processes are extremely widespread, which can be explained by the 'metropolization' of development; that is, concentration of the fastest developing sectors of the economy (specialized financial services, management functions, R&D and academic activity, entertainment and culture) in the largest cities – metropolises with a global or continental significance. Poland is in a fortunate situation because development is not concentrated only in the capital city, as there are several other big cities in its territory which can reasonably expect to achieve the status of metropolis.

Regional policy in Poland

Poland has a long history of regional policy that dates back to the 1930s, when an integrated regional development plan was formulated and implemented in the mid-central part of the country (within pre-war boundaries). This plan, known as creation of the Central Industrial District, even now should be regarded as modern and innovative. Also, from the late 1940s to late 1960s the Polish regional and spatial planning 'school' was internationally known and acclaimed. This strong position was later lost, and it is only recently that Polish spatial and regional policy is regaining its position in national strategic planning.

After 1989, there were three phases of regional policy in Poland. Similar to other countries in the region (see Bachtler, Downes and Gorzelak, 2000) in the first phase – before the creation of regional governments in 1999 and reform of the territorial organization of the state – Polish regional policy was extremely weak and subordinated to national government sectoral policies. In fact, there were only a few measures and instruments that could have been labelled as 'regional policy', such as the 16 special economic zones and special measures introduced for areas threatened by structural unemployment.

The re-emergence of regional policy

The second phase emerged together with the creation of (relatively) strong regional governments with some autonomous powers and the development of pre-accession measures. Sixteen new regional units (*Województwo*) were created in 1999 and designated NUTS 2 level regions for the purposes of EU cohesion policy (see Map 8.1). Since their creation, the regions have served as of the central government – national regional policy, weak as it was, could now be supplemented by the development policies of the 16 *województwo*. The principles of these policies were formulated in 16 regional strategies, prepared by the *Województwo* authorities in 1999 and 2000 (and recently revised to meet the needs of the 16 Regional Operational Programmes, ROPs).

Polish regional policy has been based on the principle of 'regional contracts', which are a product of two fundamental documents: the National Development Strategy (NDS), prepared by the central government (such a strategy was created for the 2001–06 period), and the regional strategies prepared by regional governments. On the basis of the NDS the government elaborates a 'support programme', which specifies the goals of national regional policy, the amounts of money that will be spent on it and the distribution of these funds among different priorities and regions. The role of the support programme has changed over time, as only after accession could EU funding be treated on equal terms with state money in the budgets of individual contracts.[2] From the very beginning, the contracts were supposed to accommodate all instruments of regional development policy, regardless of the source of funding. In general, the priorities and principles shown in Table 8.1 were adopted for the first support programme for 2001–02 (later extended to 2003, although with the same amount of money). After 2003, the priority structure was aligned with the objectives of EU cohesion policy.

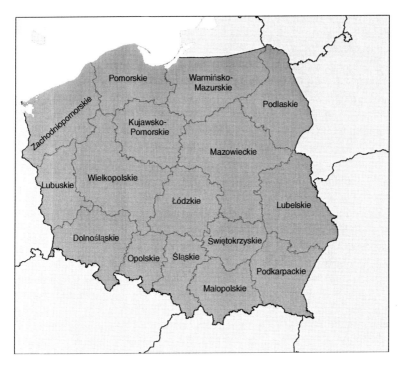

Map 8.1 Województwo (NUTS 2 regions) in Poland
Source: European Commission, DG Regional Policy.

Table 8.1 Priorities of the first support programme, 2001–03

No.	Priority	%
1	Development and improvement of infrastructure supporting the competitiveness of regions	50
2	Restructuring the economic base of regions and creating conditions for diversification	15
3	Development of human capital	12
4	Support for regions that need invigoration and are endangered by marginalization	18
5	Development of interregional cooperation	5
Total		100

Source: MRD, The National Development Strategy, 2000–06.

The total sum assigned to regional policy – rather symbolic, at only about €750 million – was distributed according to these priorities, and then divided among the regions according to the following principles:

- 80 per cent according to population;
- 10 per cent to regions which have territories (*powiats*) with per capita GDP less than 80 per cent of the national average;
- 10 per cent to territories (*powiats*) with unemployment higher than 150 per cent of the national average.

The regions knew how much money they were going to receive from the state and put foreword proposals according to the goals and tasks presented in their regional strategies, providing these proposals reflected the NDS priorities. The regional governments also proposed 'regional programmes', in which they indicated projects that were rooted in their regional strategies. The contract was then a final agreement on the regional programme between the central government and the region.

The 16 regional contracts for the period 2001–02 were signed in June 2001. *Ex-post* evaluation indicated that too much money allocated to particular regions was earmarked for projects that would have been financed anyhow, since these were the old 'central' projects previously financed from the state budget which later were rescheduled to the regional programmes. Moreover, the margin of freedom of regional governments was narrowed by the scarcity of resources assigned to national regional policy. However, the principles seemed to be interesting and promising, since at least they enhanced the importance of strategic approaches to national and regional development.

This system was simple, to some extent 'automatic', and based on very few simple criteria and generally accepted thresholds of their values.

In recent years there has been a visible trend towards marginalizing a separate national regional policy and concentrating on EU cohesion policy as the major instrument of development. This process can be seen both in the legal provisions and structure of development financing. A surprising feature of the legal framework was that the general regional development regulation of 2000[3] – the first, if not the best, attempt to create a general system that would allow for the coordination of EU and national regional policies – was soon replaced by a regulation that was intended to eliminate the inconsistencies of the previous one and allow structural operations to begin in Poland as soon as possible after accession;[4] from this point, Polish regional development law was designed around the needs of EU cohesion policy. In December 2006, a new regulation attempted to elaborate more general rules covering all development activities, including regional policy; amended the following year, it will be tested during the first year of cohesion policy implementation in the new (2007–13) programming period.[5] The quality of the laws regulating regional policy is questionable, however, and necessary institutional reforms have been slow.

In financial terms, a brief look at the structure of the cohesion policy budget in Poland reveals an underlying strategy: to maximize the influx of cohesion policy resources (85 per cent co-financing after 2006) and minimize their own contribution to the lowest level required by law (15 per cent). This, however, is a questionable approach for a country that is among the least-developed and dynamic new member states.

Spatial policy of the state

The 'Concept of the Spatial Policy of the State' was elaborated in the mid-1990s and updated in 2005 (GCSS, 2006). However, the revised document – although approved by the outgoing government in September 2006 – was not supported by the incoming government and the preparation of a new Concept was initiated.

The primary goal of Poland's spatial development is to use the well-established, polycentric functional and spatial structure of the country to dynamize its development and overcome its civilizational backwardness; this is convergent with the strategic goal set out in the NDS for 2007–13 (Government of Poland, 2006). According to the 2005 Concept, the country's spatial development should make it possible to achieve a lasting, high rate of growth of the Polish economy, which will help improve environmental quality and ensure parity of access to natural and cultural assets for present and future generations. In particular, it should facilitate the development of a knowledge-based economy and a modern, civic information society.

The 2005 Concept is based on the doctrine of polycentric concentration and diffusion. This assumes that metropolitan areas are the main links in the functional and spatial structure of the country and will remain so in the future, especially those which are most strongly connected with the networks of European metropolises. At the same time, spatial policy should support the diffusion of development from metropolitan to non-metropolitan areas, in order to enhance the chances of achieving territorial cohesion and facilitate fuller use of the country's human and material resources.

Polarization processes occur spontaneously in Poland as in most other European countries. The 2005 Concept asserts that these processes should be rationalized, to enhance the functioning of metropolitan areas, their mutual material, communication and capital relations and their links with global networks. The essence of an active spatial policy, in close conjunction with national regional policy, is to alleviate polarization processes by reinforcing the diffusion of development from areas where it is higher to those with a poorer potential for endogenous growth and fewer chances to attract external stimuli in the form of substantial market investments. Such diffusion should be enhanced by reinforcing network relations between territorial centres and systems at different levels – on the international, national, regional and local scales. At the same time, only the networks with national or international significance should remain in the sphere of direct interest of state spatial policy, while linkages and connections in smaller spatial systems should be developed and strengthened by territorial governments, possibly with indirect support from the state.

Spatial and regional policies

The relationship between spatial and regional policy is complex. At the time the National Strategic Reference Framework (NSRF) was being developed, the Concept in its 1999 version was considered outdated, and its 2005 revision non-binding. As a result, the links between regional and spatial policy were weaker than expected. Of course, a number of Concept ideas were used in preparing the NSRF and it is among the key strategic documents of cohesion policy in Poland. There are obvious differences between the two documents, however. The Concept clearly links growth to urban agglomerations and their connection to corridors, and it supports the development of regional capitals in eastern Poland in order to create development centres that can absorb surplus agricultural labour. Although these issues are mentioned as important in the NSRF, when it comes to the operational level (except for Development of Eastern Poland Operational Programme) they are not necessarily a top priority. The idea of supporting the best-developed, most competitive centres is considered by many to be contrary to the fundamentals of cohesion policy. In Poland, as in other European countries, many people continue to adhere to the old development paradigm. As a result, while strategic documents offer clear-cut, modern policy concepts and objectives, the operational level – despite the efforts of EU and national authorities – demonstrates a strong tendency to take cohesion as a synonym for equity built on infrastructure investment.

The pre-accession funds

Poland was one of the first countries to receive EU pre-accession assistance. Among the various pre-accession instruments, the PHARE programme was by far the most important source of not only funds, but also experience and knowledge about EU procedures.

There have been several projects directly connected to regional and local development, mostly within the Poland, Hungary Assistance for Economic Reconstruction (PHARE) framework. One of the first such programmes – Municipal Development and Training in Poland – helped in creating training facilities for newly elected local officials. The Structural Development in Selected Regions (STRUDER) programme, launched in 1993 in Poland as the first PHARE structural programme in the Central and Eastern European Country (CEECs), was channelled to six Polish regions that demonstrated especially serious development problems and handicaps (Pyszkowski and Kozak, 1999). The PHARE Cross-Border Cooperation Poland–Germany directed some €50 million yearly to western Polish regions *(Mapa...,* 2004). Later on, the Special Accession Programme for Agriculture and Rural Development (SAPARD) and Instrument for Structural Policies for Pre-Accession (ISPA) programmes supplemented PHARE to resemble the structure of EU funds.

To what extent did the pre-accession programmes help prepare Poland for the implementation of cohesion policy after accession? Clearly, they helped to solve a number of mostly local problems, in particular by supporting infrastructure development. On the project level, experience in project planning and management was an asset in preparation for EU structural operations. The contribution of pre-accession programmes to cohesion policy management, however, is doubtful: unlike ISPA, which resembled the Cohesion Fund, neither SAPARD nor PHARE were designed as copies of the structural funds. They were so different in organizational and procedural terms that on the day of accession they could not be integrated with them. Implemented parallel to national expenditures and kept outside the public budget, they remained non-integrated until the very end. Small wonder that they could not contribute to the transfer of management systems and best practices from the structural funds, as they were similarly different from both Polish and EU structural policies (again, except for ISPA).[6]

Operational programmes 2004–06

Upon accession Poland acquired the right to benefit from the structural and cohesion funds. Table 8.2 presents a list of Operational Programmes

Table 8.2   Operational Programmes in Poland, 2004–06

Programme	EU structural funds* €bn**	in %
Growth of Enterprise Competitiveness	1.3	16.80
Human Resource Development	1.3	16.80
Restructuring and Modernization of Food Processing Sector and Rural Development	1.1	14.30
Fishing and Fish Processing	0.2	2.60
Integrated Regional Operational Programme (IROP)	2.9	37.77
Transport – Maritime Economy	0.6	7.80
EQUAL Community Initiative	0.1	1.30
INTERREG Community Initiative	0.2	2.60
Technical Assistance	0.02	0.03
Total	7.72	100.00

Note: * Without Poland's contribution (ca 27%); Cohesion Fund excluded (€4.1 bn)
** 1999 prices.

Source: Government of Poland (2004).

(OPs) and Community Initiatives (CI) with their initial budgets. The total budget for 2004–06 (including the Cohesion Fund and domestic input) reached €18 billion.

Implementation began with some delay, as the management system turned out to be overly complicated and required time to make changes (Government of Poland, 2007a). Nevertheless, the macroeconomic objectives of Polish structural policy were reached in less than 18 months. Despite the obvious positive contribution of cohesion policy this outcome cannot be attributed exclusively – nor even mostly – to it, as an influx of FDI, income from a dynamically growing export sector, and transfers from the Polish diaspora were also of key importance.

In the end of August 2007, 98 per cent of structural funds were contracted (contracts signed with beneficiaries) and 54.3 per cent effectively spent. The most successful individual programmes were the Integrated Regional Operational Programme (IROP) (62.5 per cent of allocation disbursed), Restructuring and Modernization (62.4 per cent), Human Resource Development (53.7 per cent) and Growth of Enterprise Competitiveness (45.4 per cent); while the least successful were INTERREG (36.3 per cent), Transport (41.9 per cent) and Fishing and Fish Processing (43.3 per cent) (Government of Poland, 2007b). In the case of Cohesion Fund disbursement progress was visibly slower (26.9 per cent in March 2007), in particular in the environmental protection sector (16.9 per cent). Transport-related Cohesion Fund disbursement reached 38.9 per cent. Unlike the structural funds, the levels of funding contracted under the Cohesion Fund were relatively low: 57.4 per cent of total funding, 63.4 per cent of funding earmarked for environmental protection and 48.3 per cent allocated for transport (Government of Poland, 2007c).

The integrated regional operational programme 2004–06

When it came to regional programmes the government, after discussions with the Commission, chose a solution which is not typical for Poland; instead of creating individual regional programmes, it decided to create one large IROP managed by the Ministry for Regional Development (MRD) (with most tasks delegated), thus giving the programme a strong horizontal flavour. The most obvious reason for this decision was fear that if any independent regional programmes failed it would be difficult, if not impossible, to transfer money to more successful regions (the transfer between OPs being a complex and time-consuming procedure).

The IROP implementation system also kept regional governments at bay, by giving the responsibility for programme implementation to central government representatives in the regions (*Wojewoda*). As a result, although the IROP has been implemented to a large extent in the regions, this has mostly occurred through the *Wojewoda*; the role of regional governments (headed by the *Marszalek*), despite their responsibility for regional socioeconomic development, was reduced to not much more than project selection.

The IROP had the following priorities:

1. Development and modernization of infrastructure used to enhance the competitiveness of regions, with the following investment priorities considered the most important:

   • modernization and development of the regional transport system
   • environmental protection infrastructure
   • the facilities of tertiary education institutions
   • public infrastructure supporting the development of tourism and culture
   • Information Society infrastructure
   • development of urban public transport in the main urban centres.

2. Strengthening human resources development in the regions, concentrating on:

- development of competencies linked to regional labour market needs and lifelong learning opportunities
- equalizing opportunities through scholarships
- vocational reorientation for people leaving agriculture
- vocational reorientation of the workforce affected by restructuring
- entrepreneurship
- regional innovation strategies and knowledge-transfer

3. Local development, with assistance focused on the following areas:

- the development and restructuring of rural areas
- areas experiencing industrial decline and restructuring
- urban areas threatened by marginalization, and former industrial and military sites.

In addition, targeted investments in micro enterprise start-ups and local educational and social infrastructure have been made.

Technical Assistance was directed to the various institutions involved in IROP implementation: the IROP Managing Authority (MA) at the Ministry of Economy, Labour and Social Policy, the *Marszalek* offices, the *Wojewoda* offices, the *Województwo* Labour Offices, and regional financial institutions.[7]

The total costs of the IROP equalled €4.08 billion (almost €3 billion coming from the EU), representing over one-third of total transfers to Poland from the structural and cohesion funds in 2004–06. The least-developed regions were assigned relatively more funds than more advanced ones, reflecting the aim of accelerating their rate of growth.

While the IROP MA was the MRD, in practical terms most of the job has been done in the regions upon agreement with the central government, confirmed by a revised form of the regional contract. Against expectations, regional governments were not given full responsibility for managing structural operations; their role was limited to the selection of projects to be financed and the implementation of some minor activities (in particular through Labour Offices). Instead, the responsibility for most regional projects remained with the *Wojewoda*. As a result, for implementing the IROP two parallel administrative structures (*Wojewoda* and *Marszalek*) were used.

The projects selected by regions had to be rooted in their regional development strategies. Regional steering committees were created – composed of regional and local authorities, implementing institutions and socioeconomic partners – and given the job of recommending projects to the regional government. Unfortunately, because at least one-third of the steering committee members represented potential beneficiaries, and due to unclear rules, selected projects were not always of the highest quality. Despite this, the IROP was among the most advanced OPs in terms of implementation.

Despite its achievements, Poland does not belong to the leaders in cohesion policy implementation. As of the end of July 2007, 97.95 per cent of the total structural funds budget was committed, but only about 52 per cent was spent (Government of Poland, 2007c). When compared to other CEECs, Poland ranks in the middle as far as effective spending is concerned. As no mid-term evaluations were finalized by the time of writing, any remark on the successes and problems encountered in IROP implementation has to be treated as preliminary. It is clear that the implementation system turned out to be overly heavy and complex, which resulted in a slow and difficult start.[8] As a number of details were determined in the form of regulations, any governmental attempt to simplify things was a lengthy process. In particular, financial management was an impediment to successful implementation; due to adopted rules, less wealthy beneficiaries could not afford to finance projects, as refinancing by the system could take several months (years, for certain INTERREG projects). It should also be noted that most advanced is the implementation of small infrastructure projects, while the least advanced are those closely related to Lisbon Strategy objectives (such as regional innovation strategies and technology transfer, or entrepreneurship promotion). The shortage of own-resources for regional governments resulted in much faster implementation of local government projects having little or no regional significance. For a number of reasons, therefore, IROP implementation is characterized by a high dispersion of projects and an inability to concentrate efforts. Looking at the regional differentiation of IROP disbursement, one can hardly draw clear conclusions about the factors for success. Neither being an urban region, a western region, or a region with significant experience implementing pre-accession funds projects is important. Each of those categories covers both rich and poor regions, western and eastern, those flooded with pre-accession funding and those that were not. Most effective in spending money in July 2007 were Podlaskie, Kujawsko-pomorskie, Świętokrzyskie and Małopolskie (66–71 per cent);

least effective were Śląskie, Łódzkie and Mazowieckie (48–50 per cent) (Government of Poland, 2007d). As for results, not to mention impact, it is too early to say.

Operational programmes 2007–13

In theory, the implementation system for cohesion policy in 2007–13 should take into account experience with the previous programming period. In fact, however, when the new programming documents were developed the implementation process was not very advanced. As a result, what we see now is a compromise: the regional programmes have been decentralized (16 ROPs, each with their own regional MAs), but a centralized approach is used for the sectoral programmes managed by the MRD. However, the new implementation system operates in an institutional context which is not necessarily development oriented, and overall does not seem to be an efficient and lasting solution.

The programming exercise was completed in fall 2007. The change of government two years earlier had created some discontinuity in planning for the new programming period. However, because Poland's development priorities are in many cases relatively obvious, several ideas outlined by the previous government have been retained in the strategies prepared by the new one. In 2006, the new government undertook the enormous task of finalizing the main strategic documents of Polish regional policy, the NSRF and NDS. The pressure was immense, and preparation of Sectoral Operational Programmes (SOPs) in some cases preceded the finalization of strategic documents.

The NDS specifies the following priorities for 2007–15, when EU funding is supposed to cover the greatest part of Poland's development and modernization efforts: (1) improving the competitiveness and innovativeness of the economy; (2) improving technical and social infrastructure; (3) increasing growth and the quality of employment; (4) building an integrated social community and improving its safety; and (5) developing rural areas.

Regional development and increasing territorial cohesion

The NSRF, signed at the beginning of May 2007, structures EU intervention in Poland for 2007–13, as shown in Table 8.3. Analysis of the overall structure of activities covered by the various OPs shows that it shares with the previous programming period a strong bias towards infrastructure rather than human resource or business development.

Table 8.3 Operational Programmes in Poland, 2007–13

EU cohesion policy resources* Operational Programmes	bn €**	in %
Infrastructure and Environment	27.8	41.4
Human Capital	9.7	14.5
Innovative Economy	8.2	12.2
Development of Eastern Poland	2.2	3.3
16 Regional Operational Programmes	16.6	24.8
Technical Assistance	0.5	0.8
Reserves	2.0	3.0
Total	67.0	100.0

Note: * EU resources are supported by Poland's public and private contribution (€18.3 bn)
** 2010 prices.

Source: MRD, September 2007. <http://www.mrr.gov.pl/Dokumenty+oficjalne/Okres+
programowania+2007-2013/>.

Overall, €85.3 billion will be spent on the 21 OPs, out of which
€67 billion will come from the Commission, €11.9 billion from national
public sources and €6.4 billion from the private sector. When thinking about regional development, one should keep in mind also the
European Territorial Cooperation (ETC) programmes (€7.75 billion
from the EU), plus part of the €173.3 million of EU support to adja-
cent regions of neighbouring non-member states delivered through the
European Neighbourhood and Partnership Instrument (ENPI).

The OPs represent a high level of complexity. In particular, the
Infrastructure and Environment OP – the largest in the history of
EU cohesion policy – contains almost 20 different priorities, making successful implementation a challenge. Possibly both the size of
the programmes and experience gained in the previous programming period influenced the design of the implementation system for
2007–13, which gives the MRD huge responsibilities. Except for the 16
ROPs, where regional governments take the role of MA, programme
management is in the hands of the MRD and its departments. The
MRD is also coordinating all NSRF activities in Poland. Implementation
tasks are done either by the MRD or, in a majority of cases, delegated
to Intermediate Institutions (other government ministries). Unlike in
other new member states, the Certifying Institution in 2007 moved
from the Ministry of Finance to the MRD. Taking into account that
the latter is also in charge of strategic planning and programming,

one has to admit that its position is unique and poses great requirements for the personal skills of the Minister. Altogether, there are over
120 Intermediate Institutions (fewer than ten not financed by the state
budget). The role of Audit Institution for all OPs was given to the Chief
Inspector of Treasury Control (*Główny Inspektor Kontroli Skarbowej*) in
the Ministry of Finance.

Regional development programmes 2007–13

The NSRF for 2007–13 specifies the following goals for regional development in Poland:

1. More effective use of the endogenous potential of the largest metropolitan centres. The policies which can promote achievement of this
   goal include continued support for developing the metropolitan
   functions (including research, educational and cultural) of major
   urban centres, the development of technical infrastructure to
   enhance their attractiveness for investment, and connecting all
   urban centres via a network of motorways and dual carriageways.
2. Accelerated development of Poland's eastern regions. To ensure the
   success of cohesion policy in Poland and, in the wider European context, to include these areas in the processes generating growth and
   employment, these regions (Lubelskie, Podlaskie, Podkarpackie,
   Świętokrzyskie, Warmińsko-Mazurskie) – among the EU's poorest –
   should be given special attention. In addition to typical activities
   expected to improve the competitive positions of regions, an integrated programme of spatial, regional and sectoral policies must
   focus on accelerating structural changes which are of cardinal
   importance in view of the low attractiveness of regional economies.
   Priorities include improving the quality of human capital and the
   performance of institutions, expanding the metropolitan functions
   of the main centres of socioeconomic growth, promoting selected
   regional products and upgrading regional transport infrastructure.
3. Counteracting the marginalization and peripheralization of problem
   areas. The overriding goal of activities in problem areas is to support
   changes which can ensure sustainable development by counteracting the marginalization of selected regions, including border areas,
   areas threatened with natural disasters, and post-industrial and
   post-military zones.

Regarding the regional programmes an important decision was
made: instead of a single IROP, in 2007–13 there are 16 ROPs, one for

each of Poland's NUTS 2 regions, together consuming one-quarter of the total cohesion policy allocation for Poland. Had this decision been taken in 2004, the regional governments would now have much greater experience in managing the structural funds and the risk of mistakes or irregularities would be lower. Unlike 2004–06, the role of MA for regional programmes is performed by the regional governments themselves, headed by the *Marszalek*. The certifying function is delegated to the *Województwo* office by the main Certifying Institution, the MRD. A regional Monitoring Committee – consisting of representatives of the regional government, municipalities, the central government (relevant ministries) and the socioeconomic partners – ensures proper implementation through regular analysis of implementation reports and other relevant information.

Regional governments put a great deal of effort into preparing their ROPs, in line with their own needs and strategies. In doing so, they were obliged to observe not only the Community Strategic Guidelines on Cohesion (CSG) but also national guidelines set by the MRD. The most difficult rule for most regions was the EU requirement that a minimum of 60 per cent of Convergence objective resources be earmarked for Lisbon Strategy activities, even though new member states were not formally bound by this target. Representatives of the regions often stressed that such a rule excludes many types of infrastructure projects which in their opinion contribute to the accomplishment of Lisbon objectives. The ROPs are otherwise quite different, though most of them tend to overestimate the role of local infrastructure as a development factor. One has to note that the regions are also using every opportunity to improve their position *vis-à-vis* the central government. The implementation of cohesion policy resulted in necessary adjustments to the distribution of public finances, in order to make regional governments the real subject of regional development rather than being dependent on central government subsidies and compromises with wealthier municipalities. Thus, the regional management of ROPs in 2007–13, despite certain rules imposed by the MRD, is a further step in the process of state devolution in Poland.

The territorial distribution of funds raised significant concerns among the regions. The most influential coalition has been formed by the better-developed regions, which insisted on getting more funding as, in their opinion, less-developed *Województwo* have a low absorption capacity; they also pointed out that five poorer regions are to benefit from the special Eastern Poland Development programme. Thus, as a form of 'compensation', on 6 March 2007 an additional €570 million was distributed in equal parts among four relatively well-developed regions which had the lowest initial per capita allocations (Łódzkie, Małopolskie, Śląskie and Wielkopolskie).[9]

As mentioned above, a special programme for the five least-developed eastern regions will be launched. The programme was established on the initiative of the European Council, which wanted to give special support to the five poorest regions of the EU in 2004 (the Council slightly overlooked the fact that, after January 2007 the EU's poorest regions are now located in Romania and Bulgaria). The Polish government decided to add additional money from the structural funds and developed the programme so as not to overlap with the ROPs of the five regions. The programme, which addresses key NDS priorities (innovation and information society, support for growth poles, transport), will be managed by the Polish Agency for Entrepreneurship Development, and it will be financed from sectoral programme resources, thus not decreasing the allocation for ROPs. An additional €5.46 billion from the European Social Fund (ESF) will also be implemented regionally.[10] Taking all three items together, and estimating the GDP of particular regions in 2007–13, we can (roughly) estimate the share of funds assigned to regions relative to their prospective GDP (see Table 8.4).

As can be seen, as in the previous programming period in 2007–13 the least-developed regions will receive much greater shares of their GDP in EU assistance than those with higher GDPs. This stems from the aforementioned, rather unfortunate, allocation procedure of EU funds ('80+10+10'). This clearly indicates an equity-driven regional policy in the current programming period for Poland, which does not necessarily reflect the most recent thinking of the Commission. The regional distribution of the SOPs, which will consume another one-third of all funds coming to Poland in 2007–13, is not yet known.

When assessing the potential influence of OPs on the development of Poland and individual regions, one should take into account not only the objectives and priorities of programmes and the already-mentioned paradigm behind them. Among the key factors determining the success of development policies is the national institutional framework. Poland's is in urgent need of reform. The non-wage costs of labour are high, the labour code protects the interests of the employed rather than the unemployed and entrepreneurs, the privatization and restructuring of state-owned enterprises has come to a halt, the social and health systems are inefficient, the law is of poor quality and taxation policy seems to suffer from alienation. Corruption, as in other CEECs, is an issue that cannot be ignored. Public administration is said to have

Table 8.4 Regionally addressed EU funds as a percentage of prospective regional GDP, 2007–13

Województwo (capital city)	EU funds as % of regional GDP	Województwo (capital city)	EU funds as % of regional GDP
Dolnośląskie (Wrocław)	1.0	Podkarpackie (Rzeszów)	2.1
Kujawsko-pomorskie (Bydgoszcz)	1.2	Podlaskie (Białystok)	2.0
Lubelskie (Lublin)	2.2	Pomorskie (Gdansk)	1.0
Lubuskie (Zielona Góra)	1.3	Śląskie (Katowice)	0.8
Łódzkie (Łódź)	1.0	Świętokrzyskie (Kielce)	2.1
Małopolskie (Kraków)	1.0	Warmińsko-Mazurskie (Olsztyn)	2.4
Mazowieckie (Warszawa)	0.6	Wielkopolskie (Poznań)	0.8
Opolskie (Opole)	1.2	Zachodniopomorskie (Szczecin)	1.2
Poland			1.1

Note: * At the moment it is not possible to estimate the funds that will be channeled to particular regions from the CAP in 2007–13. These estimates were in preparation at the time of writing.

Source: Own estimates, based on the data from MRD.*

systemic weaknesses (Government of Poland, 2007a). Institutional instability was, and is, a major problem.[11]

Conclusions

EU cohesion policy has had an increasingly significant and complex impact on Polish territorial policy and governance. The institutional system designed for regional policy implementation has been increasingly adapted to the requirements of EU cohesion policy, and this adjustment has become a top priority. Although the territorial system that was created in the 1990s has many weaknesses, efforts to improve it have met with some success.

Decentralization has been a political issue in Poland since the early 1990s. Regional governments have gradually gained more influence over the implementation of EU cohesion policy, thus improving their position in the public administration structure and introducing new elements of governance. While at the time of accession the central government was not fully convinced of the need for further decentralization (the IROP, managed by the MRD, showed the reservations of both the government and the Commission in this respect), it has come to realize that this is unavoidable. Despite initial problems with the implementation system, over time improvements have been made and absorption capacity has increased, although it is still lowest for Lisbon-type projects. It is far too early to assess the impact of EU cohesion policy on regional economies, although there are good reasons to believe that most regions have stuck with the dependency concept of development – an issue of considerable importance for assessing the impact of cohesion policy on Poland and other new member states.

In Poland, as elsewhere (in the Commission's DG Regio, for instance) there is a discrepancy between the intentions and declared doctrines of cohesion policy and its actual implementation, measured by the allocation of funds between priorities. Similar to the CSG,[12] Polish strategic documents emphasize such phrases as innovation, competitiveness and growth and employment. However, when it comes to the allocation of funds rather traditional approaches to regional policy come to the fore, infrastructure development being considered the key to growth, and the poorest regions receiving the greatest share of available funding. In view of the standard regional policy trade-off between equity and efficiency, it is questionable whether the over-concentration of support on the least-developed regions – a doctrine of the traditional resource-driven paradigm of economic development – will successfully promote the goal of building a knowledge-based economy (the new development paradigm). After accession Poland benefited from a GDP growth rate exceeding 6 per cent a year. And yet, when compared to other new member states (excluding Bulgaria and Romania), it is not only the least developed but also among the three slowest in developing. In such circumstances the quality of development policy and the institutional framework for implementing it become major concerns.

Regional policy is political, and ideas formulated by development experts have to be modified by those taking the final responsibility for implementing them. The frequent result is a discrepancy between knowledge and policy that is understandable, but should not always be approved. For the time being, such a gap in the implementation of cohesion policy is not considered a problem by most Polish citizens, as recent years have brought significant GDP growth, an increased quality of life and new career opportunities both at home and abroad. However, high rates of growth may not last forever, and in any case are greatly dependent on global conditions. In the event of less favourable conditions, the utilization of accumulated reserves may not be enough to maintain high rates of growth without radical institutional reform and the shift to a knowledge-based economy.

Notes

1. It should be borne in mind that real differences in the GDP values between a large city and the surrounding area are smaller due to the fact that many people commute to work and that, in many cases, only business activity is formally registered in the city.
2. Before accession, EU funds remained the property of the EU; they could not be the subject of legal agreement between any Polish parties. Therefore, any mention of possible transfers from the EU was exclusively non-binding, informal information.
3. Principles of Regional Policy Supporting Act, 12 May 2000.
4. National Development Act, 20 April 2004.
5. Principles of Implementing Development Policy Act, 6 December 2006; amended on 29 June 2007.
6. The same implementation system for pre-accession assistance is being applied in Turkey; however, there are plans to reform it to make it as similar to EU cohesion policy as possible under local circumstances.
7. In 14 out of 16 regions this role has been played by the Regional Development Agencies (RDAs), which turn out to be much better prepared to work with entrepreneurs than the regional administration.
8. This was easy to predict before accession; see Kozak (2004).
9. Announcement of Mr Władysław Ortyl, Deputy Minister of Regional Development, http://www.funduszestrukturalne.gov.pl/Wiadomosci/Fundusze+na+lata+2007–2013/podzielono+570+na+4+woj.htm.

10. The total inflow of EU funds to Poland in 2007–13 will reach some €90 billion. This can be roughly divided into three almost equal parts: funds allocated regionally and mostly managed by the regions themselves (displayed in Table 8.4); SOPs, managed by the central government; and funds transferred within the framework of the CAP, distributed according to the area of agricultural land.

11. In the three years prior to accession the regional policy chapter of the central government moved three times, from one ministry to another. The most experienced regional development institution (the Polish Agency for Regional Development) was shut down on 31 May 2002, and the MRD was finally established in the fall of 2005.

12. This document is much less progressive and much more toothless than the Commission's original ideas on cohesion policy, published in July 2005 (http://eur-lex.europa.eu/LexUriServ/site/en/com/2005/com2005_0299en01.pdf). This change was due mainly to the influence of the member states.

9
The Czech Republic

Dan Marek and Michael Baun

Introduction

As a relatively poor new member state, the Czech Republic is a major recipient of cohesion policy funding. In 2007–13 the Czech Republic will receive nearly €27 billion in EU cohesion policy funds, making it the third largest recipient among the member states and the largest in per capita terms (MRD, 2005b). However, the implementation of cohesion policy in the Czech Republic has not been unproblematic. Institutional and administrative difficulties have hindered the efficient use of allocated funding, raising questions about absorption capacity. The management of cohesion policy has also become an issue in relations between the central government and the newly created regional governments.

This chapter examines cohesion policy implementation in the Czech Republic. It begins by discussing Czech preparations for EU regional policy in the pre-accession period. This is followed by an examination of developments since accession, focusing first on cohesion policy implementation in 2004–06, and then on the debate over cohesion policy planning for 2007–13. The next section analyzes the 2007–13 Operational Programmes (OPs) and assesses the prospects for successful implementation of cohesion policy in the current programming period. Beyond administrative and institutional problems which could have been – and were – anticipated, this chapter argues that a major factor affecting the implementation of cohesion policy in the Czech Republic has been the struggle for influence between the central government and the self-governing regions.

Preparing for accession[1]

As was the case with most of the new member states, the Czech Republic (and before 1993 Czechoslovakia) had very little experience with EU-style regional policy. To the extent that it existed, Czech regional policy in the initial period after independence lacked many of the key elements of EU cohesion policy, including its integrated, multi-sector approach, multianual programming and decentralized planning in partnership with subnational and nongovernmental actors. The Czech Republic also lacked the institutional capacity for programme monitoring and evaluation, financial management and mechanisms for co-financing that EU cohesion policy required. Thus, preparing for EU cohesion policy provided a major challenge.

Serious preparations did not begin until after the Czech Republic formally applied for EU membership in January 1996. In November of that year the Ministry for Regional Development (MRD) was established and given responsibility for coordinating the government's preparations for EU cohesion policy. Nevertheless, progress lagged in many important respects.

A major stimulus was provided by the Commission's July 1997 'Opinion' on the Czech Republic's application for EU membership; this declared that, 'The Czech Republic lacks an independent regional development policy.' In particular, the Commission noted the absence of the necessary institutional and administrative structures, including inter-ministerial coordination mechanisms at the national level, and it pointed to the absence of elected governmental bodies between the central state and local (commune) levels that could serve as partners of the national government and the Commission in implementing cohesion policy. It also noted the inadequacy of financial resources and instruments, as well as the absence of an appropriate and sufficient legal basis for cohesion policy (European Commission, 1997b, pp. 64–5, 83–4).

The 1998 Accession Partnership for the Czech Republic also identified the development of institutional capacity for cohesion policy as a key goal to be achieved before accession. The document declared it was a 'short-term priority' (to be completed immediately or taken substantially forward in 1998) for the Czech Republic to begin to set up structures needed for regional and structural policy. It designated as a 'medium-term priority' (requiring more than one year to complete, but to be achieved before accession) the 'establishment of a legal, administrative and budgetary framework for an integrated regional policy in order to participate in EU structural programs after membership' (European Commission, 1998). These goals and priorities were subsequently incorporated into the Czech government's 'National Program for Adoption of the *Acquis Communautaire*' (Czech Republic Government, 1998).

Among the main institutional requirements of EU cohesion policy is the existence of competent regional structures to manage the structural funds. Although the EU did not attempt to impose any particular model of regional organization on the candidate states, in its early remarks on this subject (contained in the 1997 Opinions and initial regular progress reports, as well as informal statements and advice) the Commission expressed a strong preference – although only 'indirectly and implicitly' – for 'democratically elected regional governments with substantial financial and legal autonomy,' which could then serve as credible partners of the Commission and national governments in managing EU structural policies after accession, in accordance with the core principle of partnership (Brusis, 2001b, pp. 12–3, 24–5).

In the Czech Republic, the Commission's preferences in this regard played a role in the December 1997 agreement to create 14 self-governing regions ('Higher Self-Governing Units'), or *kraje*, each with their own elected assemblies. The creation of the new regions was originally mandated by the 1992 Constitution; however, strong domestic opposition to regionalization, especially by the governing Civic Democratic Party (ODS) and its leader, Prime Minister Václav Klaus, delayed the implementation of this constitutional requirement. It was only after the Commission explicitly criticized the absence of 'elected bodies' between the central state and local levels in its 1997 Opinion that cross-party agreement on the new law creating the regions was finally reached. In this manner, EU pressure bolstered the domestic proponents of regionalization in the Czech Republic and accelerated the adoption of the constitutional law to create the new regions (Brusis, 2003, pp. 97–8). EU requirements also influenced the final shape of the new regional system, including the number of regions and their size. While opponents of regionalization such as Klaus favoured a larger number of smaller regions to minimize their potential political importance, proponents of regionalization backed their demand for a smaller number of larger regions with the argument that this would ensure that the *kraje* corresponded with the delineation of Nomenclature of Statistical Territorial Units (NUTS) 2 'cohesion' regions (see below).[2]

According to the law creating the new regions, each of the 14 *kraje* would directly elect their own regional assemblies, which in turn would elect a regional Governor (*hejtman*) and governing Council. After some delay, the law creating the new regions finally came into effect in January 2000. In the same year legislation was also passed establishing the rules for electing the regional assemblies and giving the new regions powers in the areas of education, culture, regional development, transport, agriculture, environment and health care. The first elections for the regional assemblies took place in November 2000, and the new regional governments began functioning in January 2001. However, resistance by central government authorities hindered the transfer of policy competencies to the regions, which was only accomplished with formal abolition of the network of central government-controlled administrative districts (*okresy*) in January 2003. Even so, continued uncertainty over financing arrangements for the regional governments has undermined their autonomy and effectiveness. While the regions have been granted a small percentage of tax revenues, they otherwise have limited resources and remain substantially dependent on central government grants for their funding. The financial weakness of the regions has raised questions about their ability to exercise their new competencies (European Commission, 2003, p. 12). It also makes it difficult for them to meet the co-financing requirements of EU-sponsored regional development projects, thus limiting their ability to effectively participate in the structural funds (McMaster, 2004b, p. 22; Ferry and McMaster, 2005, pp. 20–2).

While creation of the new regions addressed the Commission's preference for a system of regional self-governance, for the purpose of administering the structural funds the 14 *kraje* were grouped into eight larger 'cohesion regions,' designated as NUTS 2 regions in accordance with EU methodology (see Map 9.1). Each of the eight cohesion regions has their own Regional Council, consisting of representatives from each of the regional assemblies within a particular NUTS 2 region. The Regional Councils serve as regional Managing Authorities (MAs) and are responsible for preparing the Regional Operational Programmes (ROPs) necessary for receiving structural funds assistance.

Also at the NUTS 2 level, Regional Development Committees – consisting of representatives of local governments, businesses, labour unions and NGOs – exist to perform monitoring functions. However, the amalgamation of the 14 *kraje* into a smaller number of cohesion regions created potential problems. In some NUTS 2 units two or more *kraje* have been forced to cooperate in structural funds planning, placing them at a disadvantage in the competition for EU assistance with more homogeneous cohesion regions that consist of only one *kraj*. This disadvantage is exacerbated by grouping together in some of the NUTS 2 units administrative regions which have not always historically cooperated, and in some cases have even been rivals, for example the Královéhradecký and Pardubický regions in NUTS 2 Northeast (Severovýchod) (Moxon-Browne and Kreuzbergová, 2001, p. 14). The disjuncture between administrative and cohesion regions also raises questions about the role of the self-governing regions in managing the structural funds (Illner, 2002, p. 17; McMaster, 2004b, p. 19).

Preparing the 2004–06 NDP: centralization versus decentralization

As part of its accession preparations the Czech government was required to prepare a National Development Plan (NDP). This would be the main strategic planning document for cohesion policy in 2004–06, the period immediately after accession. Work on the NDP began in 1998, and a preliminary version was submitted to the Commission for approval in July 2001. It featured eight ROPs, one for each of the NUTS 2 regions, together with six cross-regional Sector Operational Programmes (SOPs): 1) strengthening the competitiveness of industry and business services; 2) development of technical infrastructure; 3) human resource development; 4) environment; 5) rural development and multifunctional agriculture; and 6) tourism. The envisaged share of financial resources between the SOPs and ROPs was 65: 35 (Blažek, 2001, p. 760).

In its evaluation of the draft NDP, the Commission recommended decreasing the number of OPs, emphasizing the need to concentrate on a lesser number of priorities and focus attention on the most pressing problems of the country's economic and social development. However, the Commission did not specify how this concentration of priorities should be achieved.

In subsequent talks with the Commission, the MRD indicated that it strongly opposed merging the SOPs, and expressed instead its preference for combining the eight ROPs into a single Joint Regional Operational Programme (JROP). Nevertheless, in the second half of 2001, as the July 2002 deadline for finalizing the NDP approached, the MRD drafted and circulated two versions of the NDP: a) one featuring the JROP and six SOPs; and b) one featuring seven ROPs plus a Single Programming Document (SPD) for Prague.

The two versions of the draft NDP also featured radically different management structures. The JROP scenario was based on the assumption that the MRD would be the primary Managing Authority (MA) for structural funds programmes, with the key position of Programme Manager being held by a high-ranking MRD official. The Regional Councils for each of the eight cohesion regions would send one representative to the MRD's Managing and Coordination Committee, and would have the right to express their views and make recommendations on any issue connected with implementation of the JROP. Nevertheless, the document made clear that primary authority lay with the MRD, declaring that the main obligation of the Regional Councils was to contribute to the effective realization of the JROP, and that the Regional Councils should act in accordance with the decisions of the MRD. This was in sharp contrast with the more decentralized management structure proposed under the second scenario, where overall management responsibility for the ROPs lay with the Regional Councils themselves (MRD, 2001).

In the ensuing debate it was clear that while the MRD favoured the first (JROP) scenario, the regions preferred the second approach. Regional leaders argued that adoption of the JROP scenario would re-centralize decisionmaking and diminish their role in administering the structural funds. Some regional officials decried the lack of communication between Prague and the regions, and expressed concern that their views were not being taken seriously by the central government.[3] Ironically, similar concerns were reflected in the Commission's 2001 Regular Report, which also criticized the lack of input from 'economic and social partners and other relevant bodies' (European Commission, 2001a, p. 82).

Nevertheless, in January 2002 the Czech government decided to adopt the JROP scenario (Czech Republic Government, 2002). In its explanatory report attached to the government resolution, the MRD justified this decision by referring to the Commission's recommendations for simplification (concentration) and its emphasis on expediency and efficiency in the use of allocated funds (MRD, 2002, p. 2).[4]

The government's decision severely disappointed regional leaders. For at least the immediate future – the three-year period covered by the NDP – the partnership principle would be applied mainly through regional representation on the centralized Managing and Coordination Committee, a system that would give the regions only a limited role in administering the structural funds. According to Jan Březina, governor of Olomoucky *kraj* and chairman of the Regional Council for the NUTS 2 region of Central Moravia, this would 'delay by several years the opportunity for the regions to gain experience with administering the structural funds' (Interview with author, March 2002). Also typical was the response of Jiří Šulc, governor of Ústecký *kraj*, who argued that '[regional policy] decisions should be taken in the regions' rather than in a centralized committee (*Euro*, 2002, p. 25). While regional leaders hoped that planning in future programming periods would make use of ROPs, they feared that the 2004–06 decision would set an unfortunate precedent and make it easier for Prague to continue with a more centralized system in the future.

In the revised NDP the Commission's recommendation for simplification was also applied to the SOPs, with the six originally envisaged
programmes reduced to four. The most logical step was folding the tourism programme (proportionally smallest of the SOPs) into the JROP. It
was also decided to merge the SOPs for environment and transport, telecommunications and postal services; together they provided the basis
for a new Infrastructure programme, with the Environment Ministry as
MA.[5] While reduction in the number of SOPs did not generate the same
friction as the ROPs versus JROP debate, there was a dispute between
the Transport and Communications and Environment Ministries over
who would be the MA for OP Infrastructure.

The Commission provided the Czech government with its comments on the revised NDP in June 2003. Formal negotiations on the
Community Support Framework (CSF) then began in early July and
concluded in September. The CSF constituted the basic strategy for
socioeconomic development of the seven cohesion regions for 2004–06,
each of whom were eligible for Objective 1 support. The Prague region,
with a per capita GDP above the EU average, was only eligible for assistance under Objectives 2 and 3 and thus was not covered by the CSF. The
CSF was implemented via the five SOPs and the JROP. Major projects
concerning transport and environment received Cohesion Fund assistance, outside the CSF but covering the entire territory of the Czech
Republic. Other assistance was provided by two Community Initiatives:
INTERREG, aimed at cross-border cooperation; and EQUAL, aimed at
combating social exclusion (MRD, 2003, pp. 1–2; see Table 9.1.).

Table 9.1   Financial allocations for structural funds operations in the Czech
Republic in 2004–06 (€ mn, current prices)

	2004–06	2004	2005	2006
Cohesion fund	945.3	316.9	266.1	362.3
Structural funds (total)	1,584.4	381.5	528.9	674.0
Objective 1 (13 *kraje* = 7 NUTS 2 regions)	1,454.3	339.0	485.5	629.8
Objective 2 (Prague)	71.3	23.3	23.8	24.2
Objective 3 (Prague)	58.8	19.2	19.6	20.0
Community initiatives (total)	100.8	28.6	32.1	40.1
INTERREG	68.7	21.0	21.4	26.3
EQUAL	32.1	7.6	10.7	13.8
Total structural operations	2,630.5	727.0	827.1	1,076.3

Source: European Commission, April 2003.

Developments since accession: cohesion policy performance in 2004–06

Accession on 1 May 2004 enabled the Czech Republic to use all the instruments of EU cohesion policy, including the five SOPs, JROP, two SPDs for Prague, the Cohesion Fund and two Community Initiatives. However, it quickly became apparent that the level of preparedness of the individual ministries responsible for implementing cohesion policy varied widely, despite many years of preparation. While some ministries were able to start programme implementation immediately after accession, others were able to do so only after significant delays. Thus, for example, the Ministry of Trade and Industry (OP Industry and Enterprise) and the MRD (JROP) announced their first calls for project proposals in May 2004, while the Ministry of Labour and Social Affairs (OP Human Resource Development) did so only in December.[6] These delays necessitated the shifting of 2004 programme allocations to the 2005 period, thus complicating their effective use.

Such delays were not the only problem affecting the early stages of programme implementation. Some ministries were strongly criticized for being ill-prepared for the project selection process. For example the MRD, regarded as the best-prepared ministry in the pre-accession period (*Euractiv*, 2004a), faced harsh criticism over project selection after the first call for proposals. In September 2004 the main regional grouping, the Association of the Regions in the Czech Republic (AKČR),[7] criticized the MRD for its inability to establish the rules for project preparation. According to František Dohnal, governor of the Vysošina region:

> We are alarmed by the fact the [MRD] constantly changes the rules for project preparation and evaluation in [the JROP] even after the deadline for project submission. The applicants are retrospectively informed that their project, prepared according to the valid rules, is no longer eligible as the rules were subsequently changed. It devalues their efforts and can lead to the creation of an environment of corruption. (*Euractiv*, 2004b)

This problem was not limited to the JROP, but was common to other programmes as well. However, while the rules for project preparation and selection were gradually perfected and clarified for all OPs, other problems persisted throughout the initial programming period. These included delays in the conclusion of contracts for successful projects, the result of ambiguities connected with the contract-making process.

Such delays were often not just a matter of weeks but several months, thus negatively impacting project realization and the efficient use of EU funds.

Problems were also caused by the existence of several different types of application forms for some programmes, and the application forms were sometimes changed during the calls for proposals. Project preparation was also hindered by superfluous documentation requirements. For example feasibility studies, typically a key document for the evaluation of investment projects, were also required under the JROP regional grant schemes for non-investment projects in the fields of social integration and tourism services, thus placing an extra burden on the applicants.

In some instances, project preparation ran up against shortcomings in the legislation. Illustrative of this problem are the restrictions in OP Human Resource Development that limited the ability of secondary and vocational schools to apply jointly with private companies for funding to support employment-increasing educational projects, all because Czech law does not permit public schools to transfer grant money to project partners from the private sector.

Project co-financing and pre-financing posed another problem. With the exception of sectors like education or social integration, grant applicants were required to ensure that EU funds had matching national co-financing. This often represented a significant burden for applicants, especially public sector institutions. Unlike many other member states, the Czech Republic did not institute continuous payment as the norm for structural funds projects. The recipients of investment projects thus had to fully pre-finance their projects, receiving the EU funding only *ex-post*, after project completion. This severely impacted disposable resources, and therefore the absorption capacity, of a vast number of financially weaker applicants, especially from the public sector.

The overall functioning of the implementation system is, to a great extent, dependent on the relationship among the key managing institutions. The MRD, as the highest MA of the CSF, was in a difficult situation as its coordinating competencies are not clearly defined in the law. It should coordinate other ministries involved in cohesion policy implementation, but its weak legal status (the MRD being equal to other ministries, not superior to them) impedes the cooperation needed for effective implementation. As a result, implementation has been hindered by insufficient cooperation and coordination between the MRD and other MAs. Effective implementation is also dependent on the sufficient availability and quality of technical personnel and financial resources. The most complicated situation concerns personnel; in many cases implementation is based on the knowledge of individual people, knowledge that is not easily transferable to new employees. The constant fluctuation of personnel, especially younger employees who often look for better-paid jobs in the private sector, poses perhaps the biggest administrative problem for the MRD and other ministries responsible for cohesion policy implementation (Potluka, Pělucha and Halámek, 2005, pp. 10–1; MRD, 2005a, pp. 102–3; MRD, 2006b; MRD, 2006c; Eurion, 2006).

The shortcomings in the implementation process were confirmed by an audit ordered by the Finance Ministry in the second half of 2004. This stated that, in the period before 31 July 2004, the implementation systems of most programmes suffered from various imperfections. Only two OPs – Industry and Enterprise, and Rural Development and Multifunctional Agriculture – received positive ratings (*Euractiv*, 2004c).

The difficulties encountered in the implementation process lowered the absorption capacity of the Czech Republic in the initial programming phase.[8] According to a mid-term analysis ordered by the MRD, the volume of contracted structural funds was only 33 per cent of the 2004–06 allocations as of 15 December 2005. Such figures led experts to warn that because of the 'n+2' rule, 'the use of approximately 15 per cent of the Objective 1 allocation for 2004 is jeopardized' (Redeco, 2006, pp. 8–9). These concerns were acknowledged by the government. The Minister for Regional Development, Radko Martínek, predicted that the country would be able to use about 80 per cent of the 2004 allocations, adding 'there is still time to improve the situation … However, we need to also realize that implementation was delayed by approximately nine months, and that it represents a very complicated process' (*Euractiv*, 2006b).

The Czech Republic's shortcomings were also noted by the Commission. While Budget Commissioner Dalia Grybauskaité declared that all new member states faced similar problems in using the structural funds, she identified the Czech Republic as the second biggest laggard among the new members, after Cyprus, as far as its ability to use EU funds was concerned. The biggest obstacle hampering the effective use of EU assistance, she argued, was 'the creation of further bureaucratic layers not requested by Brussels' (*Euractiv*, 2006c).

The MRD reacted to these criticisms by making strenuous efforts to improve the implementation system, in order to accelerate the spending of 2004 allocations. These efforts were intensified under the new Minister for Regional Development, Petr Gandalovič, who came into office in September 2006 as part of a caretaker government led by the ODS.[9] The adopted measures proved effective, and in October the MRD could announce that the 2004 allocations for the JROP and the OPs Infrastructure, Industry and Enterprise, and Rural Development and Multifunctional Agriculture would be fully spent. The biggest problem under Objective 1 continued to be OP Human Resource Development, where the implementing authorities still had to make up for significant delays in programme operation. Outside Objective 1, it also remained uncertain whether the SPDs for Prague could be fully realized by the end of 2006 (*Euractiv*, 2006d). As an Objective 2 region Prague faced less favourable conditions, having the obligation to ensure higher match funding (at least 50 per cent of total project costs, compared to 25 per cent in Objective 1).

In the end, to the relief of the government, and the MRD in particular, the 2004 money was ultimately spent in all existing programmes, including the above-mentioned problem areas. Yet despite this happy ending, the experience of the first years after accession showed that the government's preparedness for EU cohesion policy was far from adequate. However, the results achieved in 2007 confirmed that some lessons had been learned; the use of structural funds went smoother, enabling the country not only to absorb all 2005 allocations, but in three OPs – JROP, Infrastructure, and Rural Development and Multifunctional Agriculture – a significant portion of the 2006 allocations were successfully spent as well (MRD, 2008). This outcome confirmed a new trend in the use of EU funds in the Czech Republic: after weak initial performance, absorption capacity gradually improved, thus opening the way to successful utilization of allocated funding for 2004–06 by the end of 2008.

The debate over cohesion policy planning for 2007–13[10]

The Czech debate over cohesion policy in the new programming period began in early 2004, following publication of the Commission's initial reform proposals. Debate centred on the number and type of programming documents that would be used in the NDP for 2007–13. On this question, it was clear that the positions of the central government and the regions remained virtually unchanged from the previous debate over NDP 2004–06. The MRD asserted its strong preference for continuing with the JROP format, although with a larger role for the regions, while the regions restated their preference for the use of ROPs in the new programming period. In February 2005 the AKČR adopted a resolution calling for the preparation of ROPs for 2007–13 to begin at the NUTS 2 level (AKČR, 2005a).

A major problem with the ROPs approach, however, was that the Czech regions remained heavily dependent on central government grants for their finances, making it difficult for them to provide the co-financing required for structural funds projects (Ferry and McMaster, 2005, pp. 20–1). In 2004–06, this problem was circumvented by the JROP approach, which made the provision of co-financing the responsibility of the central government. In the ROPs model, however, the regions must provide the co-financing themselves, something which they had no means of doing other than borrowing or transfers from the central government. Adoption of the ROPs model, therefore, would provide an argument for creating a new system of 'own resources' for the regions, which in turn would give them greater financial independence from Prague. Seeking to use this issue as a lever to change the regional financing system, the regions declared that co-financing was a major problem that needed to be resolved in cohesion policy planning for 2007–13. According to Evžen Tošenovský, Chairman of the AKČR and governor of Moravskoslezsky *kraj*, 'without a systemic solution of this problem initiated by the central government the regions would encumber unbearable debts' (*Euractiv*, 2005).

By mid 2005, after a series of heated debates between representatives of the regions and the MRD,[11] both sides agreed to work together on preparing future programming documents in a manner that would satisfy the needs of the regions. In a major concession to the regions, the MRD agreed to support the use of ROPs, a change of position that was formally confirmed by the June 2005 Memorandum on Cooperation signed by the MRD and AKČR (AKČR, 2005b).

Thus, despite having continued reservations about the administrative capacity of the regions and their ability to play a more active role in managing cohesion policy, the MRD changed its position and opted for a consensual approach. It did so mainly because fulfillment of the MRD's primary responsibility – the implementation of regional development policy – is dependent on close cooperation with the regions, who are themselves key actors with substantial regional policy competencies. The MRD realized, therefore, that any policy that alienated the regions would undermine its ability to fulfil its own responsibilities and thus be unsustainable.

Following the agreement between the MRD and the regions on the ROPs, the revised version of the NDP for 2007–13 was presented in September 2005 and subsequently approved by the government in February 2006. The revised NDP featured a total of 24 OPs, including the seven ROPs (*Euractiv*, 2006a). However, the positions of the MRD and the regions over the distribution of funding still differed. The MRD proposed allocating 12 per cent of the total structural funds budget for the ROPs, while the regions, who in 2005 favoured a 30 per cent share for the ROPs, now argued for 20 per cent (*Euractiv*, 2006b). The MRD's position was supported by Prime Minister Jiří Paroubek, who argued that 'the share for the ROPs at 12 per cent [was] adequate' since the regions 'still lack[ed] appropriate administrative capacities' (Interview with author, February 2006).

After further negotiations with the regions, the MRD decided to increase the share for the ROPs from 12 to 13.25 per cent (MRD, 2006a). This was the upper limit the Social Democrat-led government was willing to grant the regions, most of which were controlled by the opposition ODS.[12] It was not surprising, therefore, that one of the first initiatives of the new ODS government in 2006 was to satisfy the demands of the regions by increasing the structural funds allocation for the ROPs to 18 per cent (MRD, 2006d).

The 2007–13 programmes: a basis for success?

The Czech Republic emerged a major 'winner' in the competition for cohesion policy funding in 2007–13. For this period the Czech Republic has been allocated €26.82 billion in cohesion spending, the third highest allotment among the member states and the highest in per capita terms (MRD, 2005b). The average annual allocation for cohesion funding will be about four times higher than in 2004–06, rising from an average €0.88 billion (2004–06) to €3.83 billion (2007–13). If fully utilized, the country's GDP could be increased by 3.4 per cent annually simply due to structural funds receipts in this period. All Czech NUTS 2 regions are eligible for funding under the Convergence objective of cohesion policy except for Prague, which will receive funding under the Regional Competitiveness and Employment objective (see Map 9.1).

The European Council's December 2005 agreement on the financial perspective for 2007–13 was therefore welcomed by the Czech government, and generally accepted by the major political parties as the best possible outcome. There was also consensus among the main actors that it was imperative to ensure the efficient utilization of all available

Convergence Regions
Phasing-out Regions
Phasing-in Regions
Competitiveness and
Employment Regions

Map 9.1   Structural funds eligibility, 2007–13
Source: European Commission, DG-Regional Policy.

EU funds, and a common understanding that successful utilization of
these funds depended on the quality of preparations made at both the
national and regional levels.

A key issue affecting cohesion policy implementation in 2007–13 is
the high number of OPs for this period.[13] This reflects not only the new
assertiveness of the regions, which got their way with inclusion of the
seven ROPs, but also a proliferation of thematic (sectoral) programmes.
Virtually all of the ministries whose agendas were covered by the NDP
wanted to run their own programmes, thus deviating from the practice
of 2004–06 when some of the sectoral programmes were jointly

implemented by more than one ministry. The lack of interest in horizontal, inter-ministerial cooperation resulted in the increase of sectoral programmes from four in 2004–06 to eight in 2007–13 (see Table 9.2).[14]

The NDP was a key point of departure for preparing the National Strategic Reference Framework (NSRF), which then served as the basis for negotiations between the Czech government and the Commission over the individual OPs. The decision to prepare the NDP – a document

Table 9.2   Operational programmes in the Czech Republic, 2007–13

Operational programme	Managing authority	% of total	EU Contribution (in €)
Thematic Operational Programmes		79.80	21,300,251, 251
Integrated Operational Programme	MRD	5.93	1,582,390,162
OP Technical Assistance	MRD	0.93	247,783,172
OP Enterprise and Innovation	Ministry of Industry and Trade	11.39	3,041,312,546
OP Human Resources and Employment	Ministry of Labor and Social Affairs	6.88	1,837,421,405
OP Education for Competitiveness	Ministry of Education	6.85	1,828,714,781
OP Research and Development for Innovation	Ministry of Education	7.76	2,070,680,884
OP Environment	Ministry of Environment	18.42	4,917,867,098
OP Transport	Ministry of Transport	21.63	5,774,081,203
Regional Operational Programmes		18.74	5,002,353,233
Regional Operational Programmes (7)	NUTS 2 Regions	17.46	4,659,031,986
ROP Střední Čechy		2.09	559,083,839
ROP Jihozápad		2.31	619,651,254
ROP Severozápad		2.79	745,911,021
ROP Jihovýchod		2.64	704,445,636
ROP Severovýchod		2.46	656,457,606

Continued

Table 9.2   Continued

Operational programme	Managing authority	% of total	EU Contribution (in €)
ROP Moravskoslezsko		*2.68*	*716,093,217*
ROP Střední Morava		*2.46*	*657,389,413*
OP Prague competitivness	Prague NUTS 2 Region	0.88	234,936,005
OP Prague adaptability	Prague NUTS 2 Region	0.41	108,385,242
European Territorial Cooperation		1.46	389,051,107
Cross-border Cooperation – 5 OPs	MRD	1.32	351,589,957
OP Transnational and Interregional Cooperation – 2 OPs	MRD	0.14	37,461,150
Total		100.00	26,691,655,591

Source: MRD, August 2007.

not required by the EU – was made by MRD head Martínek. Inspired by the Irish NDP, he wanted to prepare a large-scale strategic document from which priority areas to be financed by EU funds could be extracted to form a basis for the NSRF. However, in the end the NDP failed to provide an adequate basis for the NSRF, which led the MRD to prepare the NSRF as a separate document. Critics claim that this failure caused the first significant delay in NSRF preparation; according to former MRD Deputy Minister Věra Jourová, 'eight months were lost' by the decision to prepare the NDP (*Aktuálně.cz*, 2007b).

After intensive work, the fourth draft of the NSRF was approved by the government in June 2006 and sent to the Commission in July. In its response, the Commission noted that the fourth version of the Czech NSRF was significantly improved 'in all areas vis-à-vis the previous drafts' (European Commission, 2006b, pp. 31–3), but it also provided a list of recommendations for further improvement. One of the issues which the Commission 'ha[d] fundamental comments about' and identified for improvement was the OPs; it criticized the overlap among some OPs as well as other problems. However, the biggest target of criticism was the Integrated Operational Programme (IOP).[15] Some Commission officials commented that due to the lack of strategy and a systematic approach in the programme, their preference would be complete abolition of the IOP.[16] This position was confirmed, although in diplomatic language, in the Commission's NSRF position paper: 'the objective of the [IOP], its strategy and priorities as well as the added value of this grouping of unrelated activities, are still not clear. Consequently, for several proposed activities, the recommendation is to integrate them into the best appropriate programmes' (European Commission, 2006b, p. 33).

The Commission also made other recommendations, such as strengthening administrative capacity, improving the transfer of knowledge between universities/R&D institutions and the business sector, and giving more importance to the urban dimension. It also touched on the issue of an overcomplicated implementation system:

> further simplifications for the next programming period are required in order to realise a more efficient and effective system of financial flows and to increase absorption capacity, such as controlled over-booking of measures, getting rid of double approval procedures for EU and national co-financing, and pre-financing studies of important projects. (European Commission, 2006b, p. 32)

Unfortunately, however, the Czech government failed to adequately address the Commission's criticisms and make necessary changes to the overcomplicated NSRF, thus further delaying the NSRF negotiations by approximately six months.

The combination of domestic (see above) and external criticism of cohesion policy implementation led the government to consider new measures to eliminate weaknesses and bottlenecks in the implementation system. After approving most of the 24 OPs in November 2006, it began to focus on simplifying the implementation system and making it more transparent and effective (MRD, 2006e).

The final drafts of the NSRF and OPs were handed over to the Commission on 20 November 2006, and the approval process began in March 2007 when the documents were sent electronically to the Commission's information system. Formal negotiations on the NSRF between the government's negotiating team and the Commission were opened in April. The new Minister for Regional Development, Jiří Čunek,[17] expected the NSRF approval process to be finalized by the end of May so that the country could start using EU funding allocated for 2007. However, due to the Commission's continued discontent with some parts of the document the completion date was postponed, first to the end of June, and then to the end of July. The prolonged negotiations revealed that the government had not taken into consideration some of the Commission's recommendations, and thus the document had to be further revised. The painstaking revision of the NSRF, as requested by the Commission, was likened by a Czech official involved in the negotiations to 'patching a not entirely well-made product. Like repairing a [...] decommissioned, rust-eaten ship during its passage on the sea' (*Aktuálně.cz*, 2007a). The negotiations were finally completed and the document approved by Brussels on 27 July 2007 (MRD, 2007).

Approval of the NSRF opened the way to completing negotiations on the individual OPs; while these had been initiated parallel to the NSRF negotiations, they could not be finalized until agreement on the framework document was reached. The first batch of European Social Fund (ESF)-funded programmes – OP Human Resources and Employment, OP Education for Competitiveness, and OP Prague Adaptability – were approved by the Commission in October 2007. The approval of other programmes followed, and by December negotiations on all but one OP were finalized. The remaining programme, OP Research and Development for Innovation, was not approved until the first half of 2008 because of its poor preparation. This led to the resignation in October 2007 of the Education Minister, Dana Kuchtová, who had come under strong pressure from both the government and opposition politicians as well as the expert community. The intensity of this criticism, and her subsequent resignation, illustrates the high political salience of cohesion policy in the Czech Republic.

Perhaps the biggest surprise of the OP negotiations was the rather smooth approval of the ROPs. The regions thus demonstrated their capacity to prepare their own OPs, showing this to be even higher than for some central government ministries. Regional competence was further underscored by the 'courage' of regional authorities to announce the first calls for proposals in September 2007, a few months before final approval of the ROPs by the Commission. A similar strategy was adopted only by some of the better-prepared central government MAs, such as the Ministry of Industry and Trade and the Ministries of Transport and Environment. The relative competence of the regional authorities was confirmed by the Deputy Director-General at DG Regio, Katarína Mathernová, who argued that 'for many people here [in the Commission] it was fascinating to discover that the Czech Republic, which is one of the most developed and economically strongest new member states, still has such a weak bureaucracy at the state level, at the ministries.' This contrasted with her positive evaluation of the quality of the ROPs and administrative capacity at the regional level:

> Working with the regions, with governors and their teams was a real joy and I consider their plans among the best...during times of ever increasing decentralization and regionalization in Europe this [cohesion] policy helps to create teams that will manage things [cohesion policy-related]. It is therefore one of the reasons why I am happy that the Czech Republic – as opposed to Slovakia, for example – has gotten to the point that a significant part of [cohesion policy] money is in the hands of the regions. (*Respekt,* 2008)

In general, however, the Czech Republic was among the laggards, being one of the last member states to have their OP negotiations finalized. This has significantly delayed programme implementation and complicated the country's performance in the initial phase of the new programming period, which could lead to a repeat of the situation at the beginning of 2004–06. One factor that might reduce problems in using EU funds allocated for 2007 is the 'n+3' rule introduced for 2007–10. However, there is still no guarantee that in the last months of 2010, the deadline for spending 2007 allocations, the Czech Republic will not encounter similar 'drama' to what it experienced in 2006. Moreover, a recurrence of these problems would be amplified in the context of 2007–13, with EU funds for this period exceeding by several times the 2004–06 allocations.

The difficult experience with drafting the NSRF and OPs for 2007–13 and getting them approved by the Commission, and the initial experience with implementing the new OPs, point to a couple of important realities affecting cohesion policy implementation in the Czech Republic. One is the continued lack of bureaucratic competence and capacity at the central state level, especially within certain government ministries. Another is the rapid learning and increased competence of the regional governments, who, at the outset of the new programming period at least, have demonstrated a growing capacity to manage EU-funded programmes. These are factors which could have important implications for cohesion policy implementation in the Czech Republic in the future, perhaps favouring further regionalization and decentralization.

Conclusion

The Czech Republic is a major recipient of cohesion policy funding; in 2007–13 it ranks third among all member states in terms of allocated funding, and first in per capita terms. Not only is EU structural assistance of huge potential benefit to the Czech Republic, it has also aroused a tremendous amount of interest on the part of potential applicants, including municipalities, Small and Medium-Sized Enterprise (SMEs) and NGOs.

Along with other new member states, the Czech Republic made extensive preparations for implementing EU cohesion policy in the pre-accession period. Nevertheless, it has experienced major problems using EU funding since becoming a member state in May 2004. These problems are mainly administrative and institutional; they include the varying level of preparedness of relevant ministries in the first programming period (2004–06), with a continuation of this problem in 2007–13, and the lack of horizontal coordination between the MRD and other ministries managing OPs. There was also the problem of too many OPs, which in some cases were overlapping, an issue that has drawn criticism from the Commission. These administrative and institutional shortcomings have limited absorption capacity in the initial programming period after accession; problems with absorption capacity may be even bigger in 2007–13.

Unlike many member states, EU cohesion policy is a political issue in the Czech Republic. Disputes have occurred between the regions and the central government over management of the structural funds, with the newly established regions seeking to claim a larger role in administering EU assistance. There were also disputes between the government and opposition parties over the efficient use of allocated money plus related issues connected with the preparation, administration and management of the structural funds. In this manner, cohesion policy became both 'regionalized' and 'politicized' in the Czech Republic, a reflection of both the relative importance of EU assistance in economic terms, but also the fissures and still evolving nature of the Czech political system.

The problems experienced in implementing EU cohesion policy pose a major challenge for the Czech Republic; as a rapidly converging new member state in a larger and poorer EU (with the addition of Bulgaria and Romania in 2007, and the possible accession of Croatia by 2012), its cohesion policy allocation is unlikely to be as great after 2013. The inability to make effective use of current allocations, therefore, could amount to a significant wasted opportunity.

Notes

1. Part of this section draws on Baun and Marek (2006).
2. For more detailed discussion of the politics of creating the Czech regions, see Blažek and Boekhout (2000); Moxon-Browne and Kreuzbergová (2001); Jacoby and Černoch (2002); Illner (2002); and Marek and Baun (2002). Brusis (2003) gives particular attention to the relative influence of the EU in this process and the instrumentalization of EU preferences by domestic actors.
3. Interviews with government officials of the Olomouc region, December 2001–January 2002. Also see McMaster (2004b, p. 23).
4. Final approval of the NDP for 2004–06 came on 16 December 2002 (Resolution No. 1272/2002).
5. Both mergers were finalized by the government on 12 February 2003 (Resolution No. 149/2003).
6. The calls for proposals under some priorities of this programme (e.g., the Development of Lifelong Learning Priority) were announced only in early 2005.
7. The AKČR is an organization promoting the common interests of the Czech regions. It was founded in August 2001 and all 14 self-governing regions are members. It is currently the most important platform for coordinating the policies of the regions toward the central government.
8. For a detailed analysis of structural funds use in the Czech Republic in the period until February 2006, see Zahradník and Jedlička (2006).
9. The June 2006 general elections resulted in a tie. After three months of wrangling between the Civic Democrats and second strongest party – the Social Democrats – a new government came to power. The ODS at first formed a caretaker minority government (in September 2006), which did not survive a vote of confidence; subsequently, a coalition government with the Greens and Christian Democrats was approved by the Parliament in January 2007.
10. Part of this section draws on Baun and Marek (2006).
11. Interview by author of an MRD official close to the negotiations.
12. After the 2004 regional elections ODS governors headed the regional governments in 12 of the 14 *kraje* (after the 2002 elections, the mayor of Prague was also from the ODS), with a Christian Democratic governor in the lone remaining region (Jihomoravský).
13. The Czech Republic, to the displeasure of the Commission, submitted the highest number of OPs of any member state.
14. For example, the Ministry of Education, which implemented the OP Human Resource Development with the Ministries of Labour and Social Affairs (the MA), Environment, and Industry and Trade in 2004–06, has managing authority over two programmes – OP Education for Competitiveness, and OP Research and Development for Innovations – in 2007–13. In the same manner, the Ministries of Transport and Environment (the MA), who jointly ran OP Infrastructure in 2004–06, now have their own programmes: OP Transport, and OP Environment. Another example is the MRD, which after losing the JROP versus ROPs battle prepared two new programmes for 2007–13: OP Integrated Operational Programme, and OP Technical Assistance.

15. This programme was created by the MRD after losing the JROP vs. ROPs debate. In order to preserve its role in cohesion policy implementation, the MRD put together an incoherent set of priorities, ranging from support for large tourism infrastructure projects to the purchase of medical equipment and the renovation of socialist block flats.
16. Interview by author of Commission official close to the negotiations, September 2006.
17. Čunek became the Minister for Regional Development in the second ODS-led coalition government of Prime Minister Mirek Topolánek, which took office in January 2007.

10
Hungary

Gyula Horváth

Introduction: a regionally differentiated transition

Hungary is regaining its former position in Europe as it undergoes a profound transformation. These changes are not being felt equally in all regions of the country, however. Instead, economic growth has brought divergent performance and amplified disparities. Fuelled by a wave of Foreign Direct Investments (FDIs), western Hungary and Budapest and its surrounding area have been the fastest to restructure and take advantage of new economic opportunities, whereas the Northeast still struggles with the restructuring of heavy industries and mono-sectoral activities and the Great Plain and Southeast are suffering from a decline in agriculture. While northeastern regions were among the most developed during the communist period, growth has now shifted to the West. This East-West divide, the trend towards metropolization that is encouraging suburbanization around Budapest, and the exodus from rural areas and accompanying process of urbanization are all increasing territorial fragmentation. These trends are also widening income disparities between the countryside and the main cities (Horváth, 2005).

The Hungarian government has traditionally used regional policy to address disparities and foster local development, but its success has been mixed. Nevertheless, the country has considerable experience with targeting public initiatives to improve structural problems and manage crises in more backward regions (Enyedi and Tózsa, 2004).

Contrary to many Central and Eastern European Country (CEECs), Hungary has maintained a successful balance between the pace of economic transformation and the speed with which new institutions, regulatory regimes and rules of the game have been introduced. More than a hundred acts have been passed each year and twice as many decrees have been adopted. The Act on Regional Development and Physical Planning, adopted by Parliament in 1996 and amended in 1999, created a new regional level of territorial administration

Unipolar country

Disparities in income levels, unemployment and poverty are high in Hungary. The exclusion of unskilled workers from the labour market and the impoverishment of many households have created social problems. A variegated industrial mix, concentrated placements of FDIs and highly uneven R&D capacities all contribute to this lack of cohesion and tend to reinforce existing territorial dichotomies: East-West, centre-periphery, and urban-rural.

Budapest and its surrounding area have always dominated Hungary, but never so much as today. One-in-five Hungarians lives in Budapest, which possesses the country's smallest and most densely populated territory, and its highest density of economic activities and social facilities. Budapest's share of Hunagry's GDP in 2004 equalled 34.6 per cent; and although its share of the nation's industrial employees decreased significantly during the communist era (to less than 20 per cent), its share of business employees is now almost 40 per cent. In addition, industries with the highest levels of R&D and innovation still reside in Budapest. Its dominance in the service sector and high-tech industry, and its outstanding infrastructure and telecommunications facilities, are some of the reasons for the extreme weight of the capital in Hungary's spatial structure (Horváth, 2005). Even in terms of its share of social facilities, such as health services and education, Budapest is much better endowed than the relative size of its population would suggest.

In terms of territorial disparities, Hungary shares characteristics with other EU countries. Like Italy and Germany, Hungary has significant disparities between large geographical areas (East-West in Germany, North-South in Italy). However, unlike these countries, disparities are also evident at lower territorial levels. Central Hungary, Central Transdanubia and West Transdanubia are the best performing territories and are developing more rapidly than the national average. South Transdanubia, and even more North Hungary and the North and South Great Plain, however, are burdened with problems and fall short of the national average in almost all respects. The South Great Plain represents the middle in some respects, showing signs of revival and growth potential (see Table 10.1).

Table 10.1 GDP per capita of Hungarian regions, 2004

Region	GDP per capita as % of national average	GDP per capita as % of EU27 (PPS)
Central Hungary	163	106
Budapest	213	139
Middle Transdanubia	94	62
West Transdanubia	99	65
South Transdanubia	69	45
North Hungary	66	43
North Great Plain	64	41
South Great Plain	68	44
Hungary total	100	65

Source: National Statistical Office (2006).

The economic changes of the transition period have led to greater territorial disparities. Highly specialized regions with concentrations on heavy industry, mining or agriculture were negatively affected while those with a more flexible economic base recovered from the post-communist depression more rapidly and now display higher-than-average growth and employment rates. The successful regions managed to reorganize their industries, allowing them to routinely upgrade products and production processes and target competitive market niches. At the same time, their attractiveness was reinforced by new economic policies enacted during the transition which provided tax allowances for joint ventures, foreign investments and new businesses. The best-off territories include those with a high share in manufacturing, especially machinery, and a large export potential resulting from high levels of FDI. Foreign capital has been concentrated in the economic centres, especially Budapest and its surrounding areas (OECD, 2001).

The legal regulation of regional development policy

With the Act on Regional Development and Physical Planning of 1996 and its amendment in 1999, the Hungarian government introduced a regional development system whose most distinctive feature was the creation of a new regional level of administration. The seven new macro-regions (see Map 10.1), designated as Nomenclature of Statistical Territorial Units (NUTS) 2 regions in the EU's statistical categorization, are supposed to implement regional policy and assume or coordinate

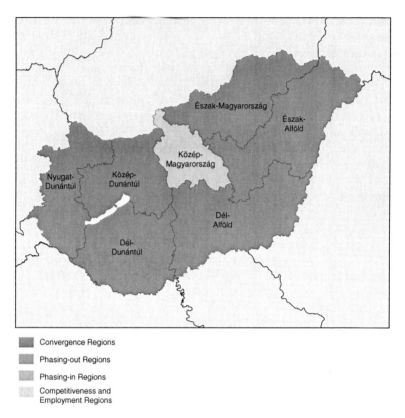

- Convergence Regions
- Phasing-out Regions
- Phasing-in Regions
- Competitiveness and Employment Regions

Map 10.1   Cohesion policy objectives in Hungary, 2007–13
Source: European Commission, DG Regional Policy.

responsibilities lying beyond the scope of the local level. The EU had a strong impact on shaping the new regional system, since it considers this an appropriate territorial level for implementing its various pre-accession programmes and the structural funds. The new regions are generally viewed as partners of the central government in implementing regional policy; some also consider them potentially the basis for a full governmental level between the central and municipal levels. However, since regional institutions operate parallel to the existing territorial-administrative framework, the new system has created some confusion. The distribution of responsibilities between new regional bodies and existing government institutions is unclear, and disputes over project implementation are quite common. Institution building remains a core issue for the decentralization of the Hungarian State (Pálné, Paraskevopoulos, and Horváth, 2004).

The present state of development planning in Hungary is characterized by a comparatively strong role for local government, a still unclear role for the new regions, and a rather traditional and partly contradictory handling of responsibilities at the national level. As mentioned above, the new regions were created in the late 1990s. In addition to delineating the seven macro-regions, the government encouraged the establishment of voluntary Regional Development Councils (RDCs). As counties were free to choose their partners for collaboration within RDCs, the statistical region (NUTS 2) system and the development region (RDC) system did not match. Furthermore, many counties belong to more than one development region. Several RDCs were established, although most of them have not been operational for long, due mainly to uncertainty about the creation of a regional level and strong resistance from the counties.

Creation of the regions has not clarified power-sharing in the Hungarian territorial governance and regional development system. One of the crucial issues of Hungary's regional development policy concerns the uncertain future role of the counties, on the one hand, and the newly created regions, on the other, as well as the role of the central state. While there is probably no reason to doubt the opportunity of maintaining and strengthening local government at county level, whether the size of the country justifies splitting up development planning and programming between county and regional levels is questionable. Efficiency considerations and the EU requirement to dispose of Operational Programmes (OPs) at the NUTS 2 level might lead to the conclusion that a single level should be responsible for preparing and implementing development plans and programmes. At local level, the practical ability to prepare and decide upon feasible programmes based on priorities determined in corresponding regional development plans depends, to a large extent, on the existing financial system. The fact that counties and regions do not dispose of sufficient financial resources to take their own decisions independently of complementary funding decisions at the national level seriously handicaps any effective decentralization (Horváth, 2001).

In sum, the creation of regions seems to be a response to weaknesses of the county level rather than the specific need for a new political level. Although most development policies can probably be implemented at county level, the geopolitical context and the need to ensure compatibility with EU policy requirements should obviously be taken into account. It is important, however, that the creation of regions does not lead to confusion over the delimitation of power between the two proximate levels. If both are to be maintained, the dual system of counties and regions needs clearly assigned tasks and policy responsibilities. Given that the counties are politically well-rooted, it is probably useful to strengthen their institutions and maintain their present responsibilities – mainly for secondary education and health care – while the regions would be basically responsible for implementing regional policy and the use of structural funds.

The goals of cohesion policy

The ultimate goal of the National Development Plan (NDP) and domestic development policies is to improve the quality of life of the Hungarian people. This depends on the income level of the population and many other aspects, including the state of the environment, the level and quality of public services, and the successful development of all regions and social groups. In the current planning period, the main goal is to reduce Hungary's income gap relative to the EU average. To a large extent, achievement of this goal depends on whether Hungary can increase its income; thus, policy actions should contribute to this overall objective (Baráth, 2004).

The NDP for 2004–06 (Government of Hungary, 2003), which was approved in 2003 and served as the basis for negotiations with the Commission on the Community Support Framework (CSF) for 2004–06, had the following specific objectives:

- Increase the competitiveness of the country and its regions both internationally and within the EU. Actions need to be taken that address low productivity, the scarcity of capital, low levels of technology, a weak Small and Medium-Sized Enterprise (SME) sector, insufficient use of agricultural potential, the low use of modern IT applications offered by new Information & Communications Technology (ICT) technologies, the weak use of opportunities presented by the information society, poor R&D activities, poor transport infrastructure and an underutilized tourism potential.
- Increase employment and develop human potential. Problems to be addressed include low participation rates in the labour market, a high level of long-term unemployment, the social exclusion of

disadvantaged groups such as the Roma, discrimination against women in the labour market, the limited flexibility and ability of education and vocational training to meet labour market needs and weak educational infrastructure, and the weakness of services that promote employability.

• Improve environmental quality, including the sustainable management of natural resources and a more regionally balanced development. This objective is justified by the need to reduce environmental costs and the large regional disparities in quality of life across the country.

Improving competitiveness and the better use of human resources are mutually reinforcing. Improving economic competitiveness increases the demand for skills and knowledge, and also helps increase the employment and economic activity rate. In turn, the successful integration of people into the labour market and improvement of their skills promotes economic competitiveness and higher value-added activities.

There are wide differences in the standard of living across Hungary. Action is required to create the conditions in which all regions benefit from economic growth by making use of their potential and available resources. This requires improvements in living conditions and the transport networks that link regions together. Creating enterprises and job opportunities and developing local skills are necessary to retain people in the regions. This will help mitigate regional differences and increase the well-being and social cohesion of the country. At the same time, an improved environment also increases the real value of income. In Hungary the environmental situation varies considerably, and governmental action can greatly contribute to the real value of income in areas where it is the worst. A cleaner environment is also necessary for sustainable development, and the NDP aims at reducing damage to Hungary's natural resources and promoting a more rational use of them. Another objective, therefore, is the achievement of a cleaner environment and more balanced regional development.

Financing cohesion policy

In 2004–06, Hungary received a multiple of its previous resources from the EU cohesion policy budget. Within the framework of the NDP, developments and investments have been completed, or are still being implemented, in nearly 2,000 communities around Hungary. About €2.85 billion of EU funds, awarded to more than 18,000 successful

Table 10.2   Cohesion policy allocations in Hungary, 2004–06 (€ mn)

Fund	2004	2005	2006	Total
Structural funds	448	620	786	1,854
Cohesion fund	340	280	374	994
Total	788	900	1,159	2,847

Source: Government of Hungary (2003a).

applicants, has contributed to the creation of nearly 50,000 new jobs around the country (Table 10.2).

Hungarian actors – local governments, entrepreneurs and NGOs – have mastered the 'ins' and 'outs' of the structural funds application process in the years since accession. The contracting authorities have also learned the intricacies of the tendering process and successfully implemented it. Step-by-step, the system is being established: the government, fully aware of the teething troubles of the tendering system, has taken the views of applicants into account when transforming and, where possible, simplifying administrative regulations.

The distribution of resources between sectoral and regional programmes is dependent on the role of the regional level. In 2004–06, the share of funds allocated for regional development was only about 18 per cent, with the remainder allocated for sectoral programmes for Human Resources Development (28 per cent), Economic Competitiveness (22 per cent), Agriculture and Rural Development (16 per cent), and Environmental Protection and Infrastructure (16 per cent) (Government of Hungary, 2003b, p. 128).

The preparation of the NDP for 2004–06 was a considerable challenge, from which some important lessons were learned. No single, coherent database had been made before. The development strategy was not in harmony with and connected to the financial planning of the NDP, and the allocation of resources among programmes was made without exact, quantified and accepted indicators of results. In a planning process driven by resource allocation, strategy-making was not target-oriented, but tools-oriented. As the structural funds use a basically regional approach, the responsibilities for respective objectives were not adequately coordinated among the sectorally organized government ministries. The task of programming was also a considerable challenge for the state administration, which was not used to thinking in terms longer than the annual budget. The experience with partnership demonstrated that poorly organized social debates and the large-scale involvement of partners having little knowledge of the structural funds could significantly slow down the planning process. Nevertheless, the experiences of 2004–06 were important for the next programming period, when Hungarian applicants have access to even greater resources from the EU.

In 2007–13 Hungary has the opportunity, with the support of the EU, to implement one of the largest-scale development programmes in its history. In this seven-year period Hungary will receive a total of €33 billion in EU funding, taking into account Common Agricultural Policy (CAP) subsidies. This includes nearly €25 billion of cohesion policy spending – the second largest in per capita terms among all member states (see Table 10.3). Cohesion policy support is supplemented by approximately €3.4 billion in EU support for rural development from the European Agricultural Fund for Rural Development (EAFRD) and the European Fisheries Fund (EEF). As a result of EU cohesion policy and rural development support, combined with domestic co-financing the resources available (at current prices) in 2007–13 are, at an annual average, triple the amount available in 2004–06.

Before finalizing its Operational Programmes for 2007–13 the government consulted with various social actors, including the Economic and Social Council, the National Interest Reconciliation Council, the National Environment Protection Council, the Council for the Disabled and Equal Opportunities, the Hungarian Academy of Sciences, the historical churches and the political parties. It also initiated consultation with the most disadvantaged regions on programmes to promote their cohesion, and with the so-called pole cities playing the role of economic development and modernization 'engines'. The government used the results of these consultations in adopting the New Hungary Development Plan for 2007–13, which contained the objectives and

Table 10.3 Cohesion policy allocations in Hungary, 2007–13

	€ bn	Percentage share
ERDF	12.6	50.8
Cohesion Fund	8.6	34.7
ESF	3.6	14.5
Total	24.8	100.0

Source: Government of Hungary.

framework for the use of more than 80 per cent of available development resources (Government of Hungary, 2006), the OPs, and the New
Hungary Rural Development Programme, which planned the use of
agricultural and rural development resources. The implementation of
these programmes spans several election periods; thus, it will require
the broadest social and political cooperation. In order to increase the
role of the political parties, the government also created a special parliamentary committee to supervise the implementation of the New
Hungary Development Plan.

Of the seven Hungarian regions, six fall under the Convergence objective and one, the Central Hungary region, under the phasing-in Regional
Competitiveness and Employment objective (See Map 10.1). The following aspects were considered when planning the distribution of funds:

- relevant EU regulations on using the cohesion and structural funds;
- the relative weight of certain types of intervention in attaining the
  main established objectives;
- obligations in the areas of environmental protection and transport
  arising from Hungary's EU membership;
- the size and relative development level of individual regions of the
  country;
- the assumed absorption capacities of individual areas of intervention.

Table 10.4 shows the funds available within the individual OPs, not
taking into account the 15 per cent national co-financing. In 2007–13

Table 10.4   Allocations for individual Operational Programmes, 2007–13 (2004
prices)

	EU contribution (€ bn)	Percentage share
Economic development	2.5	10.0
Transport	6.2	24.9
Social infrastructure	1.9	8.3
Environment and energy	4.2	16.8
Social renewal	3.4	13.7
Convergence regions	4.3	17.3
Competitiveness region	1.5	6.0
State reform and e-government	0.8	3.0
Total	24.8	100.0

Source: Government of Hungary.

sectoral programmes will receive the lion's share of resources, and the amount of spending for regional programmes will not exceed one-quarter of total allocations.

Cohesion policy and institutional change

The impact of cohesion policy on Hungary's institutional and administrative system has been significant. Among the consequences of the 1996 Regional Policy Act was the creation of a specific institution, the RDC, in reference to the partnership principle. When preparing for EU cohesion policy, a key question was whether the micro-regional (NUTS 4), county (NUTS 3) or the regional (NUTS 2) level should be the institutional basis for regional policy. The decision to utilize all three territorial levels was not ideal; the over-fragmented institutional system, and the creation of RDCs operating on all three levels, contributed to the fragmentation of development resources and resulted in conflicts stemming from the lack of a clear division of labour. The RDCs also dispose of only a portion of public development resources, which naturally caused frustration, local conflicts and finally disillusionment.

The RDCs thus became the framework for the cooperation and integration of different organizations and sectors which had previously suffered from a lack of coordination and integration. Unfortunately, the modification of the Regional Development Act in 1999 ended the membership of economic actors in the RDCs. The local egoism dominating the fragmented municipal system was channelled into the territorial framework in terms of development programming and resource distribution.

Troubles in the traditional democratic institutional system

In addition to the many positive effects of EU cohesion policy, we have to consider its questionable impact on the quality of democracy in Hungary. It is a paradox that the directly elected county assemblies have a much more limited role in the implementation of cohesion policy than the non-elected RDCs. Experience shows that a majority of RDCs have functioned in an exclusive way. A new type of elite is emerging, based on the power to redistribute economic development resources. Membership in the RDCs has created a set of personalized positions, without contributing to a real networking of institutions.

The sensitive balance between professional (technocratic and efficiency-oriented) and non-professional (equity and participation-oriented) elements has hardly been achieved in Hungary until now.

The mayors' lobby is stronger than associations of technocrats interested in economic development. As a result, resources are fragmented in a way that does not effectively promote basic infrastructure development. However, the technocrats have more opportunities to exert influence on development policy than local society.

A major contradiction of the institutional system in Hungary is the conflict between the decentralization demands of EU cohesion policy and the centralization efforts of the government. The limited scope for action of territorial bodies and the strict rules for resource division have led to the disillusionment of local actors.

Although the Regional Development Act resulted in significant progress, the problem of the territorial division of power has not yet been solved. The meso-level is 'floating', and neither professional nor political answers have been found to the question of whether the county or any other formation should be the appropriate unit for decentralization. The efficiency of regional policy implementation is thus considerably diminished by the excessive number of decision-making and distribution levels, the fragmentation of resources and general uncertainty about the role of the regions. The situation should be clarified and made unambiguous both in public administration and in the implementation of regional policy.

In 2002, the new Socialist government announced the boldest reform of public administration to date, proposing the creation of directly elected regional governments by 2006. The objective of the reform was to settle the decade-long debate over the role of counties by transferring power to the regions and eliminating the self-governing status of the counties. The regional reform has yet to be implemented, however, and its success in the long run depends largely on what the EU's attitude will be. The administrative strengthening of the regions did not take place in 2004–06 because the Commission did not want to waste time dealing with unprepared regions. Supporters of the reform were rather disappointed when the Commission encouraged Hungary to manage the first NDP at central government level, and by the fact that the regions were given only a secondary role in cohesion policy implementation.

Preparing for 2007–13, it was a basic question from the administrative point of view what role the regions should be given in programme implementation. If Hungary really wants to make determined steps towards regional reform, the regions will have to be given a much more significant role. Supporters of reform feared the political elite would not be motivated to carry out regional reform if cohesion policy implementation remained centralized in the new programming period, and thus they argued for a more regionalized approach. It is also true, however, that cohesion policy by itself does not justify the need for regional reform in Hungary, as the whole system of public administration and services should be considered when deciding what type of meso-tier the country needs.

Institutional and administrative aspects of cohesion policy

The legal regulation of regional policy spurred a significant process of institution building, with the establishment of RDCs being only the beginning. In addition to the RDCs, various working organizations or agencies were created, and they soon became the most important actors. Among the organizations represented in the RDCs (local authorities and chambers), changes also occurred and departments dealing with regional policy were established. Monitoring committees were created for the EU pre-accession programmes (Poland, Hungary Assistance for Economic Reconstruction [PHARE], Instrument for Structural Policies for Pre-Accession [ISPA] and Special Accession Programme for Agriculture and Rural Development [SAPARD]), and within the ambit of the RDCs new organizations arose, including units operating regional information systems (within the body of county assemblies), economic planning and consulting companies, and development companies and training institutions. The process of institution building slowed considerably after accession, however, due to the fact that central government organs became the programme Managing Authorities (MAs). The central authorities responsible for managing OPs were augmented by significant increases in personnel, while the capacities of regional organs were underutilized. However, there is still insufficient experience with cohesion policy management to allow for an evaluation of how the implementation system has performed.

Among the member states joining the EU in May 2004, Hungary was the first to begin implementing its NDP. The large number of project applications is a positive development and a serious challenge at the same time. Serious problems resulted from an inadequate regulatory environment. The existing laws on public procurement and VAT were especially disadvantageous for applicants, but these regulatory deficiencies were soon corrected.

In order to maximize absorption capacity, a significant decentralization of financial and management capacities is necessary. The need for regional programmes is also underlined by findings showing that NDP priorities which are difficult to reconcile with the community financing system are probably easier to manage in a relatively flexible system of regional programmes. Considering all this, Hungary has a vested interest in integrating regional programmes in the NDP. In the absence of regional reform, the institutional system for implementing regional programmes should be created by strengthening the regional development institutions that already exist. This seems a feasible solution, considering the limited budgetary resources and time available. The institutional system of regional development strengthened in this way should also be involved in implementing sectoral programmes at the regional level (Vigvári, 2005).

A significant part of national development expenditure in the coming years will be spent on programmes co-financed by the EU. The creation of a single support system thus necessitates a change to medium-term planning in the case of remaining Hungarian development resources, as the parallel use of separate methodologies would result in redundancies and a fragmentation of resources that would further decrease the efficiency of expenditures. Projects and programmes with development objectives cannot be integrated into the traditional annual budgetary system. Medium-term planning, on the other hand, allows the adequate timing of expenditures and can increase the efficiency of distribution because the future consequences of present budgetary decisions have to be taken into consideration, above all expected changes in structural factors.

In addition to a coordinated division of tasks, parallel financing should also be eliminated, in order to keep the economy on a balanced growth path and to have adequate resources for implementing objectives not financed by the EU. Developments eligible for EU support should only be implemented using EU resources, with Hungarian co-financing. In order to achieve this Hungary needs a single development policy that takes into consideration all resources from both the EU and the Hungarian budget, and this should be aligned with the process of state budget planning and the implementation of development resources. A single support system should thus be created, supported by law, which requires in the first place amendment of the state budget act and its implementation order. The state budget has made several moves in this direction in the past few years (e.g., using preliminary estimates, demonstrating obligations in the budget appendix, showing the integrated budget estimate behind the CSF), but the breakthrough has not yet occurred. The objective of creating a single development policy can be achieved by constructing a comprehensive planning system built on an adequate legal basis, adequate government decision-making mechanisms, and a mature planning terminology and methodology (Faragó, 2004). This would also insure the use of national development planning documents and the operation of horizontal coordination.

Of special importance is the need to improve the absorption capacities of municipalities, from a threefold perspective: first, an increase of own-resources; second, an improvement of planning and programming administrative and professional capacities; and third, the strengthening of internal controls.

In summation, the requirements of an efficient development policy are as follows:

- A comprehensive planning mechanism, with the application of a strategic view;
- Strong central government coordination;
- Improved horizontal (inter-sectoral) coordination;
- A strengthened strategic perspective at the ministerial level, at the same liberating it from operational tasks;
- The decentralization of development policy, based on the institutional system established in the regions;
- Expanded government interest intermediation mechanisms, promoting stronger partnership;
- Institutionalized harmony between EU cohesion policy and national development policy, including a single development financing system;
- An adequate legal foundation for development planning.

The requirements listed above make it clear that Hungary faces mainly internal learning, adaptation, regulatory and structural tasks in order to improve its institutional and administrative capacities. However, it is evident that the EU should respect the following:

- The regionalization process that has begun in the new member states can come to a halt if the EU does not assist and support the administrative and political strengthening of the regions;
- There is extremely little experience with cohesion policy implementation, so the simplification of procedures and more training and assistance for the personnel of programme MAs is necessary.
- For adapting the planning, budgetary and regulatory system to EU requirements it is of primary importance for the EU to announce its expectations as soon as possible and in the clearest possible form.

Conclusions

With the end of communism and the transition to a market-oriented system, the formerly planned economies of Central and Eastern Europe experienced the rapid emergence of regional differences. While many had hoped that market mechanisms would reduce spatial inequalities, it soon became apparent that this was not happening and that comprehensive regional policies were necessary to counter the emergence of new regional differences.

Hungary played a pioneering role in establishing the political instruments and institutions of regional policy. It was Hungary's Parliament which passed the first regional development act in Eastern Europe, and it was also Hungary which elaborated the first comprehensive spatial development concept. The Regional Development Fund (which was a rather meagre, but continuously expanding budget item) made it possible to employ up-to-date regional policy techniques. Among Hungary's different policy sectors, it was without a doubt regional policy whose goals, instruments and institutions were most in step with EU norms in the pre-accession period.

Following accession, however, Hungary lost its previous leading position among the CEECs in regional policy. Development policy based upon EU subsidies 'gobbled up' regional reforms. The preparation of national development plans occurred on the basis of sectoral and macro-political goals. These plans, which were based on the EU's standardized development handbooks, show considerable similarity among the new member states. The contents of national development documents are so generic that it is sometimes hard to ascertain exactly whose plan we are holding in our hands. Exaggerated homogenization also led to the neglect of regional specifics. This approach in development policy, as surveys of Hungarian regional development actors have demonstrated, has numerous supporters in the central government. Development policy failed to decentralize Hungary's overly centralized institutional system.

According to the results of empirical surveys, a decentralized model would invite considerable resistance from central government ministries; this can only be overcome by consistent and resolute governmental and parliamentary action, as well as constitutional safeguards. Research findings show that a majority of regional stakeholders support regionalization in principle, but aren't convinced of the appropriateness of current regional borders and centres, as their spatial ties are realized on a smaller scale. However, it would be difficult to demarcate more acceptable regional borders than those which currently exist. Moreover, it is of considerable importance that squabbles about borders and centres should not deflect attention from more substantive questions, such as the decentralization of the state and the strengthening of regional autonomy.

Unfortunately, the former are the questions *du jour* for county elites; they ignore the crucial issues, which are: What sort of functions should a region possess? And what kinds of competencies should the central government delegate? It appears the government ministries are finally becoming aware of the possibility that changes might be at hand. Why should state bureaucracies decide on the acceptance or rejection of project applications amounting to a few million forints? As they are feverishly deciding the fate of hundreds, even thousands of similar applications, the same intensity cannot be observed in discussions over strategic matters. Why doesn't the central government concern itself with preparing sectoral programmes? Why are there no elaborate long-term development concepts?

Not only operational, but also crucial strategic-planning functions may also be assigned to the regions. The more so because what the central government is currently suggesting – that tried-and-true methods from one corner of the country may be simply transplanted to another – will not be viable in the present and future programming periods. Every region must proceed along its own path. Regionally varied development trajectories – this is the recipe for the successful member states of the EU.

Reducing backwardness and regional development are among the most important strategic objectives of the EU, absorbing almost 40 per cent of its budget. Member states and their regions, depending on their level of development, receive substantial support for cohesion. But we must also recognize that despite these subsidies, changes in the regional development rankings of individual member states only occur when a consistent structural policy for the use of EU funds is followed for multiple decades. Successful regions did not concentrate on the creation of traditional infrastructure, but rather on the modern engines of regional development: innovation, business services, modern industrial organization solutions and human resource development. Those regions which expected to get along simply on the basis of EU support, and sought only to realize *de rigeur* development policy objectives, were unable to improve their relative positions.

It is now self-evident in the majority of member states that the institutions of power-sharing and multilevel governance enhance economic performance and welfare in individual regions. The lobbyist politician is replaced by his or her development-minded peer, who encourages long-term legal guarantees for autonomous local growth, cooperation on a European scale and partnerships among regional stakeholders. The successful development of numerous Western European regions shows the efficacy of this attitude, as well as its eminent role in fostering regional identity.

11
Lithuania

Vitalis Nakrošis

Introduction

This chapter examines the implementation of EU cohesion policy in Lithuania. Lithuania is one of the poorest EU member states, with a GDP per capita only 56 per cent of the EU average in 2006. As a single Nomenclature of Statistical Territorial Units (NUTS) 2 region, Lithuania was eligible to receive cohesion policy funding under Objective 1 in the 2004–06 programming period, and under the Convergence objective in 2007–13.

Support from the structural funds is considered one of the major benefits of Lithuania's membership in the EU. In 2004–06, Lithuania received about €1.38 billion (at 2004 prices) from the structural and cohesion funds. Annual receipts from the EU in this period were almost double the size of the Lithuanian State Investment Programme, and thus were highly significant in fiscal terms. In 2007–13, Lithuania should receive €6.08 billion in cohesion policy spending from the EU (at 2004 prices), about double the amount per year of the previous period.

This chapter is divided into two main parts. The first part assesses the pre-accession period, when Lithuania began its preparations for EU cohesion policy. The second assesses the implementation of cohesion policy in 2004–06, the initial programming period after accession, and Lithuania's preparations for 2007–13. Finally, the main conclusions of this chapter will be presented.

It is argued in this chapter that, like other new member states, Lithuania had a problem absorbing EU funds in the initial period after accession. However, Lithuania adopted a more strategic approach towards cohesion policy for 2007–13, making it similar to some older member states. Lithuania will also be different from most new member states in another regard: it will introduce some regionalization in the implementation of cohesion policy in 2007–13, in contrast to the centralized approach of the previous period.

Preparing for EU cohesion policy in the pre-accession period

Similar to other new member states, Lithuania lacked many of the key principles and features of EU cohesion policy (e.g., programming, partnership and sound financial management) necessary for managing the structural funds. Prior to accession, the European Commission presented a set of requirements for managing EU assistance, ranging from adequate statistical data to a sufficient 'project pipeline'. Thus, it was necessary for Lithuania to adapt to the requirements of EU cohesion policy in the pre-accession period.

After the re-establishment of independence in 1991 Lithuania, along with other transitional economies, started dismantling the system of state intervention in the economy and accorded higher priority to macro-economic stability, liberalization, privatization and other important aspects of economic transition. However, to prepare for cohesion policy Lithuania needed to define new public interventions and implementation structures through which EU money could be channelled (Nakrošis, 2003a). Domestic support instruments were particularly scarce in the business sector: in 1999–01, spending available for co-financing EU assistance amounted only to 1.5 per cent of all eligible national expenditure (Brožaitis and Nakrošis, 2002).

Stages of Lithuania's preparations to implement EU cohesion policy

Lithuania's preparations to implement EU cohesion policy began at the end of 1996, when the Commission asked the Lithuanian Government to answer its questionnaire. The preparation process can be divided into three main stages: 1996–98, 1999–2000 and 2001–03 (Nakrošis, 2003b). The main responsibility for cohesion policy preparations was initially assigned to the Ministry of Public Administration Reforms and Local Authorities (MoPARLA), which was responsible for territorial-administrative matters. However, the Ministry of Finance, which is responsible for the budget and the State Investment Programme, took over the coordination role in 2001, when MoPARLA was integrated into the Ministry of the Interior.

In the first period (1996–98), preparations were of narrow scope and slow speed. The MoPARLA engaged with two main issues: classifying territorial units according to the EU's NUTS system, and drafting a guidance document for regional policy. It took about 18 months to prepare and adopt a key legal act, the Regional Policy Guidelines. The second period (1999–2000) was characterized by the medium scope and higher speed of preparations. Major issues on the governmental agenda included the definition of a legislative framework for national regional policy as well as preparations to manage EU pre-accession assistance programmes (Poland, Hungary Assistance for Economic Reconstruction [PHARE], Special Accession Programme for Agriculture and Rural Development [SAPARD] and Instrument for Structural Policies for Pre-Accession [ISPA], with annual budgets of about €14–16 million, €29 million and €50–70 million respectively).

The third period (2001–03) saw more extensive domestic change, involving both the programming of structural funds and preparations for their implementation. Domestic change also occurred more rapidly in this period, with adoption of the main legal acts necessary for completing the negotiations on chapter 21 ('Regional policy and structural measures') in accession talks between Lithuania and the EU. Moreover, as mentioned above, this period was marked by a shift in the overall responsibility for EU cohesion policy: the Ministry of Finance became responsible for EU assistance in 2001 after adoption of the National Development Plan Concept Paper. This decision also introduced a centralized approach for implementing cohesion policy in Lithuania.

The role of the European Commission

The dynamics of change during all three stages of Lithuania's preparation for cohesion policy can be explained by the dominating role of the European Commission. However, the Commission's recommendations to Lithuania lacked consistency (Nakrošis, 2003b). In the period of 1997–99, the Commission recommended the establishment of an administrative, legal and budgetary framework for national regional policy, but in 2000–02 it emphasized the creation of a centralized system for managing EU financial assistance.

Three main factors influenced the selection of a centralized model by the Commission: the limited administrative capacities of candidate countries at the subnational level; the short duration of the first programming period (2004–06); and, the strict requirements of the structural funds, in particular the new automatic de-commitment rule (Nakrošis, 2003b). Management of the structural funds is governed by EU regulations, whose transposition into national law is not necessary. However, in the period of 1997–99 the Commission recommended establishing a national legislative framework, whose provisions would comply with the Community *acquis*. Thus, in 2000 the Lithuanian parliament passed the Law on Regional Development, which set up a regionalized framework for regional policy under the authority of Regional Development Councils (RDCs) for each county (bringing together the representatives of county administrations and all local authorities). Nevertheless, after 2001 the Commission adopted a different approach, recommending the incorporation of provisions of the *acquis* into government resolutions and viewing regional development legislation as unnecessary (Nakrošis, 2003b).

During the negotiations on chapter 21, which were opened with Lithuania in March 2001 and provisionally closed in June 2002, the Commission discussed two main issues: the institutional set-up and the administrative capacities of Lithuania for managing the structural funds. More specifically, the Commission welcomed a clear distinction between national regional policy, put under the responsibility of the Ministry of Interior, and structural funds programming and preparation, put under the authority of the Ministry of Finance (Nakrošis, 2003a). Owing to rapid introduction of the centralized approach, Lithuania was among the first candidate countries to provisionally close negotiations on chapter 21.

To assist preparations for implementing cohesion policy, the EU provided both technical and financial assistance. The main source of technical assistance was the Special Preparatory Programme (SPP), funded by PHARE. The main outputs of PHARE SPP I in Lithuania included the preparation of a National Paying Agency for accreditation, the development of a training programme for the structural funds and the preparation of a National Development Plan.

It was decided to concentrate financial assistance from the PHARE Economic and Social Cohesion 2000 component in three Lithuanian 'target' regions: Klaipėda-Tauragė, Utena and Marijampolė. This decision was made after consultation with the Commission, which insisted on designating Utena county as a 'target' region. However, after the PHARE 2000 Review the Commission proposed introducing more of a sectoral approach similar to Objective 1 of the structural funds (European Commission, 2001b). Thus, financial assistance from subsequent PHARE programmes was concentrated primarily in a sectoral manner on the development of business and human resources. Because of this change, the county administrations gradually lost their administrative capacity, which had been set up for the management of PHARE 2000 assistance.

With the introduction of a centralized approach for implementing cohesion policy, national regional development policy was reorientated towards the reduction of internal regional disparities. However, this policy lacked strong political and financial support. This came only in 2006, when it was decided to link national regional development policy with the implementation of EU cohesion policy in 2007–13.

The implementation of EU cohesion policy after accession

Design and implementation of the 2004–06 programmes

In the 2004–06 programming period EU cohesion policy was implemented through one large national programme – the Single Programming Document, or SPD – and two smaller Community Initiative programmes (INTERREG and EQUAL). The 2004–06 SPD, which was adopted by the Commission in June 2004, was co-financed from all the structural funds, providing €0.895 billion of the total budget of €1.207 billion.

The SPD was prepared by the Ministry of Finance through a special SPD working group, involving the main sectoral ministries and some socioeconomic partners. The economic development strategy until 2015 and other wider national strategic documents were used as a loose strategic framework during the first programming process. However, the partnership process was characterized by some supply side problems: despite the partnership efforts of the government, the capacity of socioeconomic partners to provide input into the SPD was rather limited. Also, consultation with the main stakeholders concerned primarily the vertical priorities and measures of the SPD; there was little discussion about horizontal priorities (sustainable development, equal opportunities, information society and regional development).

As previously mentioned, Lithuania adopted a centralized system for implementing EU cohesion policy, without any delegation of power to the subnational level (the counties and local authorities). This fit well with the national investment policy, under which about 90 per cent of relevant investment expenditures was managed by sectoral ministries at the central level. A rather complex three-level administrative system was set up in Lithuania for managing the structural funds, involving one Managing Authority (MA), the Ministry of Finance, eight intermediate bodies (seven ministries and one government committee) and six implementation agencies.

Lithuania's performance in the 2004–06 programming period

In general, the functioning of the Lithuanian government is characterized by relatively good performance on the input side, but poorer performance on the outcome side, both at the EU and national level (Nakrošis, 2007). For example, although Lithuania has one of the lowest deficits in transposing EU directives among all member states, it is unlikely to meet its targets under the Lisbon Strategy at the outcome level.

The implementation of cohesion policy in Lithuania is fairly similar to the general functioning of the Lithuanian government. In 2004–06 priority was accorded to spending EU money according to all rules and procedures. This is not surprising because Lithuania (along with other new member states) had no previous experience with implementing programmes funded by the structural funds, whereas its experience with managing EU pre-accession assistance (in a regionalized framework and on the basis of PHARE rules) was not very relevant.

One can assess Lithuania's performance in implementing the 2004–06 SPD in terms of financial absorption, meeting aims and targets, main evaluation results and general public perception.

Absorption

By the end of 2006, more than 950 operations had been granted assistance from the European Regional Development Fund (ERDF) and more than 700 from the ESF. 38.6 per cent of the total ERDF allocation and 26 per cent of the European Social Fund (ESF) allocation (including advance payments) had been paid out from the Commission to Lithuania by this time (CEC, 2007c). In the middle of 2007, Lithuania's record in absorbing EU assistance was similar to the average of the ten new member states (about 45 per cent of total allocations). After taking some measures to accelerate financial absorption (changes to the programme complement, re-allocation of assistance among and within measures, some simplification of procedures and regular monitoring of financial progress), the pace of absorption increased somewhat and reached about 57 per cent towards the end of 2007.

The rather slow absorption of the structural funds became an important political issue in the Lithuanian government. The Lithuanian Commissioner Dalia Grybauskaite˙, the Commissioner responsible for financial programming and the budget, repeatedly criticized the Lithuanian government: 'I have the money, but I receive no invoices for payment' (Delfi, 2007b). Prime Minister Gediminas Kirkilas argued that the use of structural funds is not a 'socialist competition' with other countries: all that matters is to completely absorb the money by the end of 2008 (Balsas, 2008).

Administration of the ESF was particularly slow, because of many small operations and overly bureaucratic procedures. Lithuania still requires that every payment request from a project beneficiary be checked before payment from the ESF is approved. A responsible servant from one intermediate body said: 'As far as I know, no other EU country checks all 100 per cent of [ESF] expenditure. In our country finding an error of LTL 1 could cost one LTL 100' (Lietuvos rytas, 2007, p. 12).

The implementation of environmental projects financed from the Cohesion Fund also suffered from excessively long preparation periods (an average of four years from granting assistance to the start of actual physical work). Such delays were associated with many bureaucratic requirements, inadequate cooperation between the Ministry of Environment and municipalities and the shortage of qualified staff for preparing big investment projects. Because of these and other environmental problems the opposition in the Lithuanian parliament even called for the resignation of the responsible minister several times; after surviving a vote of confidence by only one vote in late 2007, he decided to resign at the beginning of 2008.

Meeting aims and targets

It is possible to assess the implementation of EU cohesion policy on the basis of the main aims and targets of the 2004–06 SPD. However, the Commission assumes that such assessment on the basis of monitoring information will not be possible until at least three years after the start of implementation. According to a 2007 Commission report: 'it is as yet difficult to assess the actual impact of the assistance and attainment of the general objectives of the programme since the programme started only in 2004' (CEC, 2007c, p. 84).

Preliminary monitoring information for 2007 shows that about 90 per cent of all beneficiaries of the 2004–06 SPD achieved their targets at the project level. At the programme level it is likely that only a few targets will not be achieved. However, it is necessary to mention a few caveats: some monitoring indicators are not 'SMART' (specific, measurable, achievable, reliable and timely) and it was possible to adjust some targets during project implementation. Therefore, any quantitative assessment of achievements is rather difficult. Nevertheless, the achievement of planned results is likely to be mixed under the measure of direct business assistance: although this measure will attract more private capital (the so-called leverage effect) than expected, the indicator of gross jobs created will probably not be reached. This monitoring evidence, combined with some evaluation findings (see below), raises doubts about the effectiveness of EU assistance to the business sector.

Evaluation results

The *ex-ante* assessment of Lithuania's 2007–13 Operational Programmes (OPs) found that EU assistance in 2004–06 contributed to economic growth and the modernization of Lithuania's economy. However, it urged that 'direct support to business enterprises be maximally reduced in order to avoid competitive distortions' (EKT, 2006, p. 56). It was argued that the allocation of more assistance for human resource development and R&D would increase the impact of the structural funds on economic growth, depending on their efficient use.

The assessment of horizontal priorities during implementation of the 2004–06 SPD also showed mixed results. Although the ESF-financed priorities contributed primarily to the creation of equal opportunities (achieving a rating of 90 out of a possible 100 on a specially created effectiveness index), the ERDF-financed priorities contributed more to the implementation of sustainable development (a rating of 85) and regional development (67.5). The horizontal priority of equal opportunities was the least mainstreamed outside of ESF assistance during implementation of the SPD. Lithuania applied a rather compliance-based approach in 2004–06, with limited mainstreaming of horizontal priorities in various SPD measures and projects (Public Policy and Management Institute, 2008).

The territorial effect of the 2004–06 SPD on Lithuanian counties and local authorities was uneven. The region of the Ignalina nuclear power plant, the single Lithuanian region selected for special assistance under the 2004–06 SPD, attracted 162 per cent of the total project value per inhabitant (see Table 11.1). However, some poorer regions, which were named as main regional development centres in the 2005 regional development strategy, received less than 100 per cent (e.g., the counties of Tauragė and Telšiai received only 88 and 72 per cent respectively).

The fact that some regional projects (e.g., energy-efficiency operations in the public sector such as the renovation of public schools and hospitals) were selected by central authorities in the capital city of Vilnius without consulting subnational authorities created tensions between the national and subnational levels. Thus, after some discussion it was decided to introduce a more regionalized approach to managing EU cohesion policy in 2007–13.

Table 11.1 Structural funds allocations according to territorial units in 2004–06

Territorial unit of Lithuanian regional policy	Total project value, %	Total project value per inhabitant in LTL (% of national average)
Alytus county	7	1,783 (133)
Kaunas country	16	1,072 (80)
Klaipėda county	12	1,440 (108)
Marijampolė county	6	1,603 (120)
Panevėžys county	10	1,589 (119)
Šiauliai county	11	1,382 (103)
Tauragė county	3	1,177 (88)
Telšiai county	4	970 (72)
Utena county	7	1,766 (132)
Vilnius county	24	1,264 (90)
Main regional development centres (five municipalities)	7	1,128 (84)
Ignalina nuclear plant region (three municipalities)	3	2,166 (162)
Problem territories of social development (14 municipalities)	16	1,659 (124)
Total	100	1,339 (100)

Source: Public Policy and Management Institute (2008).

Public perception

According to surveys, about 40 per cent of the Lithuanian population (age 18 and above) saw the SPD logo and 12 per cent know of the SPD as a programme (Europos socialiniai, 2007, p. 8). Despite rather good and increasing visibility, other surveys show that management of the structural funds in Lithuania is not transparent enough. For instance, about one-third of all respondents agreed that Lithuanian companies, institutions and persons which received EU structural assistance make unofficial pay-backs to civil servants and politicians. The procedures of project assessment, selection and grant award were found to be the most corrupt in implementing the 2004–06 SPD (Transparency International, 2006).

There have been some legal disputes and resignations linked to the lack of openness in the management of EU assistance in Lithuania (in particular in the business support sector). The Vilnius city court banned a former deputy director of the Lithuanian Business Support Agency – one of Lithuania's implementing agencies – from being employed in the civil service for two years because of his misconduct in office. He was found to be involved in increasing the score from 62 to 65 in one project assessment on behalf of a project applicant seeking a grant award (Delfi, 2007a).

Also, a former Economics Minister from the populist Labour Party, Viktor Uspaskich, was blamed for the corrupt management of EU money. He was forced to resign from the cabinet in 2005, when the Lithuanian Higher Service Ethics Commission decided that he breached conflict-of-interest rules by initiating the establishment of a joint company in Russia (Delfi, 2005b).

Administrative and institutional capacity

The nature of Lithuanian administration can largely explain its performance in implementing EU cohesion policy. Lithuania has a rather small civil service, employing about 25,000 civil servants at the end of 2006. However, its size has been increasing since 2004, due largely to the growing demands of managing EU assistance. Previously, there was a shortage of staff to implement cohesion policy and existing staff were overloaded with many administrative tasks. However, new units have been set up to manage EU assistance and additional staff has been recruited for various institutions. Additional staff was being recruited in 2007–08 for implementation of the 2007–13 OPs.

More stability has been achieved in the administrative system after Lithuania's accession to the EU. In general, politicization of the civil service has been decreasing in recent years (turnover was estimated to be about 30 per cent after the 1996 general elections). Previously, there was a large turnover of staff responsible for the structural funds; for example, following MoPARLA's integration into the Ministry of Interior only one civil servant from its Regional Development Department was retained (Nacionalinė regionų plėtros agentūra, 2002, p. 62). However, in recent years employment in the civil service has become less attractive and the morale of civil servants is decreasing because of internal factors, including problems of leadership and remuneration, and opportunities in an expanding private sector.

Moreover, the capacity of Lithuanian institutions that are responsible for cohesion policy implementation remains uneven. A regionalized selection of EU-financed projects in 2007–13 (especially under one priority of the Cohesion Promotion OP) poses a risk because neither the Ministry of Interior (as a new intermediate body) nor the county administrations have previous administration experience. Unlike most new member states, Lithuania needs to design new mechanisms for regional project selection for the 2007–13 OPs.

Inter-institutional coordination and partnership

The relationship between responsible institutions became more stable after some tensions in the administrative system while implementing the 2004–06 SPD. In 2005 the Economics Ministry (the intermediate body) decided to stop taking applications for three categories of operations without consulting the Ministry of Finance (the MA). This decision was justified in terms of a widening gap between the volumes of requested and available assistance in the area of business support. The Economics Minister from the Labour Party argued, 'I have the right to stop [taking the applications], and no one can prove that I do not.... Let them [the Ministry of Finance] monitor. Yet leave business-making to those, who understand it' (Verslo žinios, 2005).

Later the Ministry of Finance, which was headed by a minister from the Social Democratic Party, changed the administrative procedures, eliminating the procedure of continuous project selection.

There have also been tensions over the role of different ministries in the new implementation system for 2007–13. The Labour Party wanted three ministries to be Managing Authorities (one for each OP), but the Social Democratic Party insisted on continuing with one MA, the Ministry of Finance (Delfi, 2006). After some discussion the Ministry of Finance was at last appointed by the Lithuanian government to be the single MA for all 2007–13 OPs.

The 2004–06 SPD made some contribution to partnership in Lithuania. According to monitoring data, about only 12.3 per cent of all SPD projects were jointly implemented by the partners. Such partnership projects were mostly designed for seeking better quality of operations, but some respondents understood partnership in more formal terms, for meeting the requirements of various documents or for receiving EU assistance (Public Policy and Management Institute, 2008, p. 52–3).

Remaining problems in implementing
EU cohesion policy

One of the main problems in implementing EU cohesion policy in Lithuania is its overly bureaucratic procedures. According to one survey, the main obstacle in Lithuania is the 'large workload of administration' (47.1 per cent of all respondents agree) (Public Policy and Management Institute, 2008, p. 36). There were a few simplifications during implementation of the 2004–06 SPD and further simplifications were planned for the 2007–13 OPs. Although some simplifications originated at the EU-level (e.g., the eligibility rules), most are of a domestic nature, including the electronic application process.

Another problem is associated with national processes of planning and public procurement. Sometimes it is difficult to obtain construction permits owing to the complex requirements of land use, planning and design. There have also been many complaints during the tendering process with litigation in the courts. This has delayed the implementation of EU-financed projects, often forcing Lithuanian courts to make quick decisions.

Moreover, rising inflation and market prices frequently disrupt project implementation (especially the work on projects financed from the ERDF). To solve this unanticipated obstacle, it became necessary for the Lithuanian government to allocate an additional €23 million for ongoing projects in 2007. In addition, to meet new financial constraints, the scope of work will be reduced for several ongoing projects. Seven projects have been cancelled because of insufficient funds, including a €4 million project, the Northtown Technology Park in Vilnius. According to its director, 'the project promoters overestimated their ability to implement the project' owing to increasing prices (Veidas, 2008, p. 21).

Preparations for the 2007–13 programming period

Cohesion policy reform and its implications for Lithuania

The 2006 reform of EU cohesion policy aimed at increased simplification, decentralization and effectiveness of the structural funds, similar to the aims of previous reforms. A new reform aim was the strategic orientation of cohesion policy, linking the structural funds to the Lisbon Agenda and other EU strategies.

As a new member state, Lithuania agreed to most of the Commission's proposals and those of the EU presidency concerning the new regulations for cohesion policy in 2007–13 and the Community Strategic Guidelines (CSG). However, a major Lithuanian interest was the eligibility of private housing projects for EU funding. Because of the large number of energy-inefficient apartment blocks in Lithuania, the Lithuanian government, together with other new member states, successfully argued that their renovation should be eligible for funding from the ERDF.

The new member states will have more favourable conditions for absorbing EU assistance in 2007–13, thanks to lower rates of co-financing

(85 per cent for new member states) and application of the 'n+3' rule until 2010. The Lithuanian government welcomed these proposals made by the British EU Presidency in the debate over the 2007–13 financial perspective. They will reduce the volume of necessary national co-financing and mitigate the risk of a de-commitment of funds during the implementation process.

In general, the Lithuanian government was rather satisfied with the main outcomes of the negotiations on the 2007–13 financial perspective. However, former Lithuanian Prime Minister, Algirdas Brazauskas, admitted that Lithuania, unlike other Baltic states, failed to receive additional side-payments for its Convergence regions (despite two Lithuanian vetoes during the negotiations). Although Lithuania clearly preferred such side-payments under EU cohesion policy, it received additional assistance for decommissioning the Ignalina nuclear power plant instead. The Prime Minister claimed that 'the nuclear power plant is not a Lithuanian problem, but an EU commitment' (Delfi, 2005a). However, there was an informal agreement at the European Council to allocate an additional €120 million for Lithuania from the EU budget.

The design of the NSRF and OPs and their adoption

To implement cohesion policy in 2007–13, the Lithuanian authorities prepared the National Strategic Reference Framework (NSRF) and four OPs (two ESF-financed and two ERDF-financed, see Table 11.2). There was an initial proposal to prepare up to five OPs, but their number was later reduced to three; however, a fourth OP, Technical Assistance, was

Table 11.2 Cohesion policy allocations for Lithuania by OP, 2007–13

Operational Programme	% of the total assistance	Source of assistance
Human Resource Development	13.80	European Social Fund
Economic Growth	45.72	European Regional Development Fund, Cohesion Fund
Cohesion Promotion	39.08	European Regional Development Fund, Cohesion Fund
Technical Assistance	1.40	European Social Fund
Total	100.00	

Source: Ministry of Finance, 2007, <http://www.esparama.lt/lt/pasirengimas/>.

added towards the end of the programming process. This is a rather small number compared with other new member states (Poland – 21, the Czech Republic – 17, Hungary – 15). Nevertheless, some Objective 1 member states managed to prepare even fewer (Cyprus – two, Estonia – three, Latvia – three, Malta – two, Slovenia – three). Lithuania did not use the option of programming a national performance reserve (consisting of 3 per cent of its total allocation under the Convergence objective) whose amount would have been decided by the Commission on the basis of its mid-term assessment in 2011.

The 2007–13 NSRF and OPs were discussed and negotiated with the Commission. As with other new member states one of the most important issues during the negotiation process was the selection of indicators for monitoring the physical outputs and outcomes of EU assistance. This shows increased emphasis on the effectiveness of this assistance, which can be measured on the basis of such indicators. Also, the Commission suggested that Lithuania should divide its broad priority of quality employment and social inclusion within the ESF-financed OP into three separate priorities (including a separate social inclusion priority). However, the Lithuanian authorities, who sought greater flexibility in the implementation process, refused to change the overall structure of its strategy in this OP. The Commission approved Lithuania's three OPs in August–September 2007.

In Lithuania, the NSRF was regarded as a new strategic document, necessary only for the purposes of implementing EU cohesion policy. The NSRF was prepared on the basis of existing national strategic documents: in particular the State Long-Term Development Strategy and its first two priorities of knowledge society and competitive economy. However, Lithuania still has no integrated approach to investment management: the NSRF co-exists with several national strategies, and the new OPs with the State Investment Programme and the budget programmes.

In 2006 the Ministry of Interior proposed designing an Integrated Regional Operational Programme (IROP) for 2007–13. However, an agreement was made in the Lithuanian government to partially regionalize management of the 2007–13 OPs through one sub-priority for urban development in the Cohesion Promotion OP (amounting to about 5 per cent of Lithuania's total allocation) and a special 'regional dimension' under some other priorities (amounting to about 7 per cent of the total allocation). Thus, the volume of financial assistance to be channelled through regional structures and mechanisms constitutes about 12 per cent of total EU assistance to Lithuania in 2007–13. This

regionalized assistance will be concentrated in 5–7 regional development centres and about 14 problem territories according to the national
regional development strategy (see Map 11.1).

The distribution of financial assistance among the ministries and
certain sectors of the economy was an important issue during preparation of the OPs. One of the main changes compared with the previous
programming period was the government's decision to allocate 10 per
cent of the total ERDF allocation to R&D. Prime Minister Kirkilas, who
brokered the deal in the cabinet, announced, 'I am sure that we should
increase these [R& D] resources' (Alfa.lt, 2006).

However, the health sector, which is publicly perceived as being the
main target of the structural funds in Lithuania (Veidas, 2008), will

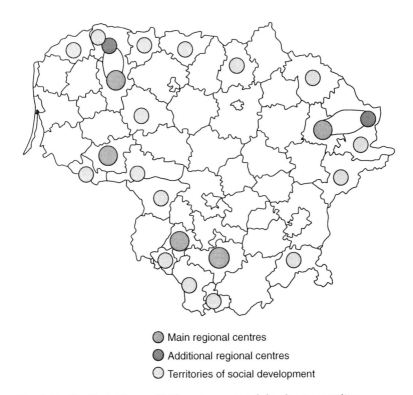

⬤ Main regional centres
⬤ Additional regional centres
◯ Territories of social development

Map 11.1   Territorial focus of Lithuanian regional development policy
Source: Lithuanian Ministry of the Interior, 2006.
<http://www.esparama.lt/ES_Parama/strukturines_paramos_2007_1013m._medis/
titulinis/files/VRM_Grumadas.ppt>.

receive much lower financing from the ERDF. Also, the OPs feature a few new priorities: a new ESF-financed priority of administrative capacity and public administration efficiency (ineligible in 2004–06) and a sub-priority of urban regeneration at the regional level (not financed in the 2004–06 SPD).

The 2007–13 programming process was marked by a more differentiated approach towards the partnership principle. Unlike preparation of the 2004–06 SPD, there were no partners represented on the inter-institutional commission responsible for the structural funds for 2007–13. Socioeconomic partners were involved in preparing the 2007–13 OPs through lower-level working groups and broad partnership forums. However, the Lithuanian parliament was consulted in preparing both the NSRF and the 2007–13 OPs to a much greater extent than in 2004–06. This was due to the increased importance of EU cohesion policy in the legislature as well as the introduction of a more strategic approach for 2007–13 (see below).

Links between cohesion policy and the Lisbon agenda

There are mixed links between EU cohesion policy and the Lisbon Strategy in Lithuania. At the level of broad aims there is a good deal of consistency. The priorities of the Lithuanian NSRF (human resources for knowledge society, competitive economy and the quality of life and cohesion) are well aligned with the Lisbon Strategy. Also, Lithuania earmarked about 55 per cent of its 2007–13 allocation for Lisbon-oriented activities. Although this falls below the mandatory target of 60 per cent for Convergence regions in the old member states, the share of assistance for R&D as well as transport is particularly high: about 16 and 17 per cent respectively (see Table 11.3). In its 2007 assessment the Commission acknowledged 'substantial support earmarked for R&D, innovation and information society as well as for the improvement of transport networks' (CEC, 2007b).

As mentioned above, allocating 10 per cent of total ERDF assistance for R&D implies that the Lisbon Strategy has had a considerable impact on national spending priorities. This assistance will certainly contribute to Lithuania's ambitious target of 2 per cent of GDP for R&D by 2010, thus partly implementing the Commission's recommendation that Lithuania 'strengthen [its] science and technology base' (CEC, 2006c, p. 6). However, there are serious problems for its effective utilization. Lithuania has a rather fragmented system of R&D institutions (14 universities, 17 independent institutes and 19 other institutes), whose performance results are rather poor if compared with the EU average on the basis of such indicators as

Table 11.3 Share of EU funding earmarked for Lisbon-oriented activities in Lithuania, 2007

Priority theme	% of the EU assistance
Transport	17.20
Research and development, innovation and entrepreneurship	16.21
Improving human capital	5.50
Information society	3.54
Energy	5.41
Increasing the adaptability of workers and firms, enterprises and entrepreneurs	3.17
Improving access to employment and sustainability	2.05
Improving the social inclusion of less-favoured persons	0.88
Environmental protection and risk prevention	0.60
Total share of EU assistance earmarked for Lisbon-related activities	54.60

Source: Government of Lithuania (2007, p. 61).

international scientific publications or patents. Despite these shortcomings, the reform of Lithuanian higher education has been delayed several times in recent years. Also, Lithuania still has no research council which would be ready to grant assistance to research projects or researchers.

However, there is less coherence between EU cohesion policy and the Lisbon Strategy in Lithuania at the level of measures. This is associated with the nature of the Lisbon process at the domestic level. The Lithuanian National Reform Programme (NRP) resembles more a framework programme – bringing together objectives and measures from other strategic documents within the areas of the Lisbon Strategy – rather than a new reform programme, which would enjoy a strong political priority and higher status in the hierarchy of strategic documents (IIRPS, 2006). The NRP is coordinated by the Economics Ministry, while the SPD and the OPs are coordinated by the Ministry of Finance with rather limited involvement of the Government Office in both processes.

Implementation of the Lisbon Strategy in Lithuania is also very process-orientated. Its main results have occurred in the administrative set-up (e.g., new units, commissions and working groups). More ambitious measures of microeconomic policy (particularly in the area of R&D) remain unimplemented compared with some ongoing measures of macroeconomic and employment policy which are less ambitious (IIRPS, 2006). Thus, any contribution of the structural funds to these reform measures would not have been effective in Lithuania.

Preparations for implementation

Management experience accumulated by Lithuania in 2004–06 has been utilized for the programming and implementation of EU assistance in 2007–13. A new MA was set up in the Ministry of Finance, separate from an existing department in charge of coordinating EU cohesion policy. The 2007–13 administrative system will remain rather centralized. However, as previously mentioned, Lithuania plans to use existing regional development structures (10 RDCs involving the county administrations and all local authorities at the county level) for managing some regionalized assistance; but new mechanisms for regional project selection will be created.

There have also been changes in the role of intermediate bodies: in the new programming period their role is enhanced in the area of planning EU assistance for certain projects, but they are less involved in its administration. In 2007–13 about 75 per cent of all EU assistance for Lithuania will be used for state and regional projects planned in certain strategic documents. This is in sharp contrast to the previous programming period, when almost all assistance was considered 'opportunity financing' available to many types of applicants through open calls-for-proposals. Most ministries are trying to align EU-financed measures with national measures through the preparation of specific planning documents (e.g., national programmes and action plans).

Moreover, it is likely that the Lithuanian parliament will more closely scrutinize the implementation of 2007–13 OPs than it did the 2004–06 SPD. In the middle of 2007, the parliament approved a list of nine economic projects important for the state in the area of knowledge and innovation infrastructure. Despite their 'project' title, they represent the broad directions of EU assistance: upgrading and developing R&D infrastructure, preparing and implementing a lifelong-learning programme, setting up a network of science, studies and business, setting up a risk capital fund, preparing and implementing a 'brain-drain' programme, preparing and implementing an investment promotion programme (including the development of industrial parks and free economic zones), the implementation of R&D programmes, the development of a broadband network in Lithuanian rural areas and the reform of higher education.

Although the programme complement is not mandatory in the new programming period, Lithuania (together with many other new member states) decided to prepare a national programming document similar to that for 2004–06. This was approved by the Lithuanian government at the end of 2007. Also, in early 2007 the Lithuanian government had already approved the implementation of some public projects whose expenditures will be reimbursed from the structural funds. 65 such projects are being implemented, and two projects (development of the Vilnius and Palanga airports) were already completed (Veidas, 2008). This shows the willingness of the Lithuanian government to begin using new EU assistance as soon as possible.

Increasing co-financed expenditure in the context of increasing fiscal constraints

The lack of integration of EU co-financed and non-co-financed expenditure is becoming increasingly problematic in Lithuania. The volume of government expenditure has increased particularly in EU co-financed sectors (e.g., transportation and other economic affairs, by 75 and 93 per cent respectively in the 2008 draft budget compared with 2007) because there has been no corresponding reduction in the volume of non-co-financed expenditure. Until 2008 EU assistance was budgeted separately in so-called special budget programmes. However, this dual approach was found to be inefficient, and it was decided to eliminate the special programmes by integrating all EU-financed measures into other budget programmes from 2008.

A rapid increase in government expenditure is becoming a fiscal problem. It is difficult for the Lithuanian government to reduce the fiscal deficit (seeking a balanced budget by 2009) while financing other important needs (especially the salaries of teachers, doctors, police officers and other public-sector employees). The Lithuanian Free Market Institute called for zero-based budgeting and reducing government expenditure in some sectors of the economy (Lietuvos laisvosios rinkos institutas, 2007). However, a more efficient use of the structural funds (producing more or better goods and services with less money) could also contribute to the objective of a balanced budget in Lithuania.

Conclusion

The decision of the Lithuanian government to use a centralized system for implementing cohesion policy proved successful in terms of the fast completion of negotiations with the Commission in the pre-accession period. However, it did not guarantee a rapid absorption of EU funds in the post-accession period. Nevertheless, a decentralized system would probably have been even worse.

Although implementation of the PHARE programme in the pre-accession period was regarded largely as a technical issue, the implementation of cohesion policy in the post-accession period became a partisan political issue in Lithuania. Because of the large amount of EU assistance and implementation difficulties, the Lithuanian government was subjected to criticism from both the Commission and the opposition. The participation of the populist Labour Party in the government in 2004–06 also led to internal tensions over the use of EU money. The next general elections in 2008 pose another political challenge for the implementation of cohesion policy in Lithuania. The election of certain populist parties and the appointment of their representatives to the government could bring corruption and inefficiency to management of the structural funds.

It is interesting that the main obstacles to implementing cohesion policy in Lithuania are of a domestic or even global nature. They are not transferred from Brussels, which is often blamed for a great deal of red-tape in Lithuania. The large volume of EU assistance basically aggravated many existing problems at the domestic level. The small Lithuanian administration and some weaker project beneficiaries were not capable of dealing with the rather bureaucratic requirements of EU assistance. Also, increasing prices in Lithuania are linked to inflationary trends in global markets for commodities and services. This increasingly highlights the need for domestic reforms such as deregulation, the simplification of public administration, reforming the civil service and better programme and project management inside the public sector. This would improve not only the implementation of cohesion policy, but also the global competitiveness of Lithuania's economy.

The new member states face similar obstacles in implementing EU cohesion policy. Almost all of these countries undertook certain measures to accelerate the absorption of EU assistance. Absorption capacity will remain a challenge for Lithuania, in particular at the subnational level after some regionalization of cohesion policy implementation in 2007–13. Despite these absorption difficulties, maintaining the volume of EU assistance remains the top priority of the Lithuanian government's EU policy. Lithuania, along with other new member states, sought additional assistance during negotiations on the 2007–13 financial perspective. It is likely that these countries will stress the importance of the structural funds for Convergence regions during the upcoming mid-term review of the EU budget.

The implementation of EU cohesion policy has helped improve the quality of governance in Lithuania. This is especially evident in the area of programme and project management in the public sector. In 2000 the Commission argued that the capacity to prepare projects for the structural funds in Lithuania was insufficient and the culture of project management in its infancy (CEC, 2000). Nevertheless, Lithuania managed to develop enough projects to absorb all EU assistance in the first programming period after accession (about 3,000 projects under the 2004–06 SPD). However, the application of new interventions in the business sector produced some corruption and competitive distortions in the market.

In 2007–13 a large share of EU assistance will be used strategically for certain state and regional projects. This shift from 'opportunity financing' to strategic delivery entails the risk of politicization at the ministerial level and requires strong delivery bodies in the public sector. Moreover, such strategic use of EU assistance in Lithuania lacks clear domestic reform and policy commitments, in particular in the areas of education and health care. It also remains necessary to better integrate implementation of the Lisbon Strategy with the 2007–13 structural funds at the operational level. Thus, it is uncertain if a more strategic implementation of EU cohesion policy in Lithuania will produce better societal effects in the new programming period.

Another challenge for Lithuania is more efficient management of the structural funds and domestic expenditure in an environment of slower economic growth and increased fiscal constraints. There was some alignment of the 2007–13 OPs with domestic public policies at the central level. However, calls for greater efficiency are likely to become even stronger in the future. Interestingly, this is a similar challenge for some old member states, who are increasingly concerned with the integration of EU and national expenditures and their cost-effectiveness.

Another favourable trend in Lithuania is growing attention to the effectiveness of EU assistance through such evidence-based methods as monitoring and evaluation. Although Lithuania already generates a lot of monitoring and evaluation information, there is a need to improve its quality and use in decisionmaking. Improved methods of monitoring and evaluation have the potential for contributing to both the strategic use and increased efficiency of the structural funds in Lithuania.

12
Romania
Jozsef Benedek and Réka Horváth

Introduction

With 22 million inhabitants, Romania is the seventh-largest EU member state, and the second-largest in the eastern part of the EU. Although the country has experienced strong economic growth in recent years (6.4 per cent annually from 2003 to 2006), it remains among the poorest member states, with GDP per capita reaching only about 35 per cent of the EU average in 2005. Romania has a particular situation among the Central and Eastern European Country (CEECs) because it was not part of the first wave of Eastern enlargement in May 2004. Romania formally applied to join the EU in June 1995, and began accession negotiations in February 2000; however, accession was delayed – as also for Bulgaria – until January 2007, a situation that impacted the country's level of preparedness for implementing EU cohesion policy. This chapter emphasizes these preparations. It also examines various factors that have influenced or played a role in Romanian regional policy: regional disparities; regional policies during the pre-accession period; basic national planning documents; EU pre-accession funds; the implementation of regional policy after accession; and finally, the question of political parties and regionalism.

Creating the institutional basis for EU cohesion policy

Adoption of the Nomenclature of Statistical Territorial Units (NUTS) system – a basic requirement of EU cohesion policy – was based on the existing territorial-administrative structure of Romania, consisting of two levels: communes (groups of villages) and towns in the lower level, and counties in the upper. Law no. 215/2001 regulates local autonomy, as well as the organization and functioning of local public administration. The basic principles of the latter are: decentralization, local autonomy and the decentralization of public services. However, the law also specifies that these principles cannot 'offend the national, unitary and indivisible character of the state of Romania' (Article 2/2). Local autonomy is understood as 'the right and effective capacity of the local public administration authorities to solve and manage public duties, on behalf of and in the best interest of the communities they represent' (Article 3/1). This right is exerted by the local councils, mayors and county councils. The law defines local administrative and financial autonomy as well, which 'concerns the organization, functioning, competencies and prerogatives, as well as the management of resources which, by law, belong to the commune, town, city or county' (Article 4/2). Both local and county councils have competencies related to social and economic development. For example, the local council approves strategies for the economic, social and environmental development of the administrative unit, and the county council adopts strategies, prognoses and county economic, social and environmental development programmes.

EU accession was an important factor affecting the creation of regional policy in Romania. During the accession process, the European Commission drew up reports on the progress made by Romania in preparing for accession. The first progress report in 1998 explicitly mentions the impact of accession preparations on the legislative basis for regional policy in Romania, declaring that 'a Law on Regional Development, drafted with EU assistance and approved in July 1998, has created a framework for the development and implementation of regional policies' (CEC, 1998, p. 38). Romania also had to comply with other aspects of the EU *acquis* in the area of cohesion policy; for instance, it was expected that candidate states create an economic development system based on the regional principle.

Negotiations with the EU on the cohesion policy chapter were opened in June 2002, and as a result, a new Law on Regional Development (Law no. 315/2004) was adopted. This establishes the objectives, institutions, competencies and instruments of regional policy in Romania. According to the law, the main objectives of regional policy are: the reduction of regional disparities; the preparation of an institutional framework for regional policy in accordance with EU criteria and those of the structural funds; the correlation of government sectoral policies on the regional level; and support for domestic, international, interregional and cross-border cooperation, in order to promote the economic and institutional development of the regions.

Territorially, a new regional level was created – without juridical personality, meaning the regions are not administrative-territorial units – by grouping the 41 counties, according to several criteria, into eight development regions, equivalent to the EU's NUTS 2 level (Map 12.1). The regions have a framework function for the establishment, implementation and evaluation of regional development policies, as well as a technical function as basic territorial units for the collection of statistical data according to EU Statistics Office (EUROSTAT) regulations. The boundaries of the new regions follow the boundaries of the counties and the City of Bucharest.

A new institutional network for administering the NUTS 2 regions was created, consisting of: the National Council for Regional Development (NCRD), eight Regional Development Councils (RDCs) and Regional Development Agencies (RDAs).

The NCRD is a partnership-based institution for drawing up and implementing the objectives of regional policy. The state has a strong position in this institution because its chair is the Ministry for Development,

1. North-East, 2. South-East, 3. South-Muntenia 4. South-West Oltenia,
5. West, 6. North-West, 7. Center, 8. Bucharest-Ilfov

Map 12.1   Development (NUTS 2) regions and counties (NUTS 3 regions) in Romania

Source: Benedek (2004); adapted by author.

Public Works and Housing (MDPH), the Secretariat is held by the same ministry, and government representatives are members of the NCRD in equal number with representatives (the presidents and vice-presidents) of the eight RDCs. The NCRD is designed to: approve the national strategy for regional development and the National Development Plan (NDP); approve the criteria and priorities for using the national Regional Development Fund (RDF); and approve projects proposed by the RDAs. Before accession, it was also tasked with proposing the use of EU pre-accession funds allocated to Romania for the purposes of regional development.

The eight RDCs are territorial structures for regional development. They are deliberative bodies at the level of every NUTS 2 region, without juridical personality. They are responsible for analyzing and deciding on regional development strategy and programmes; approving regional development projects; and approving the criteria, priorities, allocation and destination of resources from the RDF.

The RDAs are territorial structures for regional development established within each NUTS 2 region. They are nongovernmental, nonprofit public institutions, with juridical personality. RDAs are assigned the following main tasks: formulate and propose regional development strategies, programmes and plans, and funds management plans, to the RDC for approval; implement regional development and funds management plans; and manage the RDF.

We would like to stress two problems related to Romanian regionalization. First, the criteria underlying regionalization are heavily disputed and not thoroughly applied. The four main criteria are: population, surface space, culture and economic interrelations. But the created regions are too large in population and size (above the EU average for NUTS 2 regions); one region is culturally heterogeneous;[1] and in many cases county representatives want another classification because of stronger economic links to other regions.

There was little effort by the state to create new territorial symbols or use already existing ones. For example, the names given to the NUTS 2 regions mainly reflect their geographical position (North-East, South-East, West, North-West, and Center); only three names also reflect historical-cultural backgrounds: South-West Oltenia, South-Muntenia and Bucharest-Ilfov.

A second problem is that the regions have very limited powers of decisionmaking and they are financially weak. They have no executive or legislative powers and they are subordinated to the central government, which distributes financial resources to them. Regionalization in Romania was done in a top-down fashion, and only a very limited number of actors were consulted.

Regional disparities in Romania

Regional disparities in Romania, as in other countries, constitute a fundamental feature of society, with changes conditioned by such factors as the size of inter-regional disparities, development trajectories, and the social and economic positions of specific regions. The differences in development between cultural and historical regions, reproduced at the level of NUTS 2 regions, have their roots in the different historical and economic evolutions of these regions (Benedek and Jordan, 2007). Thus, during the modern age, the regions of Central and Western Romania (Transylvania, Bucovina, Maramureş, Crişana and Banat) experienced early industrialization (eighteenth century) and the formation of proto-industrial regions based on mining and metallurgy, the textile industry and a relatively diverse urban economy. In the Southern and Eastern parts of Romania, however, the first proto-industrial regions only developed in the nineteenth century. Following the Union of Principalities in 1859, the capital city of Bucharest experienced a period of uninterrupted cumulative development. The Prahova oil region and several ports (Galaţi, Brăila, and later Constanţa) also began their development. The trajectory of convergent development for these territorial units began after the First World War, a moment when regional differences in development were considerable (Popescu, 2000).

The development policy of the communist period (1945–89) recomposed to a certain extent the previous regional hierarchy; it promoted the equalization of development (Iara, 2005), but did not produce any spectacular changes in the hierarchy of regions.

The Romanian regions reacted differently to the new political and economic framework after 1989, in accordance with their economic capabilities, competitiveness and institutional networks. The transition 'winners' were the urban agglomerations with a developed service sector, the coastal region, and the border regions of western Romania, while the big losers were the remote mountain regions, rural regions and industrial districts (Ianoş, 2006).

Cultural background remains an important factor influencing regional development in Romania. The 'pole of underdevelopment' is still Moldova (NUTS 2 region North-East); Dobrogea, Muntenia and Oltenia (NUTS 2 regions South-East, South and South-West) are situated on an intermediate level; while Transylvania, Banat and Crişana (NUTS

2 regions Center, West and North-West) together with Bucharest constitute the 'pole of development' (Sandu, 1999; Benedek, 2004).

The Green Chart of Regional Development (Government of Romania and European Commission, 1997) offers a global index of development, calculated by aggregating 17 indicators, grouped into four categories (economy, infrastructure, demography and standard of family life). According to the resulting values, the counties of Botoşani and Vaslui (both with general poverty and few material resources), and Ialomiţa, Călăraşi, Giurgiu and Teleorman (all with cultural poverty – that is, a low level of education – infant mortality and weak sanitary conditions) have the lowest level of development. In 2005, the disparity index between the region with the highest GDP per capita – the West Region (excluding Bucharest, which has a much higher level than other regions) – and the region with the lowest (North-East) was 1.671. At the NUTS 3 level, the disparities are growing but still not dramatic: the top five counties have average values which are 2.4 times higher than the bottom five.

Regional policy in the pre-accession period

In Romania, the delimitation of territorial spaces with specific problems, having a particular juridical status and a functioning regime, took place with the designation of 'disadvantaged areas' in 1998. These are geographical regions defined on the basis of local administrative units (towns and communes) corresponding to one of the following conditions: a rate of unemployment at least three times higher than the national rate (calculated for the latest three months before drawing up the documentation for granting disadvantaged area status); inadequate means of communication; and poor infrastructure. 38 disadvantaged have been delimited (Map 12.2), together having about 1.5 million inhabitants.

The status of 'disadvantaged area' may be held for 3–10 years, with the possibility of extension. The functioning regime for these areas has a fiscal character, with facilities for companies that are majority privately owned, and for Romanian corporate bodies which are headquartered and pursue activities in disadvantaged regions.

The purpose of designating disadvantaged areas is to increase the attractiveness of these regions for capital investments which generate jobs, horizontal linkages in the local economy, and economic growth. Target areas for investment are established for each area (e.g., agriculture, production, service provision, commerce, environmental protection, environmental

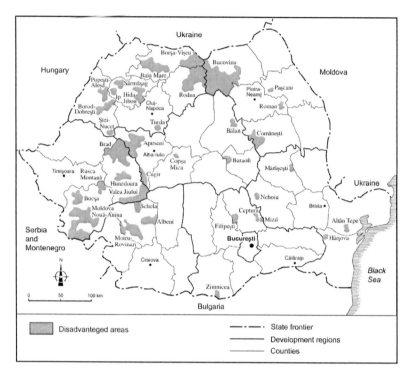

Map 12.2   Disadvantaged areas of Romania in 2002
Source: Benedek (2004); adapted by author.

restoration) depending on the regional economic profile and territorial and sectoral disadvantages. A number of factors have been identified as reasons for reduced levels of investment in disadvantaged areas. First, underdeveloped transport and public utilities infrastructure has hindered the mobility of production factors and the integration of these areas into larger production chains. Second, the lack of entrepreneurial knowledge in the population has led to a low level of local firm creation. And third, the lack of a skilled labour force, as well as a skeptical attitude towards training, has inhibited the adaptation of regional labour markets to new economic conditions (Government of Romania, 2001).

The fiscal facilities for disadvantaged areas disappeared in 2002 with the approval of new tax legislation, but there is already an alternative concept of 'assisted areas'. There will be no fiscal facilities for investors in these areas, but irredeemable financing programmes for development projects on a short-to-medium term (6–10 years), drawn up by local public authorities (local and county councils).

An adaptation of the concept of old industrial areas and relevant regional policies to existing conditions in Romania took place by defining and delimiting 'areas of industrial restructuring' with a potential for economic growth. These areas are defined as geographical concentrations of settlements with a high level of unemployment, environmental pollution problems and a potential for economic growth. Altogether 11 such areas have been delimited (Map 12.3), incorporating 25.7 per cent of the Romanian population.

Public and private sector investment projects in the 11 industrial restructuring areas were selected according to Poland, Hungary Assistance for Economic Reconstruction (PHARE) procedures, in accordance with the development priorities of the NDP (see below),

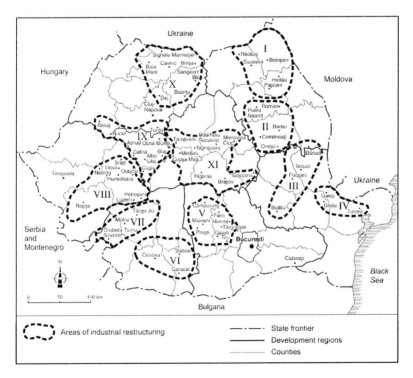

Map 12.3 Areas of industrial restructuring in Romania
Source: Benedek (2004); adapted by author.

and approved by the European Commission for financing through the 2001 PHARE programme. The industrial restructuring areas have been included in various other financing programmes, and seem to have become one of the basic pillars of regional policy in Romania.

The national development plan

There were three NDPs for Romania before it joined the EU. The first was for the 2000–02 period; it was drafted at the request of the Commission as part of Romania's preparations for EU accession.

The second NDP, for 2002–05, included the regional and sectoral development strategies of various government ministries. It specifies that the NDP is the basis for Romania's requests for EU funding to support development programmes. Although this aspect of the NDP is stressed, the document also mentioned that the NDP comprises the government's general development strategy (Government of Romania, 2001).

The third NDP, for 2004–06, states that 'it is the first document that performs a multiannual planning and programming of public investments' (Government of Romania, 2003). A gradual increase in the complexity of national development plans and methodology is observable.

The 2000–02 NDP declares that 'the development priorities identified within the framework of the NDP are in compliance with the tasks and necessities determined by the [Accession Partnership] and by the Romanian National EU Integration Program' (National Agency for Regional Development, 1999). The total NDP budget amounted to €4.8 billion, 86 per cent of which consisted of EU funds. It is interesting to note that, according to the NDP, the financing chart for the year 2000 was established in agreement with the European Commission. This chart differentiates NUTS 2 regions of first (North-East, South-East, South, North-West) and second-level priority (South-West, West, Center, Bucharest-Ilfov). According to the charts, €94.7 million was allocated for three priorities in first-level regions: supporting Small and Medium-Sized Enterprise (SMEs), development of human resources and development of regional and local infrastructure. For second-level regions, €43.2 million was provided for the following objectives: supporting SMEs, development of human resources, development of regional and local infrastructure, development of tourism, supporting technical development and innovation, development of the private sphere and the promotion of investments.

It is interesting to remark that the NDP for 2002–05, in the conception of its writers, 'is part of the management of change'. The need for upgrading the document is mentioned, as the NDP is regarded as the basis of the annual Action Plan of the government. The NDP identifies seven priority axes, out of which six are sectoral (development of the production sector, improvement of infrastructure, reinforcement of human resources potential, support for agriculture and rural development, environmental protection, stimulation of research and technological development), while the seventh is regional (improvement of the economic structure of the regions and support for a balanced and sustainable regional development). One should remark that the seventh priority axis contains the first six priority axes as fields for intervention, it being clearly specified that 'axis 7 represents a territorial distribution of priority national development objectives and of funds materializing these objectives' (Government of Romania, 2001, p. 375).

Elaboration of the 2004–06 NDP was basically the result of the pre-accession process. This is clearly underlined in the introduction, which among other things mentions that the NDP has a double purpose: an instrument for fundamenting and financing the national, sectoral and regional development priorities from funds provided by the state budget and local budgets, on the one hand, and an instrument of fundamenting the access of the country to financial assistance from the pre-accession structural and cohesion funds granted to Romania by the EU within the accession partnership, on the other.

Financing sources for the NDP were given as follows: 16 per cent EU funds, 5 per cent national co-financing of EU funds, 56 per cent Romanian public funds, 15 per cent loans from international financing institutions, 9 per cent private funds and resources (Government of Romania, 2003).

The national plan for territorial development

Another basic document for territorial development in Romania is the National Plan for Territorial Development (NPTD). This is the most important planning document at state level. The institutions responsible for its editing and application are the Parliament, the government, the counties and local public administrations. At the time of writing, five sections of the NPTD had been drafted: means of communication, water, protected areas, network of settlements and natural risks. There is no official document which clarifies the relationship of the NPTD and the NDP. We can only assume that during the process of drafting the NDP the development goals established by the five sections of the NPTD were taken into consideration.

A high priority of the NPTD is the construction of six new motorways and completion of the existing one between Bucharest and Piteşti (Law no. 203/2003). The motorways will link Bucharest with other important urban centres (Constanţa, Braşov, Timişoara, Arad and Ploieşti), while another road will form the Bucharest City ring. Two of the motorways will connect with trans-European transport systems: Piteşti-Sibiu–Sebeş–Deva–Arad–Nădlac and Braşov–Târgu Mureş–Cluj-Napoca–Borş. They will increase the central role played by Bucharest in the hierarchy of settlements and help integrate neighbouring regions in the urban area of the Capital. The main issue is related to the timing of these projects. By themselves they are not enough to ensure economic growth. If other development measures are not applied at the same time, some regions would simply become transit corridors for the transportation of goods from the western and central part of the continent to its eastern part, on the one hand, and between the major growth-centres of Romania, on the other.

The second section of the NPTD (Law no. 171/1997) stipulates the achievement of objectives in an area of public infrastructure that has thus far received scant attention: the provision of water for people and the economy. The problem is especially serious in rural areas. In 2000, only about half of all communes had a public network for distributing drinkable water, and only about 55 per cent of the rural population had access to such networks. During the last decade, planning activity in this field has concentrated on rural areas, where the water network expanded by 35.7 per cent compared to 1990.

The third section (Law no. 5/2000) includes lists of protected natural areas of national interest, natural monuments and cultural objectives of national value. Presently, however, these areas are regulated by a special law that is yet to be revised. Another problem is that most of these areas do not have an exact delimitation of territory, at the level of land parcels. There are 827 protected natural areas altogether, covering an area of about 1,230,000 ha (5.2 per cent of national territory, according to NDP 2002–05).

The fourth section (Law 351/2001) regulates the network of settlements. One of the most important achievements of this law is the 'hierarchization of Romanian settlements' according to six ranks, which will also be the basis for establishing growth poles. This ranking will have significant practical implications, as taxes and duties will be established according to rank.

The fourth article of the law stipulates that the government and local public authorities should become involved in 'areas without towns for a radius of 25–30 kilometers'. This means they should allocate resources aiming at modernizing certain rural settlements that provide services and have an area of influence. The purpose is to declare new towns by supporting the institutional development of some rural settlements. Two observations should be made upon the text of the law. First, the term 'rural settlements that provide services' is not clearly defined. Their selection will probably be made at lower spatial levels, probably the county level. Thus, there is a free field of action for regional planners, which is a positive thing, as it is difficult to precisely define generally valid terms at the national level for such settlements. Second, we do not believe that the declaration of new towns may be solved only by setting up institutions, because the law establishes precise criteria for declaring new towns. These criteria go beyond the institutional sphere to include economic, social and infrastructure criteria. In all, 17 areas without towns for a radius of 25–30 kilometers have been established, encompassing an impressive number of communes (452) and a total population of about 1.5 million.

The law also stipulates the solution of several 'conflicts related to the administrative organization of the territory'. Thus, it establishes that the transfer of rural settlements from one administrative unit to another is to be done using local referendums. Another regulation of even greater importance concerns the criteria for establishing new towns and cities. This appears for the first time in 50 years in the form of a legal text. Analyzing these indicators, the population criterion (at least 5,000) is not high compared to the practice of southern European countries (Spain, Italy) or the Netherlands, but is high compared to northern European countries. This is the simplest criterion, and a relatively large number of rural settlements meet its demands (Benedek, 2004). The population criterion is augmented by economic, social and infrastructure criteria. Meeting these criteria will be the greatest challenge for prospective new towns. In fact, a series of existing towns do not meet many of the demands established by the law. Meeting these criteria would require significant financial efforts to upgrade the infrastructural endowment of settlements and good settlement management to increase economic attractiveness. The establishment of these criteria aims at creating future urban centres that should become real centres for the provision of services to the population of an area made up by a number of settlements, as the indicators cover almost the entire field of public services (health, culture, education, sports, tourism).

The introduction of indicators reflecting environmental protection activities (e.g., purifying stations, controlled waste storage yards, green spaces) provides an ecological dimension to the urban space, which is very important from the perspective of balanced and sustainable development.

On the other hand, the law does not regulate a series of other conflicts which have emerged in the last decade; most importantly, the transfer of settlements from one county to another and the creation of new counties (NUTS 3 units). As the law does not explicitly address these issues, they will remain subjects for debate in the future.

Finally, the last section of the NPTD (Law 575/2001) refers to areas with natural risks. It addresses three such risks – earthquakes, floods and landslides – while other risks (such as air, water and soil pollution) are to be regulated by other laws. During the years to come, the implementation and success of this law depends largely on overcoming methodological problems related to the delimitation and designation of areas with natural risks, as well as concrete measures to prevent and reduce the occurrence of natural catastrophes. One also needs to consider the large territorial coverage of these phenomena: floods affect 1,351 administrative units and landslides 987 (out of a total of 2,951).

EU pre-accession funds

In the run-up to accession Romania benefited from three pre-accession funds: PHARE, Instrument for Structural Policies for Pre-Accession (ISPA) and Special Accession Programme for Agriculture and Rural Development (SAPARD). Table 12.1 shows the amounts allocated from different funds to Romania between 1998 and 2005.

Romania was the second-to-last country to begin implementation of the SAPARD programme; because of delay in accrediting the SAPARD Agency, the first calls for projects were issued only in August 2002. Nevertheless, this late start did not hinder Romanian authorities from

Table 12.1 EU pre-accession aid to Romania by programme and year (€ mn)

	1998	1999	2000	2001	2002	2003	2004	2005	Total
PHARE	155.2	215.2	254.83	286.69	278.8	283.06	422.3	455.5	2,351.58
ISPA			239.2	246.0	255.0	260.8	315.0	348.0	1,664.0
SAPARD			153.2	156.3	160.6	162.2	158.6	175.2	966.1
Total	155.2	215.2	647.23	688.99	694.4	706.06	895.9	978.7	4,981.68

Source: European Commission, PHARE, ISPA and SAPARD official documents.

using all funds meant for rural infrastructure development for the entire programme period (European Court of Auditors, 2004).

The Commission's 2004 annual report noted: 'In Romania, by the end of 2004, the SAPARD agency approved 1096 projects accounting for €452.4 million of EU funds. This figure corresponds to 57 per cent of the SAPARD allocation for the years 2000–04' (European Commission, 2005b, p. 4).

In Romania, as well as other candidate countries in the pre-accession period, ISPA concentrated on two main fields: environment and infrastructure. The main purpose in the former category was the support of large investments related to the application of EU environmental directives. In the latter, priority was given to investments which contributed to the integration of Romania's transport system into Trans-European networks (TENs) and the EU transport system.

According to the Commission's 2005 report, PHARE financing in Romania between 1990 and 2004 showed the following results: €2.7 billion was given to Romania by different PHARE financing memorandums; contracts existed for €1.9 billion and €1.6 billion had been paid. There were still PHARE programmes in progress at the time of the report, however, and as a result there were still parts of some signed contracts that had not yet been paid.

The data regarding pre-accession funds in Romania are not fully assembled and available, and some programmes are still ongoing. Because of this, it is quite difficult to render a more detailed analysis of the results of pre-accession funding for the whole period. We know, for example, that the percentage of payments of commitments for the PHARE-Economic and Social Cohesion programmes implemented in 2000–02 was 26.6 per cent. We also know that the share of payments of commitments for ISPA Romania in 2000–05 was low, about 23 per cent (Government of Romania, 2006). Once again, however, we must remember that in 2005 there were still programmes in progress with some signed contracts that had not been fully paid.

Among the problematic issues related to the implementation of pre-accession programmes in Romania are the following: poor coordination between partners in developing programmes; high staff turnover; inadequate sustainability of projects; inadequate implementation structures; weak administrative capacity to manage EU funds; insufficient monitoring mechanisms; and poor project preparation (European Court of Auditors, 2006). For example, in its audit of the 2000 national

PHARE programme in Romania, the European Court of Auditors found the following problems:

> For over half of the investment projects audited, assets were not, or only partially, being used for the intended purpose. Outputs and results lagged considerably behind schedule, sometimes by up to two years. These shortcomings were due to the continuing lack of both administrative capacity and national resources, the technical viability of the investment goods is not assured and their longevity is at risk (European Court of Auditors, 2006, p. 3).

At the same time, the Court also criticized the Commission's overall management of investment projects, citing its overestimation of the management capacity of public authorities and neglect of the principles of sustainability and co-financing.

Regional policy after accession, 2007–13

In the introduction of the NDP for 2007–13, the references to EU cohesion policy and its requirements are ubiquitous. This document formed the basis for drawing up the National Strategic Reference Framework (NSRF) for 2007–13. At the same time, it states that the NDP is not a national strategy for economic development; instead, it only indicates 'the public investment priorities for development' (Government of Romania, 2006, p. 4).

The NDP for 2007–13 sets the goal of raising Romanian GDP per capita to 41 per cent of the EU average by 2013. It also establishes three major objectives: the Romanian economy should become more competitive in the long run; basic infrastructure should be developed to European standards; and domestic human capital should be better trained and more efficiently used. Six priorities are set to help achieve these objectives: increased economic competitiveness and the development of a knowledge-based economy; the development and modernization of transportation infrastructure; protection of the environment and improved environmental quality; the development of human resources, including the promotion of employment and social inclusion and the improvement of public administration capacity; development of the rural economy and increased productivity in the agricultural sector; and decreased economic disparities between the regions (Government of Romania 2006, pp. 242–3).

The NDP foresees €58.7 billion in financial resources available for 2007–13 (compared to only €12.1 billion for NDP 2004–06). EU funds are listed among these resources, although it is emphasized that the amounts represent only 'indicative allocations', as EU funding is granted according to the NSRF and Operational Programmes (OPs). The following distribution of types of financing resources is envisaged: 43 per cent EU funds; 48 per cent national public sources, some of them necessary for co-financing EU funds; 9 per cent private sources exclusively provided for the co-financing of EU funds (Government of Romania 2006, pp. 350–2). Thus, EU funding and Romanian co-financing combined represents more than half the resources planned for in the NDP.

While NDP 2007–13 establishes six priorities, the NSRF defines only four: the development of basic infrastructure at European standards; growth of the Romanian economy and its increased long-term competitiveness; development and more efficient use of human capital; and the consolidation of an efficient administrative capacity. The stress laid on infrastructure development is obvious, if one takes a look at the financial estimates, which assign 60 per cent of the total budget for this priority subject (Government of Romania, 2007, p. 153). The NSRF also defines a territorial priority: the promotion of balanced territorial development. The main objective of the NSRF is to reduce economic and social disparities between Romania and other member states, by generating a 15–20 per cent increase of GDP by 2015 (Government of Romania, 2007, p. 85).

Romania will receive assistance in 2007–13 under two of the three objectives of EU cohesion policy: Convergence and European Territorial Cooperation (ETC) (see Table 12.2). All of Romania's regions meet the Convergence criteria of GDP per capita less than 75 per cent of the EU average. Seven OPs have been drawn up within the Convergence objective, one regional and six sectoral. The following OPs have been defined for the ETC objective: Cross-border Cooperation OPs (Romania-Bulgaria, Romania-Hungary, Romania-Hungary-Slovakia-Ukraine, Romania-Ukraine-Moldova and Romania-Serbia), Transnational Cooperation OPs (South-Eastern Europe, the Black Sea) and Inter-regional Cooperation OPs (URBACT II, INTERREG IVC, ESPON 2013, INTERACT II).

The implementation of the cohesion policy, or better said, the mechanism which allows the money allocated to Romania for the Convergence and ETC objectives to get to the beneficiaries, is quite complex and organized on several levels. There is a difference between NSRF coordination and the authorities responsible for managing the OPs. The NSRF has four coordination institutions (Government of Romania, 2007). First, the National Coordination Committee for Structural Instruments, which is an interministerial board, presided

Table 12.2 Cohesion policy allocations for Romania, 2007–13

Operational Programme Convergence objective	EU contribution in €	% of total
SOP Increased Economic Competitiveness	2,554,222,109	12.99
SOP Transport	4,565,937,295	23.22
SOP Environment	4,512,470,138	22.94
Regional OP	3,726,021,762	18.94
SOP Human Resources Development	3,476,144,996	17.67
OP Administrative Capacity Development	208,002,622	1.06
OP Technical Assistance	170,237,790	0.87
Total Convergence objective	19,213,036,712	97.69
ETC objective	454,610,340	2.31
Total	19,667,647,052	100.00

Source: Government of Romania (2007); EU documents.

over by the Minister of Economy and Finance. Its members are the ministers responsible for the Management Authorities (MAs) and the Certifying and Paying Authority. The Committee is responsible for coordinating the implementation of EU structural instruments and for coordination between the cohesion policy OPs and programmes financed by the European Agricultural Fund for Rural Development (EAFRD) and European Fisheries Fund (EFF). Second, the Management Coordination Committee, which will coordinate administrative and management issues between the different OPs. Its members are the heads of the OP MAs and the Certifying and Paying Authority. Third is the Thematic Working Groups, which are set up whenever necessary. Such groups already exist, for instance for developing the Single Management Information System (SMIS). And fourth, Regional Coordination Committees for Structural Instruments, which are organized in each region as a consultative authority that analyzes the implementation of the European programmes in the region.

The Ministry of Public Finance is the MA for the Community Support Framework (CSF), coordinating the implementation of structural funds in Romania. For every OP, MAs and also intermediate bodies have been designated. The latter are, most of the time, ministries or bodies coordinated by ministries. The Regional Operational Programme (ROP) is the only one with RDAs as the intermediate bodies. In this capacity, the RDAs are given the authority to: provide information to project applicants; participate in preparing appeals for project proposals; receive and register applications, and analyze their administrative conformity and the eligibility of financing applications; organize technical and financial assessment sessions of registered projects with the help of independent evaluators; conclude financing contracts; receive payment applications; check the correctness of expenses; and, in their role as Secretary, chair the Regional Committee of Strategic Assessment and Correlation (see below). The ROP Managing Authority is a unit of the MDPH. Among other tasks, the ROP MA prepares the ROP, is responsible for achieving the ROP's objectives and ensuring its implementation, develops partnerships, proposes changes in the ROP, drafts the criteria for selecting and assessing projects, and approves the projects selected by the RDAs. Thus, the RDAs are the institutions which will have the most direct contact with the potential beneficiaries of structural programmes.

The Monitoring Committee of the ROP (MC ROP) is made up of three categories of members: eight representatives of central government ministries (the MAs of the ROP and six Sectoral Operational Programme (SOPs), the Ministry of Public Finance, and the MA of the national programme for rural development); eight representatives of the RDCs, who are the presidents of county councils; and eight representatives of the business and academic communities and civil society, named by the RDCs. The president of MC ROP is the Minister of Development, Public Works and Housing.

Among the prerogatives of MC ROP are the following: approve the selection criteria for projects drawn up by the ROP MA; approve implementation reports; propose revisions of the ROP by the ROP MA; and approve proposed changes to the financial assignments of the ROP. Based on its composition, it is apparent that the RDCs may (theoretically, at least) exert a strong influence within MC ROP.

Apart from these national structures, a Regional Committee for Strategic Assessment and Correlation is set up in every NUTS 2 region. Among other tasks, it assesses regional projects from a strategic point of view and establishes priority among them, and it approves the list of priority projects for each region proposed for financing within the ROP.

The ROP and four SOPs – Increased Economic Competitiveness, Transport, Environment, and Human Resources Development – represent more than 95 per cent of the cohesion policy funds allocated to Romania in 2007–13. Priority axes have been established for each of them, representing the main directions for development and investment for the next seven years.

The SOP Increased Economic Competitiveness has five priority axes: the development of an innovative and ecologically efficient production system; research, technological development and innovation for competitiveness; information technology and communications technology for the public and private sector; the increase of energy efficiency and security in the context of climatic changes; and technical assistance (Ministry of Economy and Finance, 2007a).

The SOP Transport has only four priority axes: the modernization and development of TEN-T priority axes aiming at a sustainable transport system integrated with EU transport networks; modernization and development of the national transport infrastructure outside the TEN-T priority axes aiming at a sustainable national transport system; modernization of the transport sector aiming at a higher degree of environmental protection, human health and passenger safety; and technical assistance (Ministry of Transport, 2007).

The SOP Environment has six priority axes: extension and modernization of water and wastewater systems; development of integrated waste management systems and rehabilitation of historically contaminated sites; reduction of pollution and mitigation of climate change by restructuring and renovating urban heating systems to meet energy efficiency targets in identified local environmental hotspots; implementation of adequate management systems for nature protection; implementation of adequate infrastructure for natural risk prevention in the most vulnerable areas; and technical assistance (Ministry of Environment and Sustainable Development, 2007).

The ROP has the following priority axes: supporting the sustainable development of urban growth poles; improvement of the regional and local transportation infrastructure; improvement of social infrastructure; strengthening the regional and local business environment; sustainable development and promotion of tourism; and technical assistance (MDPH, 2007).

The SOP Human Resources Development has seven priority axes: education and training for the growth and development of a knowledge-based society; linking lifelong learning and the labour market; increasing the adaptability of workers and enterprises; modernization of the Public Employment Service; promoting active employment measures; promoting social inclusion; and technical assistance (Ministry of Labour, Family and Equal Opportunities, 2007).

Political parties and regionalism

Despite the existence of strong regional identities in different historical regions of Romania, only a low level of political regionalism exists
(Benedek, 2008). As a consequence, there is little internal pressure for
devolution and decentralization. Two factors play a huge role in this situation. First, the law on political parties makes the registration of regional
parties very difficult, because the list of party supporters should include
at least 25,000 founding members who reside in at least 18 counties and
Bucharest City, with at least 700 persons in each county and Bucharest
City. According to some political scientists (Waele, 2004; Delwit, 2005),
the one Romanian party which may be conceived of as a regional or
autonomist party is the Democratic Alliance of Hungarians in Romania
(DAHR). However, this party represents mainly the Hungarian minority of Romania and not a particular region. That Transylvania is highlighted in the discourse of DAHR members or within its programmes
is due to the territorial concentration of the Hungarian minority, with
98.88 per cent of them living in Transylvanian counties.

Second, the programmes of the main parties do not reflect questions
related to regionalization. Among the parliamentary parties, only the
DAHR has a large chapter on the regional issue.[2] In fact, the regional
issue appears twice in the DAHR's programme. Among the aims of the
chapter on local public administration and democracy is the following: 'regions should be based on a willing association; the economic
development region should appear in the Constitution.' The DAHR's
programme also contains a chapter on 'the regional interests of DAHR,
regional and territorial development', according to which, 'the region
is not an administrative unit, but an association based on economic
development'. The programme speaks about the need to change the
present NUTS 2 regions, because certain economic, historical and geographical aspects were not taken into consideration when they were set
up.[3] As for the National Liberal Party, the chapter on regional and local
development taken from the ideas and principles of the party[4] speaks
only about the reduction of regional disparities. The programme of the
Democrat Party, on the other hand, speaks generally about support for
a federal Europe.[5]

Thus, regionalization is not a central issue of public debate in
Romania. However, that does not mean that regional issues are not dis-
cussed at all. For instance, on many occasions the National Union of the
County Councils of Romania has spoken out for reorganizing the NUTS

2 regions, with effective involvement of the counties, thus reflecting the interests of those communities. In 2007 the question of reorganizing the NUTS 2 regions was on the political agenda, as an issue in the European Parliament elections. The DAHR presented a proposal for reorganizing the NUTS 2 regions, but serious discussion was hindered by widespread fears that regional reform would lead to separatism and active regionalism in Romania (Jordan, 1998; Benedek, 2008).

Conclusions

This chapter provides a number of basic insights into regional policy in Romania. It suggests that the greatest challenge for regional policy in Romania is the country's limited capacity to absorb EU assistance. The country monitoring report for 2005 mentioned the need for implementation structures for EU cohesion policy to become functional and for administrative capacity to be strengthened (European Commission, 2005b). The 2006 monitoring report also mentioned the need to increase administrative capacity to absorb EU funds (CEC, 2006d). As a requirement of EU accession, Romania has created an institutional framework to manage EU assistance, which includes a range of administrative structures and monitoring mechanisms. In this very early stage of cohesion policy implementation after accession in 2007, it is hard to make judgments about how efficiently EU funds have been used.

We emphasize that in Romania, EU cohesion policy has played a key role in establishing regional policy. The role of regions was strengthened by EU-mandated regionalization and the creation of NUTS 2 regions, while the NUTS 3 units (counties) and local administration were also part of a decentralization process. However, the NUTS 2 regions are only statistical regions and basic units for implementing EU cohesion policy. There is evidence that what has emerged is a hierarchical, top-down pattern of multilevel governance, where collaboration and partnership is rather formal and declarative. In accordance with national political traditions, and due to Commission support for the centralized administration of EU structural assistance, no decentralized management structures have been created. Even the designated intermediate bodies are, most of the time, government ministries or bodies coordinated by ministries.

Finally, we cannot underestimate the high expectations regarding the economic effects of EU cohesion policy. The new NUTS 2 regions correspond to interregional economic disparities which were consistent in the 1920s, decreased during the long period of state-controlled economy, and finally were reinforced after 1989 by the opening up of the Romanian economy and its integration into global networks of production and consumption (Benedek, 2004). A positive impact of EU structural spending on economic convergence and growth is expected. According to the latest estimates of the Ministry of Economy and Finance, both the developments of recent years and projections for 2008 indicate that economic disparities between regions will be maintained in the short term (Ministry of Economy and Finance, 2007b). The GDP per capita ratio between the wealthiest (West) and poorest (North-East) regions remains steady at around 1.7 (the comparison excludes the Bucharest region, which has a very high GDP per capita). For 2008, projected trends for the North-East region, with growth levels equal to or above the national average, and the West region indicate that the disparity index will decrease slightly compared to 2005, reaching a level of 1.66. Thus, as regional disparities are no longer increasing, the basis for reducing discrepancies after 2008 is created, especially in view of the anticipated positive effects of EU cohesion policy.

Notes

1. The South-East region, with counties from three different cultural regions: Moldavia, Muntenia and Dobrogea.
2. In Romania, the regional issue appears in political discourse mainly when the DAHR brings up the question of regional autonomy or regionalization.
3. The DAHR Programme, 2007 <http://www.rmdsz.ro>.
4. 'Ideas and Principles: The Economic Policy of the National Liberal Party' <http://www.pnl.ro>.
5. 'Prosperous Romania – Democratic Romania', The Democrat Party's Political Programme, 'Our Europe' <http://www.pd.ro>.

13
Conclusion

Dan Marek and Michael Baun

This volume has examined the implementation of EU cohesion policy after enlargement and the 2006 reform of cohesion policy, utilizing ten country case studies equally weighted between old and new member states. In this concluding chapter, we summarize our findings and provide answers to the questions posed in the first chapter of this book. The next two sections discuss specific questions facing old and new member states when it comes to implementing EU cohesion policy, followed by an analysis of how member states have responded to the common challenges posed by Lisbonization and the 2006 reform of cohesion policy. The subsequent section discusses the role of domestic mediating factors in shaping cohesion policy implementation in EU countries. We then conclude with some thoughts about the future of cohesion policy in a larger and more diverse EU.

arg. reason for S. and G finance crisis

Old member states: coping with reduced funding

While most of the EU15 faced a sharp reduction of funding after 2006, the extent of this reduction varies considerably across countries. Among the old member states examined in this book, Spain was hit with a 42 per cent reduction of its cohesion policy allocation (the biggest loss in absolute terms among the EU15 at €23 billion) and the United Kingdom a 46 per cent reduction, while Germany suffered only a 19 per cent cut in cohesion policy receipts and Greece 26 per cent. Ireland is the biggest 'loser' in percentage terms, not just among the five countries studied in this book but also among the EU15 overall, suffering an 80 per cent reduction of its cohesion policy allocation.[1]

The loss of EU funding has had a significant impact on cohesion policy implementation in all of the old member states examined in this volume. One area affected by the loss of funding is structural programming, with most countries seeking to concentrate more limited funding on certain types of projects and priorities. In the United Kingdom (most notably in Scotland), funding in 2007–13 is focused on a smaller number of larger projects; there is also an increased focus on efficiency and the best use of more limited resources. In Ireland, less funding, and the loss of eligibility under the Convergence objective, means less investment in infrastructure and more on R&D and competitiveness. It has also led to a narrower policy focus on the Lisbon goals – which, according to McMaster, 'aims to maximize the impact of reduced funding, by focusing on a more limited range of interventions and rationalizing the administrative burden of working with the Funds over a wide range of activities' – as well as concentration on a smaller number of 'niche' investments. In Germany, the loss of funding has not necessarily led to fewer funding priorities (this varies across regions, with no clear link between an increase or decrease of funding priorities and the level of funding). However, Sturm and Schorlemmer note a narrower range of specific funding targets in 2007–13 compared to the previous programming period. Also in Germany, the loss of funding has led to a concentration of resources, for example by increasing the focus on 'clusters' of growth-oriented companies that could develop into growth poles with a broader positive impact on economic growth, and more support for projects with broader positive effects for economic and social development. There is also an increased focus on the urban dimension and the role of cities as regional economic engines. The loss of funding would seem to pose the most serious problems for Spain and Greece, two less wealthy cohesion countries among the EU15. Indeed, Morata and Popartan note a clear reorientation by the Spanish government and regional governments towards the Lisbon priorities as a strategy for dealing with reduced levels of funding, as well as a greater emphasis on efficiency and partnership. According to Paraskevopoulos, however, the loss of funding poses less of a problem for Greece than the reorientation of development activities towards the Lisbon priorities and the continued need to increase administrative performance and efficiency.

Reduced funding has also affected implementation and management structures, leading in most cases to rationalization in an effort to make them more efficient and cost-effective. In the United Kingdom, for example, there has been a rationalization of implementing structures in the direction of regionalization and decentralization and an overall reduction in the number of MAs. Ireland has also introduced increased decentralization and regional participation in cohesion policy planning and implementation. However, it is unclear whether reduced funding plays a role in this (although in 2000–06 Ireland began regionalization – the creation of two Nomenclature of Statistical Territorial Units (NUTS) 2 regions and the use of Regional Operational Programme (ROPs) – as a deliberate strategy to maximize structural funds receipts), or whether it is more reflective of broader national efforts at administrative decentralization and local economic development. In Spain, the decentralization of cohesion policy implementation appears to be a response both to domestic political demands for regionalization as well as the search for efficiency gains in the face of reduced funding. Germany and Greece present a different picture, however. In Germany, reduced funding and Lisbonization have promoted the centralization and standardization of cohesion policy implementation at the *Land* level, reinforcing a trend that began in the second half of 2000–06 in an effort to achieve greater efficiency. In Greece as well, reduced funding appears to have reinforced the existing trend towards greater centralization of cohesion policy implementation (and the adoption of a more technocratic approach) as a means of improving efficiency and performance. These two countries appear to counter the trend towards regionalization and decentralization of management structures as a means of rationalizing cohesion policy implementation in the old member states; however, it is also important to note that centralization in Germany has occurred at the *Land* and not the federal level.

Reduced funding also seems to have had an impact on partnership, apparently increasing the importance of this basic governance principle in most cases. In the United Kingdom, according to Chapman, greater emphasis is now given to projects that are explicitly partnership-based in design. At the same time, she notes, the shift of focus to Lisbon growth and competitiveness themes could affect the nature of partnership, 'rationalizing' or narrowing the scope of partnership arrangements by reducing the engagement of third-sector (civic and voluntary) actors in favour of business and economic actors. In Ireland, reduced funding has promoted efforts at more effective partnership and cooperative working in order to make better use of more limited resources. Similarly in Spain, Morata and Popartan argue that reduced funding has made partnership and more cooperative modes of governance even more important to ensure efficient and creative use of funding, the goal being 'to achieve more results with less funding'. They report that in planning for 2007–13, and especially when designing Operational Programmes (OPs), the Spanish government sought to involve a wider range of social partners than ever before, including more private-sector and nongovernmental actors. In Germany, by contrast, the centralization of cohesion policy implementation at the *Land* level – in part the result of less funding – has reduced, in Baden-Württemberg at least, the involvement of local actors (e.g., regional chambers of commerce) in the selection of EU-funded projects. In Greece – another country in which cohesion policy implementation has been centralized – effective partnership arrangements have been undermined more by a weak civil society and low levels of social capital – and also by a clientelistic political culture – than by reduced levels of funding.

Reduced funding appears to have affected the link between EU cohesion policy and national economic development policies, although in different ways in different countries. In the United Kingdom, there is now a closer alignment of EU cohesion policy with domestic regional and economic development policies, in order to ensure the maximum use of EU funds and support for existing domestic policies. This contrasts with Ireland, where the result has been a decoupling of EU and domestic policies; in contrast to the previous highly integrated approach, EU and domestic policies are now programmed separately. According to McMaster, this decoupling is designed to maximize the impact of EU funds and ensure the achievement of EU targets; at the same time, decoupling has freed domestic policies from the need to adhere to strict EU regulations, thus creating more flexibility. In Germany, it is the reorientation of cohesion policy towards the Lisbon goals, rather than reduced funding, that has reinforced the trend towards decoupling that was already underway due to the growing incompatibility of the goals and targeting of EU cohesion policy and national regional policy. In these (relatively wealthy) countries, at least, both responses suggest a 'nationalization' of cohesion policy, with governments seeking to enhance flexibility and/or link EU policy to the achievement of pre-determined national goals. In Spain, however, reduced funding and Lisbonization appear to have had little impact on the relationship between EU cohesion policy and national regional policy, and the same can be said for Greece. In these relatively poor countries the importance of EU funding has meant, and continues to mean, that EU cohesion policy largely determines the goals and direction of national regional policy.

New member states: up to the task?

In all of the new member states, EU accession was a catalyst for establishing a full-fledged regional policy. Prior to accession national regional policies in most Central and Eastern European Country (CEECs) were rather marginal in both size and scope and lacked many of the key elements of EU cohesion policy (e.g., integrated multiannual programming, partnership, sound financial management). In some countries, such as Romania, regional policies were established only in relation to the utilization of EU pre-accession assistance. A key question for the new member states, therefore, is how they have performed in implementing cohesion policy since joining the EU in 2004 (or 2007) and whether their institutional and administrative capacities have been up to the task? Another important question concerns the impact of EU cohesion policy on multilevel governance in the new member states.

Institutional and administrative capacity

As expected, all of the new member states examined in this book faced difficulties in implementing EU cohesion policy after accession, with negative consequences for their ability to absorb EU funds. In fact, it is very likely that none of them will be able to fully utilize the funds allocated for the 2004–06 programming period. In the case of the Czech Republic, experts estimate that only 75–90 per cent of allocated funds will be used by the end of 2008, the deadline for spending 2006 allocations. In Poland, where an 'overly heavy and complex' implementation system has contributed to a 'slow and difficult start', Gorzelak and Kozak report that 98 per cent of allocated structural funds were contracted in August 2007 but only 54.3 per cent 'effectively spent'. In Lithuania, about 57 per cent of allocated funds had been spent by the end of 2007. In most of the countries studied, initial failures led to improvements in administrative procedures and implementation systems, in the attempt to ensure the full usage of funds. These improvements have led to better results. In February 2008, the Commission reported that the average 'absorption rate' for the 2004 entrants (EU10) had improved to 75 per cent by the end of 2007, with Hungary the best performer at 82 per cent; this compared to an average absorption rate for the EU15 over the same period of 84 per cent (*Euractiv*, 2008). Nevertheless, problems with administrative capacity will likely continue to undermine the absorption capacity of most new member states in 2007–13.

Generally speaking, cohesion policy implementation suffered from a number of problems in the new member states, including overly complex bureaucratic procedures, institutional instability and the lack of sufficient numbers of well-trained and qualified officials. All of the new member states examined in this book have had difficulty handling the demanding horizontal coordination of OPs in various stages of the implementation process, with a typical problem being the thematic overlap of different programmes; in fact, this was one of the main criticisms voiced by the Commission during negotiations with the new member states on the National Strategic Reference Framework (NSRFs) and OPs for 2007–13. In the Czech Republic, the unwillingness of individual government ministries to co-manage joint inter-ministerial programmes, each wanting to run their own, resulted in a proliferation of OPs in 2007–13. Weak central direction and the lack of inter-ministerial coordination are problems for most of the new member states. In Poland, this resulted from institutional instability, with the shift of responsibility for regional development policy from one ministry to another until the Ministry of Regional Development (MRD) was finally established in fall 2005. The lack of inter-ministerial cooperation has been a problem in Hungary and Lithuania as well, in the latter case despite the formal central coordinating role of the Ministry of Finance.

Problems have also stemmed from the varying levels of preparedness and uneven capacities of individual MAs (ministries). In the Czech Republic, this delayed the start of some OPs after accession and resulted in the shifting of programme allocations for 2004 to the following year, thus complicating their effective use. In both the Czech Republic and Hungary, uncertain rules for project preparation, application and selection caused delays; ambiguities in the contract-making process also delayed the conclusion of contracts for successful projects in many OPs.

Shortcomings in the legislation also created hurdles for potential applicants. In the Czech Republic, for example, the law did not permit public schools to transfer funds to private-sector actors, thus limiting their ability to apply jointly with private companies for funding to support job-creating educational projects. In Hungary, the laws on public procurement and VAT proved disadvantageous for potential applicants, while continued uncertainty about the distribution of competencies among different levels of government (especially at the regional level) have hindered the effective implementation of EU cohesion policy. In Lithuania, problems with public procurement laws and complex procedures for obtaining construction permits have delayed the implementation of EU-funded projects.

Problems have also occurred with the co-financing and pre-financing of projects. In the Czech Republic in 2004–06, for instance, the lack of a system of continuous payment meant that beneficiaries had to fully pre-finance projects and could only be reimbursed upon project completion, thus discouraging applications from smaller and financially weaker organizations as well as the public sector. Similarly in Poland, refinancing rules discouraged less wealthy beneficiaries from participating in projects because they would not be reimbursed for several months (or even years in the case of Interregional cooperation programme (INTERREG) projects). In Poland, the Czech Republic and Hungary, the limited financial resources of regional authorities precluded their effective participation in EU-funded projects; in Poland, this tended to favour the selection of projects promoted by local governments which had little regional coherence or significance.

The new member states have responded to these difficulties by seeking to modernize and improve their administrative capacities and implementing systems. One response has been to centralize Managing Authority (MA) at the national government level, focusing responsibility within a particular ministry – the MRD in the case of both Poland and the Czech Republic. Poland has gone farthest in this direction, with the MRD also being named the Certifying Institution for EU-funded projects, rather than the Ministry of Finance as in other new member states. In the Czech Republic, however, Marek and Baun note that the MRD's ability to carry out this coordinating function could be hamstrung by its formal legal equality with other government ministries, thus limiting its ability to give instructions to other ministries. In Lithuania, problems with inter-ministerial coordination in 2004–06 led to the decision to designate the Ministry of Finance as the single MA for all OPs in 2007–13.

Multilevel governance

EU cohesion policy appears to have had a definite effect on multilevel governance in the new member states. Despite the centralized administration of EU cohesion policy at the national level, especially in the management of horizontal or sectoral programmes, there is a notable trend towards the decentralization or regionalization of cohesion policy implementation in most of the new member states examined in this book in the 2007–13 programming period.

In the initial period after accession (2004–06), cohesion policy implementation in the new member states was heavily centralized. Even the instruments for regional interventions (ROPs) were managed by central governments in Poland, the Czech Republic, Hungary and Lithuania. Regional actors played only a secondary role. The reasons for this included the relatively small level of EU funding provided; the limited administrative experience and capacity of regional actors and their limited financial resources for co-financing projects; and the desire of national governments to fully utilize available funding in a short period of time (the usual 'n+2' rule applying to the accession states in this programming period). In Poland, according to Gorzelak and Kozak, a key consideration supporting the use of a single Integrated ROP rather than separate ROPs for each region was the difficulty of transferring funds among OPs in the event that a particular region or regions failed to implement their programmes. Central government representatives in the Polish regions (*Wojewoda*) also played the main role in implementing programmes rather than democratically elected regional governments.

However, in most of the new member states examined in this volume cohesion policy in 2007–13 is being implemented in a more decentralized manner. Poland, the Czech Republic and Hungary have all prepared separate ROPs for their individual NUTS 2 regions. Regional governments are also the MAs for the ROPs in Poland and the Czech Republic, rather than national government ministries as in 2004–06. In Hungary, non-elected Regional Development Councils (RDCs) have been given a larger role in cohesion policy implementation and resource allocation in 2007–13. Lithuania, due to its small size (the country represents one NUTS 2 region), does not utilize ROPs. Nevertheless, Nakrošis reports that Lithuania is also using a more decentralized management system in 2007–13, utilizing the existing structure of RDCs and local and county administrations; however, the total volume of financial resources to be channeled through regional structures remains limited (only about 12 per cent of total), in part because of continued doubts about the administrative capacity of these structures. Romania, having only joined the EU in 2007, has prepared one centralized ROP for the whole country, following a similar strategy to that adopted by some EU10 countries for the 2004–06 programming period.

The reasons for this decentralization or regionalization trend are several. While the increased emphasis on decentralization and subsidiarity in the 2006 cohesion policy reform undoubtedly plays a role, also important is the increased amount of funding for new member states in the new programming period, making more money available for use by regional actors, and the increased experience of regional and subnational actors with managing EU funds. Domestic administrative reforms in the new member states are another key factor, motivated in some cases by demands for greater governmental decentralization. In the Czech Republic and Poland, democratically elected regional governments (*kraje* and *województwo*, respectively) have sought an enhanced role in implementing cohesion policy and greater autonomy in using EU funds to address regional priorities. In Hungary, by contrast, Horváth argues that demands for decentralization have been countered by the centralization efforts of the national government, leading to a heightened 'disillusionment among local actors'. Even so, in Hungary there are plans for regional authorities (the RDCs) to be given a larger role in programme management and implementation. In Romania, Benedek and Horváth note that calls for greater decentralization, including the reorganization of NUTS 2 regions to take greater account of certain historical, economic and geographical factors, run up against governmental fears of political regionalism and separatism, and thus far have not yielded any results.

This decentralization trend suggests that EU cohesion policy is having an impact on territorial politics and multilevel governance in the new member states. In Poland and the Czech Republic, democratically elected regional governments have used the structural funds as leverage in their struggle with national governments for greater competencies and resources. In both countries, regional governments have argued for a revision of the public financing system to end their dependence on central government grants and enable them to independently co-finance EU-funded projects. In Poland, according to Gorzelak and Kozak, the regionalization of cohesion policy implementation and management 'is a further step in the process of devolution of the state'. As Horváth notes, EU cohesion policy has fueled a debate about regional reform in Hungary, although a 2002 proposal by the Socialist government to create democratically elected regional governments has yet to be realized. In Romania, Benedek and Horváth claim that cohesion policy has led to the creation of a system of territorial multilevel governance, although one that is 'hierarchical' and 'top-down', 'where collaboration and partnership is rather formal and declarative'.

EU cohesion policy also appears to be having an impact on 'horizontal' multilevel governance in the new member states, leading to increased efforts by governments to consult with nongovernmental and economic and social partners in the implementation of cohesion policy. However, the development of horizontal (type II) multilevel governance appears to be lagging behind the progress of vertical (type I) multilevel governance in most of the new member states examined in this book. In part, this is due to weak traditions of public-private partnership and state consultation with nongovernmental actors in these countries. Similar problems have been found in EU15 cohesion countries such as Spain and Greece, however, and we can expect improved partnership performance in the new member states in the future as a result of increased experience with EU policies and governance norms, economic and social development – which should lead to stronger and better organized civil society – and learning by both the state and social actors. In Hungary, for example, Horváth reports that there has already been a flourishing of nongovernmental actors (although not much progress in government-private sector partnerships), and of 'quasi-governmental' and 'quasi-nongovernmental organizational forms' as a consequence of EU cohesion policy.

Aside from the issue of multilevel governance, EU cohesion policy also appears to be having a positive impact on the quality of governance in the new member states more generally. In the Czech Republic, a major appeal of EU cohesion policy, in addition to the economic development resources it provides, is its positive impact on governmental norms, practices and efficiency; as Marek and Baun report, such positive effects are already being observed. In Hungary, Horváth claims that cohesion policy has led to the development of more flexible and quicker-acting organizational forms of public administration; it has also promoted efforts to improve management efficiency and the search for ways to measure and evaluate it. In Lithuania, as in other new member states, there is growing attention to the effectiveness of EU-funded programmes through monitoring and evaluation, as required by the EU. Benedek and Horváth claim that cohesion policy has also had a positive impact on the quality of governance in Romania.

Lisbonization and the 2006 reform

The reorientation of EU cohesion policy towards the goals and priorities of the Lisbon Agenda, or 'Lisbonization', has had a major impact on cohesion policy implementation in all member states. In most of the EU15 countries examined in this book, Lisbonization has been welcomed – at least rhetorically – as a positive change. The main exception is Germany, where Lisbonization was not enthusiastically welcomed due to fears that it would reduce national flexibility in implementing regional policy and addressing critical regional needs. According to Sturm and Schorlemmer, philosophical differences between German authorities and the Commission over the targeting of regional aid also played a role in the critical reaction to Lisbonization. In Spain, by contrast, Morata and Popartan claim that Lisbonization has been embraced as a strategy to cope with reduced EU funding and a way of getting greater benefits from less money. Paraskevopoulos also reports a rather uncritical reception of Lisbonization in Greece, arguing that it fits well with Greece's growing competitiveness and integration into EU and global markets. Nevertheless, Lisbonization appears to contradict the emphasis on large-scale infrastructure projects in Greek regional and cohesion policy since the mid-1990s.

In all of the old member states examined in this book, a review of the NSRFs and OPs for 2007–13 shows a high level of compliance with Lisbon 'earmarking' requirements; in most cases the Lisbon targets (60 per cent of spending for Convergence regions, and 75 per cent for Competitiveness regions) have been exceeded.[2] In the United Kingdom, there has been a shift of cohesion policy spending towards meeting the Lisbon goals and the adoption of a narrow approach to the Lisbon themes of competitiveness, growth and employment, although this varies somewhat across regions according to the volume of funds available (e.g., compare the OPs in NE England against those in Scotland and West Wales). According to Chapman, however, this reorientation of spending has reduced funding for activities traditionally supported by cohesion policy; in Scotland, for example, it is anticipated there will be 'less support for large-scale infrastructure projects in transport, tourism and economic development' in favour of a greater focus on activities such as workforce development, encouraging enterprise, business growth, support for innovation and commercialization of research development. Lisbonization has also reduced spending on 'social inclusion and capacity building activities' and programmes aimed at the regeneration of disadvantaged communities, such as the Community Economic Development (CED). In Ireland, the new thematic orientation of cohesion policy appears to be a good fit with national economic strategies, and therefore adaptation has been relatively unproblematic. The positive reception of Lisbonization in the United Kingdom and Ireland contrasts with the critical response in Germany, where concerns that new EU rules could reduce flexibility in implementing regional policy and limit the ability of governments to address critical regional needs have promoted the decoupling of national regional development policies and EU cohesion policy. Perhaps surprisingly, given their less wealthy status and previous focus on traditional infrastructure projects, Spain and Greece have embraced the new Lisbon orientation of cohesion policy and met or exceeded the earmarking requirements for Convergence and Competitiveness funding. In fact, Spain (along with Portugal, another EU15 cohesion country) has the highest level of earmarked investments for Convergence regions of any member state, at 80 per cent of the total (European Commission, 2007b, p. 5).[3]

Lisbonization has also affected the implementation of EU cohesion policy in the new member states, although adherence to the Lisbon earmarking requirements is not compulsory for these countries in the current programming period. All of the new member states surveyed in this volume have sought to address the Lisbon goals in their NSRFs and OPs for 2007–13, in some cases (Poland for Convergence regions, and the Czech Republic for Regional Competitiveness and Employment [RCE] funding) even exceeding the established targets. For the new member states overall, the Commission reports an average of 59 per cent of spending earmarked for both Convergence and Competitiveness regions, while noting that 'all new Member States have engaged in the earmarking exercise, albeit to varying degrees' (European Commission, 2007b, p. 7).

Nevertheless, programming in the new member states still leans heavily towards traditional infrastructure projects rather than human resource or business development projects, as might be expected for relatively less-developed countries with extensive basic infrastructure needs. In the case of Poland, Gorzelak and Kozak note the resistance of regional governments to the Lisbon targets in favour of infrastructure projects; they also claim that absorption capacity is most limited in the case of Lisbon-oriented projects, such as promoting innovation, entrepreneurship and R&D. Overall, they argue, cohesion policy in Poland still favours the traditional infrastructure and equity approach despite rhetorical commitment to the Lisbon goals of growth and competitiveness. In Romania, according to Benedek, 60 per cent of the regional policy budget for 2007–13 is dedicated to infrastructure projects, while balanced territorial development is another major priority. The heavy investment in basic infrastructure by new member states is by-and-large accepted by the Commission, which nevertheless notes that countries like Poland and Romania, 'with extensive investment needs in basic national, regional and local infrastructure, have decided to concentrate a significant proportion of [EU] resources on Lisbon-related priorities' (European Commission, 2007b, p. 5).

Strategic planning and multilevel governance

Cohesion policy implementation has also been affected by changes to implementation rules introduced by the 2006 reform, including the new focus on strategic planning, with the requirement that member states prepare NSRFs in alignment with the Community Strategic Guidelines to guide the use of EU funds. Overall, the impact of strategic planning appears to be positive. In the United Kingdom, for instance, Chapman claims that a greater emphasis is now given to the 'strategic fit and sustainability of projects'. Also in the other EU15 countries examined in this book, the new strategic orientation of cohesion policy appears to have introduced a longer-term perspective and increased awareness of the links between cohesion policy and other EU goals and policies.

The impact on development planning in the new member states appears to be somewhat less, however. In most of the new member states examined in this book, there is still a need for long-term, integrated national development planning which links EU-funded programmes to other national development policies. In Lithuania, for example, Nakrošis argues that separate programming for cohesion policy is simply aimed at spending available EU money. In Hungary, according to Horváth, there remains the need to go beyond an annual budget perspective to multiannual planning; a system of comprehensive, strategic development planning is still lacking, he complains. In the Czech Republic as well, the difficult and lengthy process of drafting the NSRF for 2007–13 and getting it approved by the Commission revealed the continued lack of a systematic and strategic approach to development planning, as well as continued problems with administrative capacity. Thus, despite formal adaptation to EU strategic planning requirements, it appears that deep or 'thick' learning in this crucial area of cohesion policy has yet to occur.

The new policy governance rules introduced by the 2006 reform – including the increased emphasis on decentralization and subsidiarity, and on the inclusion of nongovernmental and civil society actors in horizontal partnership arrangements – also seem to be having some effect on multilevel governance in EU countries, although it may be too early to say much about this. In both the United Kingdom and Ireland, the cohesion policy emphasis on decentralization fits well with established national trends in the direction of increased decentralization and partnership. In the United Kingdom, Chapman reports the shift of programme management responsibilities downwards, to the regional and local levels. At the same time, however, she notes that the shift from smaller-scale, 'bottom-up' projects to more top-down, higher profile ones –a consequence of the new strategic orientation of cohesion policy – could result in the exclusion of smaller organizations from participation in EU-funded programmes, thus undermining somewhat the goal of increased partnership. In Ireland as well the trend is towards decentralization, with a greater role for regional and local actors in cohesion policy implementation. Morata and Popartan report that decentralization below the regional level is a goal in Spain, but this is being hampered by the underdevelopment and weak capacity of local government actors. In Germany, by contrast, the decentralization of cohesion policy management below the regional (*Land*) level has been inhibited by a countertrend towards centralization at the *Land* level that began in the second half of 2000–06. In Greece, Paraskevopoulos notes the government's wide consultation of regional and local authorities and social and economic partners in preparing the National Strategic Development Plan for 2007–13, which later became the basis for the 2007–13 NSRF, but nevertheless acknowledges the limits to partnership and decentralization posed by political culture and tradition; in fact, there has been a recentralization of cohesion policy implementation in Greece since the mid-1990s in response to the ineffectiveness and waste of the decentralized system used previously. In all of the EU15 countries examined in this book, there appears to be recognition of the need to build stronger horizontal partnerships and include nongovernmental and local actors in cohesion policy implementation if the growth and competitiveness goals of the Lisbon Agenda are to be realized. As discussed in the next section, however, the extension of multi-level governance in these directions is inhibited or facilitated in these countries by various domestic mediating factors.

As discussed above, the new cohesion policy emphasis on decentralization and subsidiarity may be a factor in the decision of several new member states to regionalize and decentralize the implementation of EU cohesion policy in 2007–13, although other factors (increased funding and improved regional administrative capacities, domestic politics) also undoubtedly play a role. However, the development of horizontal multilevel governance has made less progress in these countries, despite the new emphasis on this dimension of partnership in the 2006 cohesion policy reform. Thus in Hungary, Horváth reports, economic and social partners were only consulted in the final stages of the process of drafting the NSRF and OPs for 2007–13; while in Lithuania, according to Nakrošis, socioeconomic partners were only included in lower-level planning bodies in preparations for 2007–13, in part a consequence of their limited capacity to provide input into planning for the previous programming period. Nongovernmental groups and social and economic partners also do not appear to have played a major role in programme planning for 2007–13 in Poland, the Czech Republic or Romania.

Explaining variation: domestic mediating factors

The country case studies of this book reveal considerable variation in the implementation of cohesion policy, despite common EU regulations, strategic guidelines and the central coordinating role of the Commission. This variation occurs in such areas as planning and structural programming, the design and functioning of management structures, and the implementation of partnership, including the nature and extent of partnership arrangements. Such variation is consistent with one of the main findings of the literature on Europeanization, which is the differential pattern of national adaptation to EU policy requirements and pressures. The Europeanization literature also emphasizes the role of 'domestic mediating factors' in accounting for this differentiation. In Chapter 1, we drew from this literature to identify several domestic factors that might affect the implementation of EU cohesion policy and account for national variation: established governmental structures and arrangements, governmental and administrative traditions, political-cultural values, and domestic politics and partisan contestation. In the remainder of this section, the impact of each factor is examined in turn, before we then discuss the relative influence of domestic and EU factors in cohesion policy implementation.

Governmental structures and arrangements

As discussed in Chapter 1, previous studies have found that established governmental structures and arrangements are a major factor affecting cohesion policy implementation, especially its impact on multilevel governance. This was also found to be the case in the countries examined in this book. In the only formally federal system examined, Germany, cohesion policy is implemented in a regionalized fashion, with most EU spending administered through separate ROPs under the control of the 16 *Länder*. At the *Land* level, however, cohesion policy is implemented in a fairly centralized fashion, with only limited roles for sub-regional and local actors; in fact, as Sturm and Schorlemmer point out, centralization at the *Land* level has increased since the second half of the 2000–06 programming period. Germany's federal system also favours the decoupling of EU and national regional policies because the *Länder* enjoy the autonomy (control over resources, direct access to the Commission) provided by EU cohesion policy and thus seek to keep it independent from federal government policies.

In the centralized unitary states examined in this book – Greece, Ireland, Lithuania, Hungary and Romania – cohesion policy is implemented in a more centralized fashion by national governments, despite varying efforts at decentralization in most of these countries. Decentralization has gone the furthest in Ireland, where regional actors have been given a greater role in implementing cohesion policy since

2000. In Greece, by contrast, an initial experiment with decentralized management of cohesion policy proved ineffective due to clientelism and politicization and was thus ended in the mid-1990s; cohesion policy has been implemented in a more centralized and technocratic fashion ever since. It is in decentralized or regionalized unitary states – the United Kingdom, Spain, Poland and the Czech Republic – where the trend towards regionalized or decentralized management of cohesion policy is most notable, following the prior devolution of power to regional governments or in response to the demands of democratically elected regional governments for more competencies, resources and autonomy. It must be noted, however (see the chapters on the United Kingdom, Ireland and Spain), that decentralizing cohesion policy implementation is not always the result of bottom-up political pressure; it is also done for pragmatic reasons of enhanced efficiency and effectiveness. In Ireland, for example, McMaster argues that decentralization was a 'pragmatic response to changing economic conditions in the country'.

Governmental and administrative traditions

The case studies in this book also show that governmental and administrative traditions are an important factor affecting cohesion policy implementation. In Ireland, for instance, a strong tradition of social partnership and consultative policymaking facilitated adaptation to the EU's partnership requirements. Similarly in the United Kingdom, Chapman argues that the already strong involvement of nongovernmental partners in the implementation of cohesion policy meant that Britain was 'ahead of the game' when it came to third-sector engagement; as a consequence, few changes were required in order to comply with the extended definition of partnership in the 2006 cohesion policy reform. In Germany, a dense culture of consensus; common understandings, attitudes and beliefs; and strong networks of informal coordination among civil servants have limited variation in the way that cohesion policy is implemented in the 16 *Länder*; these same factors also contribute to good inter-ministerial coordination at the *Land* level and facilitate the multilevel implementation of cohesion policy in Germany, at least when it comes to the *Länder* governments. Multilevel governance in Germany does not extend much beyond the *Land* level, however, at least when it comes to the implementation of EU cohesion policy, perhaps owing to the strong tradition of 'cooperative federalism' in Germany as some previous studies have argued (Kelleher, Batterbury and Stern, 1999; Thielemann, 2000; Bache, 2008, pp. 63–5). Sturm and

Schorlemmer also note that governmental and administrative norms pose a problem for adaptation to EU requirements in another sense, as Germany's bureaucratic culture is challenged by the 'efficiency philosophy' of the new Lisbon-oriented cohesion policy; German bureaucrats are simply not used to thinking in economic categories, they argue. In Spain, by contrast, Morata and Popartan claim that the 'persistence of old, hierarchical modes of governance' at the local level impedes the more active participation of local actors in cohesion policy, as required by the 2006 reform. Statist governmental traditions have also inhibited decentralization and the building of partnership networks in Greece.

Governmental traditions have also affected cohesion policy implementation in the new member states. In Hungary, according to Horváth, the dynamic growth of nongovernmental groups in recent years has not been matched by progress in establishing public-private partnerships, largely because of the persistence of traditional governmental attitudes. A similar picture can be painted in most of the new member states, where traditions of centralized government and administration – to some extent reinforced by the post-communist transition and EU accession processes, because of the premium placed on expediency and efficiency in the completion of top-down reforms – have resulted in slow adaptation to the EU cohesion policy requirements of regionalization, decentralization and partnership. In fact, the centralized management of EU funds was even advocated by the Commission after 2000 for pre-accession programmes and in the initial (2004–06) programming period for cohesion policy after accession, as it is in 2007–13 for Romania. Nevertheless, the (at least partial) decentralization of cohesion policy implementation in Poland, the Czech Republic, Hungary and Lithuania in 2007–13, together with the increased (although still inadequate) efforts of governments to involve social partners and build partnership networks, indicates a process of learning that goes beyond simple instrumental or formal adaptation to EU rules.

Political-cultural values

The case of Greece perhaps shows the impact of political-cultural values most clearly. In Greece, as Paraskevopoulos notes, a clientelistic political culture and low levels of social capital have inhibited the development of multilevel governance and the building of partnership networks. Low levels of social capital have also inhibited the policy learning process, when it comes to both 'learning from past successes and failures' and 'learning from abroad'. In Spain as well the persistence of traditional hierarchical norms of governance has limited the decentralization of cohesion policy implementation. Weak or underdeveloped civil society has also limited the spread of horizontal partnership and multilevel governance in the new member states. In Lithuania, for instance, Nakrošis argues that the development of horizontal partnership has been inhibited by the limited capacity of socioeconomic partners to participate in programme planning for cohesion policy, what he terms a 'supply side' problem for the partnership process. On the other hand, well-established norms of social partnership, consultative government and third-sector engagement in Ireland and the United Kingdom have facilitated adaptation to the EU's new policy governance requirements of greater local involvement and horizontal partnership.

Domestic politics and partisan contestation

Domestic politics appear to have had an important impact on the implementation of cohesion policy in some of the countries examined in this book, but not in others. Among the EU15, it appears to have had little impact in Ireland and Germany, where EU cohesion policy appears to not be an issue in domestic politics; in Germany, in fact, Sturm and Schorlemmer note the complete lack of public interest in attempts to organize a 'bottom-up' or 'deliberative' planning process for the 2007–13 NSRF. Party politics and the composition of government also do not seem to have affected cohesion policy implementation in these countries. Domestic politics was a factor in the United Kingdom, however, where the electoral victory of the Labour party in 1997 led to the devolution of significant governmental powers to the Scottish and Welsh regions. As Chapman argues, governmental devolution in the United Kingdom influenced the decentralization of programme management in 2007–13; the increased maturity of devolved regional arrangements was also a key factor in the closer alignment of EU cohesion and domestic regional policies after 2006, she claims. Chapman also notes that the Labour government (in part a reflection of its traditional social-democratic ideology) was more open to cooperation with social and economic partners, which in turn bolstered partnership and the spread of horizontal multilevel governance in the United Kingdom.

Domestic politics has also played a role in Spain, where governmental regionalization and demands for greater regional autonomy have gone hand-in-hand with the increased regionalization of cohesion policy implementation. Party politics has also affected cohesion policy implementation in Spain. According to Morata and Popartan, the election of a Socialist government in 2004 led to increased cooperation between the central state and self-governing regions (Autonomous Communities

[ACs]), perhaps motivated by the inclusion of small regionalist parties in the government coalition, but also due to the greater openness of Prime Minister Zapatero and his party to regional autonomy and decentralization. In Greece, management of the structural funds was a central issue in domestic politics in the 1980s and early-1990s, due to the inefficient and politicized implementation system introduced by the Pan-Hellenic Socialist Movement (PASOK) government, but it has become much less so with the increased centralization and technocratic orientation of cohesion policy management since the mid-1990s.

The role of domestic politics also varies in the new member states. In both Poland and the Czech Republic, the creation of democratically elected regional governments has led to a partial politicization of cohesion policy, with the newly created regions seeking a greater role in implementing and managing the structural funds. In both countries, cohesion policy became intertwined with the debate about governmental devolution and decentralization. In Hungary as well, the debate over creating a new regional tier of government, stimulated by the accession process and the regionalized focus of EU cohesion policy, has been a domestic political issue that remains unsettled. Allegations of corruption and mismanagement in the administration of EU funds aside, cohesion policy does not appear to be a domestic political issue in relatively small Lithuania, a country with no serious regional divisions or identities. In larger and more diverse Romania, however, regionalism – especially the autonomy demands of the Hungarian population concentrated in the west of the country and Transylvania – could potentially lead to the politicization of EU cohesion policy.

Domestic mediating and other factors

While the impact of domestic mediating factors on cohesion policy implementation is clear, somewhat less clear is the relative importance of domestic and EU (as well as non-EU) factors. The United Kingdom is a good example of a country in which domestic factors appear to be more important than EU requirements when it comes to cohesion policy implementation, at least in recent years. Chapman argues that the reorientation of regional policy in the United Kingdom towards the Lisbon themes was not just a response to the EU, but was in keeping with national or domestic preferences; if anything, she claims, the Lisbonization of cohesion policy might be an example of the 'uploading' of domestically determined preferences to the EU level. The same is true when it comes to decentralization and the horizontal extension of partnership, where the United Kingdom is already 'ahead of the game' in terms of third-sector engagement. Thus, because of the overall 'good fit' between new trends in cohesion policy and domestic preferences and developments, there is relatively little EU adaptational pressure; hence, domestic policies and preferences seem to play a larger role in determining cohesion policy priorities in the United Kingdom than the other way around.

Ireland is another country in which domestic factors seem to be predominant. While there has been some regionalization of cohesion policy implementation, McMaster asserts that this is not the result of EU pressures but rather Irish governmental efforts to increase efficiency and effectiveness; decentralization in Ireland, she argues, is a 'pragmatic response to changing economic conditions in the country'. Ireland's strong tradition of consultative policy making and its focus on human resource development and economic competitiveness also makes it a 'good fit' for EU cohesion policy, especially in its new Lisbonized form.

Germany is a bit more complicated. While its federal system and traditions of coordinated government appear to make it a natural fit for EU cohesion policy, this same system has created problems in adapting to the extended definitions of decentralization (to the sub-regional and local levels) and partnership (to include social, private-sector and nongovernmental actors) embodied in the new cohesion policy. As Sturm and Schorlemmer also point out, the traditional bureaucratic culture of Germany is not well-suited to the 'efficiency philosophy' of the Lisbonized cohesion policy, and the economic development and infrastructure needs of the country's poor regions (the eastern *Länder*) have also clashed with the new growth and competitiveness focus of cohesion policy. Thus, Germany may be less of a 'good fit' for EU cohesion policy today. Nonetheless, because of its relative wealth, Germany has the option of delinking its national regional development policies from EU cohesion policy in response, thus minimizing the impact of EU requirements and preserving some flexibility in responding to domestic needs and preferences.

In comparison, the EU exerts much greater influence in the less wealthy EU15 and new member states, because of their greater resource dependency on Brussels and the 'less good fit' of EU cohesion policy – with its requirements of regionalization, decentralization and partnership, and its reorientation towards the Lisbon Agenda goals – with national conditions (inadequate administrative and institutional capacity, statist governmental traditions, and weak civil society and social capital) and needs (basic infrastructure and economic development). In other words, adaptational pressures are higher, and non-EU options (e.g., to decouple national development policies from EU cohesion policy) are fewer. If there is a simple pattern or rule of thumb here, it appears to be this: domestic factors are more important than EU pressures to the extent that: a) there is a strong 'goodness of fit' between domestic preferences and EU requirements; and b) EU cohesion policy resources are not so important.

The future of EU cohesion policy

While enlargement has clearly had an impact on EU cohesion policy, it is also true, as Allen suggests in Chapter 2, that it will not be until 2013–14 and the conclusion of negotiations on the next financial perspective that we can fully assess EU cohesion policy after enlargement. Even at the beginning of the 2007–13 programming period, as member states began to implement the new Lisbonized cohesion policy agreed to in 2006, preparations for these negotiations and the accompanying debate about the future of EU cohesion policy were underway. In September 2007 the Commission organized a 'Fourth European Forum on Cohesion' in Brussels, intended to launch an EU-wide consultation process on the future of cohesion policy. This was followed in April 2008 by a conference on the future of cohesion policy organized by the Slovenian EU presidency. A mid-term review of cohesion policy spending and the budget will be launched in 2009, and further reform of cohesion policy will be on the agenda as debate on the post-2013 financial perspective begins.

While it is still too early to say for sure what the issues on this agenda will be, they are likely to include renewed efforts by wealthier net contributors to limit or reduce EU spending, a move that will be strongly opposed by the main net beneficiaries of cohesion policy. The United Kingdom and other net contributors will also undoubtedly renew their demand that cohesion policy be 'renationalized', with the bulk of cohesion policy spending shifted to poorer countries and wealthier member states being given greater responsibility for dealing with their own regional imbalances (and freedom from Commission interference in doing so). Debate is also likely to focus on the 'value added' of cohesion policy and whether it continues to merit its current share of the EU budget. Here the linkage of cohesion policy to the Lisbon and Gothenberg goals could play an important role in legitimizing the current level of spending and building support for maintaining it, assuming that a significant contribution of cohesion policy to achieving these goals can be demonstrated. As the Commission has also suggested, debate is likely to focus on the contribution of cohesion policy to dealing with a host of 'new challenges' including globalization, climate change, energy security and demographic change (European Commission, 2007a, pp. xvii–xx; 2008b, pp. 5–9).

It is also far too soon to say what the outcome of this debate will be, although it is unlikely that EU cohesion policy post-2013 will differ dramatically from its present form, both in terms of its basic design and orientation and the level of spending and percentage of the EU budget that it accounts for. One reason for this is the nature of EU intergovernmental bargaining and politics. As Allen argues in Chapter 2, cohesion policy over the years has played an important role in facilitating EU enlargement and major new EU strategic developments, such as the Single Market, Economic and Monetary Union (EMU) and the Lisbon Agenda. To the extent that cohesion policy continues to play this politically useful facilitative role, it is likely to survive without major changes or substantial reductions of funding well into the future. Other reasons for keeping cohesion policy basically as it is include the continued existence of significant regional disparities in the EU, possibly exacerbated by further enlargements to come, as well as the continued relevance for the EU and its member states of the basic norms of cohesion, solidarity and consensus. It is also certain that the future reform of EU cohesion policy will be strongly influenced by the experience with cohesion policy implementation in 2007–13, the first full programming period following the 2004 enlargement and 2006 cohesion policy reform. It is to a better understanding of the implementation of cohesion policy in an enlarged and more diverse EU that this book has sought to contribute.

Notes

1. Calculated from European Commission (2006d–g) and CEC (2006a).
2. This reflects the situation for the EU15 overall. As of December 2007, 74 per cent of expenditures under the Convergence objective had been earmarked for the achievement of Lisbon objectives, and 83 per cent of expenditures under the RCE objective (European Commission, 2007b, p. 4).
3. As of December 2007, before submission of the final versions of all OPs for 2007–13.

Bibliography

Adshead, M. (2005) 'Europeanisation and Changing Patterns of Governance in Ireland', *Public Administration*, vol. 83, no. 1, pp. 159–78.

Adshead, M. (2002) *Developing European Regions? Comparative Governance, Policy Networks and European Integration*, Aldershot: Ashgate.

Adshead, M. and Quinn, B. (1998) 'The Move from Government to Governance: Irish Development Policy's Paradigm Shift', *Policy and Politics*, vol. 26, no. 2, pp. 209–25.

AKČR (2005a) 'Zápis z 2. zasedání Rady Asociace krajů České republiky v jejím 2. funkčním období. Špindlerův Mlýn', 11 February, Website: http://www. kr-urady.cz/vismo/dokumenty2.asp?u=450022&id_org=450022&id=78479.

AKČR (2005b) 'Zápis ze 4. zasedání Rady Asociace krajů České republiky v jejím 2. funkčním období', Praha, 24 June, Website: http://www.kr-urady.cz/vismo/ dokumenty2.asp?u=450022&id_org=450022&id=92106.

Aktuálně.cz (2007a) Miliardy z Bruselu ohroženy, Čunek nestihl další termín, Prague, 27 June, Website: http://aktualne.centrum.cz/domaci/politika/clanek. phtml?id=457167.

Aktuálně.cz (2007b) Čunkův náměstek: Trable eurodotací začal Lachnit, Prague, 15 October, Website: http://aktualne.centrum.cz/domaci/politika/clanek. phtml?id=510786.

Alfa.lt (2006) *Lietuvos mokslui – 2 mlrd. Litų ES paramos*, 19 September, Website: http://www.alfa.lt/straipsnis/57082.

Allen, D. (2000) 'Cohesion and the Structural Funds: Transfers and Trade-Offs', in H. Wallace and W. Wallace (eds), *Policy-Making in the European Union*, 4th Edition, Oxford: Oxford University Press, pp. 243–66.

Allen, D. (2005) 'Cohesion and the Structural Funds: Competing Pressures for Reform', H. Wallace, W. Wallace and M. Pollack (eds), *Policy-Making in the European Union*, Fifth edition, Oxford: Oxford University Press, pp. 213–41.

Anderson, J. (1990) 'Sceptical Reflections on a Europe of Regions: Britain, Germany and the ERDF', *Journal of Public Policy*, vol. 10, pp. 417–47.

Anderson, J. (2002) 'Europeanization and the Transformation of the Democratic Polity: 1945–2000', *Journal of Common Market Studies*, vol. 40, no. 5, pp. 793–822.

Armstrong, A., Wells, P. and Woolford, J. (2002) Research Working Paper Number 1: 'The Role of the Third Sector in the Governance of Regional Policy in South Yorkshire', Sheffield: The University of Sheffield.

Bache, I. (1998) *The Politics of European Union Regional Policy: Multi-Level Governance or Flexible Gatekeeping?* Sheffield: Sheffield Academic Press.

Bache, I. (1999) 'The Extended Gatekeeper: Central Government and the Implementation of the EC Regional Policy in the UK', *Journal of European Public Policy*, vol. 6, no. 1, pp. 28–45.

Bache, I. (2003) 'Europeanization: A Governance Approach', paper presented at the EUSA 8th International Biennial Conference, Nashville, 27–9 March.

Bache, I. (2004) 'Muliti-level Governance and EU Regional Policy', in I. Bache and M. Flinders (eds), *Multi-Level Governance*, Oxford: Oxford University Press, pp. 165–78.

Bache, I. (2007) 'Cohesion Policy', in P. Graziano and M. Vink (eds), *Europeanization: New Research Agendas*, Basingstoke: Palgrave, pp. 239–52.

Bache, I. (2008) *Europeanization and Multilevel Governance: Cohesion Policy in the European Union and Britain*, Lanham: Rowman & Littlefield.

Bache, I. and Bristow, G. (2003) 'Devolution and the Gatekeeping Role of the Core Executive: The Struggle for European Funds', *British Journal of Politics and International Relations*, vol. 5, no. 3, pp. 405–27.

Bache, I. and Flinders M. (eds) (2004) *Multi-Level Governance*, Oxford: Oxford University Press.

Bache I. and Jones R. (2000) 'Has Regional Policy Empowered the Regions? A Study of Spain and the United Kingdom', *Regional and Federal Studies*, vol. 10, pp. 1–20.

Bache, I. *et al.* (1996) 'The European Union, Cohesion Policy and Sub National Authorities in the UK', in L. Hooghe (ed.), *Cohesion Policy and European Integration: Building Multi-Level Governance*, Oxford: Oxford University Press, pp. 294–319.

Bache, I. and Jordan, A. (eds.) (2006) *The Europeanization of British Politics*, Basingstoke: Palgrave Macmillan.

Bachtler J., Downes R. and Gorzelak G. (eds) (2000) *Transition, Cohesion and Regional Policy in Central and Eastern Europe*, University of Strathclyde: Ashgate.

Bachtler, J. and McMaster, I. (2008) 'EU Cohesion Policy and the Role of the Regions: Investigating the Influence of Structural Funds in the New Member States', *Environment and Planning C: Government and Policy*, vol. 26, no. 2, pp. 398–427.

Bachtler, J. and Mendez, C. (2007) 'Who Governs EU Cohesion Policy? Deconstructing the Reforms of the Structural Funds', *Journal of Common Market Studies*, vol. 45, no. 3, pp. 535–64.

Bachtler, J. and Wishlade, F. (2004) *Searching for Consensus: The Debate on Reforming EU Cohesion Policy*, European Policy Research Paper No. 55, European Policies Research Centre, University of Strathclyde, November.

Bachtler, J., *et al.* (2007) *The 2007–13 Operational Programmes: A Preliminary Assessment*, IQ-Net Thematic Paper No. 19 (2), Glasgow: European Policies Research Centre.

Badiello, L. (2001) 'La Accion Exterior de las Comunidades Autonomas', in F. Morata (ed.), *Gobernanza Multinivel en la Unión Europea*, Madrid: Fernandez de Casadevante.

Bailey, D. and De Propris, L. (2004) 'A Bridge too Phare? EU Pre-Accession Aid and Capacity Building in the Candidate Countries', *Journal of Common Market Studies*, vol. 42, no. 1, pp. 77–98.

Balsas, G. (2008) *Kirkilas nesijaudina dėl lėto ES lėšų įsisavinimo*, 13 February, Website:http://www.balsas.lt/naujiena/183184.

Baráth, E. (2004) 'A Magyar Nemzeti Fejlesztési Terv (The Hungarian National Development Plan)', *Területi Statisztika*, 3, pp. 203–17.

Barua, D. and Morata, F. (2001) 'La europeización de las Politicas regionales de desarrollo agrícola y rural', in C. Closa (ed.), *La europeización del sistema político español,* Madrid: Istmo.

Bauer, M. W. (2006) 'Co-managing Programme Implementation: Conceptualizing the European Commission's Role in Policy Execution', *Journal of European Public Policy*, vol. 13, no. 5, pp. 717–35.

Baun, M. (2002) 'EU Regional Policy and the Candidate States: Poland and the Czech Republic', *European Integration*, vol. 24, pp. 261–80.

Baun, M. and Marek, D. (2006) 'Regional Policy and Decentralization in the Czech Republic', *Regional and Federal Studies*, vol. 16, no. 4, pp. 409–28.

Benedek, J. (2004) *Amenajarea teritoriului şi dezvoltarea regională*, Editura Presa Universitară Clujeană, Cluj-Napoca.

Benedek, J. (forthcoming, 2009) 'The Emergence of New Regions in Transition Romania', in J. Scott (ed.), *De-coding New Regionalism: Shifting Socio-political Contexts in Central Europe and Latin America*, Ashgate: Urban and Regional Planning and Development Series.

Benedek, J. and Jordan, P. (2007) 'Administrative Dezentralisierung, Regionalisierung und Regionalismus in den Transformationsländern am Beispiel Rumäniens', *Mitteilungen der Österreichischen Geographischen Gesellschaft*, 149 Jg., pp. 81–108.

Benz, A. and Eberlein, B. (1999) 'The Europeanization of Regional Policies: Patterns of Multi-level Governance', *Journal of European Public Policy*, vol. 6, no. 2, pp. 329–48.

Blažek, J. (2001) 'Regional Development and Regional Policy in the Czech Republic: An Outline of the EU Enlargement Impacts', *Informationen zur Raumentwicklung*, Heft 11/12.2001, pp. 757–67, Website: http://www.reg-dev.org.md/library/regdev_ CzechR.pdf.

Blažek, J. and Boekhout, S. (2000) 'Regional Policy in the Czech Republic and the EU Accession', in J. Bachtler, R. Downes and G. Gorzelak (eds), *Transition, Cohesion, and Regional Policy in Central and Eastern Europe*, Aldershot: Ashgate Publishing.

Blom-Hansen, J. (2005) 'Principals, Agents and the Implementation of EU Cohesion Policy', *Journal of European Public Policy*, vol. 12, no. 4, pp. 624–48.

BMW Regional Assembly (2006) *Submission to the Department of Finance on the NDP 2007–13*, Ballaghaderreen: BMW Regional Assembly, April.

BMW Regional Assembly (2007) Draft BMW Regional Operational Programme for 2007–2013, Ballaghaderreen: BMW Regional Assembly, 13 July.

BMW Regional Assembly & Western Development Commission (2005) *Submission from the Border, Midland & Western Regional Assembly to the National Economic and Social Council (NESC), More Effective Regional Policy & the Social Partnership Process*, Ballaghaderreen: BMW Regional Assembly, June.

Boldrin, M. and Canova, F. (2001) 'Inequality and Convergence in Europe's Regions: Reconsidering European Regional Policies', *Economic Policy: A European Forum*, no. 32, pp. 205–45.

Börzel, T. (1999) 'Towards Convergence in Europe? Institutional Adaptation and Europeanization in Germany and Spain', *Journal of Common Market Studies* vol. 37, no. 4, pp. 573–96.

Börzel, T. (2001) 'Europeanization and Territorial Institutional Change: Toward Cooperative Regionalism?', in M. G. Cowles, J. Caporaso and T. Risse (eds), *Transforming Europe: Europeanization and Domestic Change*, Ithaca, NY: Cornell University Press, 137–58.

Börzel, T. (2002) *States and Regions in Europe: Institutional Adaptation in Germany and Spain*, Cambridge: Cambridge University Press.

Börzel, T. and Risse, T. (2000) 'When Europe Hits Home: Europeanization and Domestic Change', EUI Working Paper RSC, No 2000/56.

Börzel, T. and Risse, T. (2003) 'Conceptualising the Domestic Impact of Europe', in K. Featherstone and C. Radaelli (eds) *The Politics of Europeanization*, Oxford: Oxford University Press.

Boyle, M. (2000) 'Euro-Regionalism and Struggles over Scales of Governance: The Politics of Ireland's Regionalisation Approach to Structural Fund Allocations 2000– 2006', *Political Geography*, vol. 19, no. 6, pp. 737–69.

Brožaitis, H. and Nakrošis, V. (2002) *Lithuania's Capacity to Absorb the EU Structural and Cohesion Funds Assistance: Summary*, Vilnius: National Regional Development Agency.

Brunn, G. (2002) *Die Europäische Einigung*, Stuttgart: Philipp Reclam, June.

Brusis, M. (2001a) 'Institution Building for Regional Development: A Comparison of the Czech Republic, Estonia, Hungary, Poland and Slovakia', in J. Beyer, J. Wielgohs and H. Wiesenthal (eds), *Successful Transitions: Political Factors of Socio-Economic Progress in Post-socialist Countries*, Baden-Baden: Nomos, pp. 223–42.

Brusis, M. (2001b) 'Between EU Eligibility Requirements, Competitive Politics and National Traditions: Re-creating Regions in the Accession Countries of Central and Eastern Europe', paper presented at the Bi-Annual Conference of the European Union Studies Association, Madison, WI, 30 May–2 June.

Brusis, M. (2003) 'Regionalisation in the Czech and Slovak Republics: Comparing the Influence of the European Union', in M. Keating and J. Hughes (eds), *The Regional Challenge in Central and Eastern Europe: Territorial Restructuring and European Integration*, Brussels: P.I.E.-Peter Lang, pp. 89–105.

Bulmer, S. and Burch, M. (1998) 'Organising for Europe: Whitehall, the British State and European Union', *Public Administration*, vol. 76, no. 3, pp. 601–28.

Bulmer, S. and Burch, M. (2002) 'British Devolution and European Policy-Making: A Step Change Towards Multi-Level Governance', *Politique Europeene*, vol. 6, pp. 114–36.

Bulmer, S., *et al.* (2002) *British Devolution and European Policy-Making: Transforming Britain into Multi-Level Governance*, London: Palgrave.

Bulmer, S. and Lequesne, C. (eds) (2005) *The Member States of the European Union*, Oxford: Oxford University Press.

Bulmer, S. and Radaelli, C. (2005) 'The Europeanization of National Policy', in S. Bulmer and C. Lequesne (eds), *The Member States of the European Union*, Oxford: Oxford University Press, pp. 338–59.

Büning, S. (2007) 'Die Milliarde kommt. Als erste Region in Westdeutschland erhält die strukturschwache Gegend um Lüneburg jetzt die maximale Förderung der Europäischen Union', *Die Zeit*, 4 April, p. 31.

Bundesministerium für Arbeit und Soziales (2007) *Operationelles Programm des Bundes für den Europäischen Sozialfonds. Förderperiode 2007–2013*, as of 22 March 2007, Berlin.

Bundesministerium für Wirtschaft und Arbeit (2005) *Nationales Reformprogramm Deutschland. 'Innovation forcieren – Sicherheit im Wandel fördern – Deutsche Einheit vollenden'*, Berlin.

Bundesministerium für Wirtschaft und Technologie (2007) *Nationaler Strategischer Rahmenplan für den Einsatz der EU-Strukturfonds in der Bundesrepublik Deutschland 2007–2013*, Berlin, Website: http://www.bmwi.de/BMWi/Navigation/Europa/EU-Strukturpolitik/nationaler-strategie-rahmenplan-07–13.html.

Burch, M. and Gomez, R. (2006) 'The English Regions', in I. Bache and A. Jordan (eds), *The Europeanization of British Politics*, Basingstoke: Palgrave Macmillan, pp. 82–97.

Caporaso, J. (1996) 'The European Union and Forms of the State: Westphalian, Regulatory or Post-Modern?' *Journal of Common Market Studies*, vol. 34, no. 1, pp. 29–52.

CEC (1989) *First CSF 1989–93, Greece*. Luxembourg: OOPEC.

CEC (1993) *Second CSF 1994–99, Greece*. Luxembourg: OOPEC.

CEC (1996) *Social and Economic Inclusion Through Regional Development. The Community Economic Development Priority in European Structural Funds Programmes in Great Britain* (The Lloyd Report), Luxembourg: Office for Official Publications of the European Communities.

CEC (1998) *Regular Report from the Commission on Romania's Progress Towards Accession*, Brussels: European Commission.

CEC (2000) *2000 Regular Report from the Commission on Lithuania's Progress Towards Accession*, Website: http://europa.eu.int/comm/enlargement/report_11_00/.

CEC (2001) *Unity, Solidarity, Diversity for Europe, Its People and Its Territory: Second Report on Economic and Social Cohesion*. Luxembourg: OOPEC.

CEC (2004a) *A New Partnership for Cohesion, Third Cohesion Report*, Brussels: European Commission.

CEC (2004b) *The Commission's Assessments of National Reform Programmes for Growth and Jobs: Ireland*, Brussels: European Commission.

CEC (2006a) Inforegio Factsheet: Cohesion Policy 2007–2013 – The United Kingdom, European Commission, October, Website: http://ec.europa.eu/regional_policy/atlas2007/fiche/uk_en.pdf.

CEC (2006b) *Communication from the Commission to the Spring European Council: Implementing the Renewed Lisbon Strategy for Growth and Jobs*, December.

CEC (2006c) *Communication from the Commission to the Spring European Council: Implementing the Renewed Lisbon Strategy for Growth and Jobs. Lithuania: Assessment of National Reform Programme*, Website: http://ec.europa.eu/growthandjobs/pdf/1206_annual_report_lithuania_en.pdf.

CEC (2006d) *Monitoring Report of the State of Preparedness for EU membership of Bulgaria and Romania*, Brussels: European Commission.

CEC (2007a) *United Kingdom: Cohesion Policy 2007–2013*, European Commission, Website: http://ec.europa.eu/regional_policy/atlas2007/uk/index_en.htm.

CEC (2007b) *Communication from the Commission to the European Council: Strategic Report on the Renewed Lisbon Strategy for Growth and Jobs. Lithuania: Assessment of National Reform Programme*, Website: http://ec.europa.eu/growthandjobs/pdf/european-dimension-200712-annual-progress-report/200712-annual-progress-report-LT_en.pdf.

CEC (2007c) *Commission Staff Working Document. Annex to the Report from the Commission: 18 Annual Report on Implementation of the Structural Funds (2006)*, Brussels, Website: http://ec.europa.eu/regional_policy/sources/docoffic/ official/reports/pdf/annex/ 2006_sf_annex_en.pdf.

Central Statistical Office (2004) *County Incomes and Regional GDP*, Dublin: Government of Ireland.

Chapman, R. (2004) 'Europeanization of the Third Sector', paper presented at the ESRC/UACES conference 'Britain in Europe and Europe in Britain: The Europeanization of British Politics', Sheffield Town Hall, 16 July.

Chapman, R. (2005) Third Sector Empowerment and Legitimacy in a Multi-Level Polity, unpublished PhD Thesis, Sheffield: The University of Sheffield.

Chapman, R. (2006) 'The Third Sector', in I. Bache and A. Jordan (eds), *The Europeanization of British Politics*, Hampshire: Palgrave Macmillan, pp. 168–86.

Chubb, B. (1992) *The Government and Politics of Ireland*, 3rd edition, London: Longman.

Closa C. and Heywood P. (2004) *Spain and the European Union*, Houndsmill: Palgrave Macmillan.

Conzelmann, T. (2002) *Große Räume, kleine Räume. Europäisierte Regionalpolitik in Deutschland und Großbritannien*, Baden-Baden: Nomos.

Cowles, M. G., Caporaso, J. and Risse, T. (eds) (2001) *Transforming Europe: Europeanization and Domestic Change*, Ithaca: Cornell University Press.

CRG (2003) *Mid Term Evaluation of the Objective 1 Programme for West Wales and the Valleys: Final Report*, Website: http://www.wefo.cymru.gov.uk/resource/ Objective1MidTermEvaluation-MainReport.pdf (accessed 18 September 2005).

Crosbie, J. (2006) 'From the Dirt Poor to the Filthy Rich', *European Voice*, 1–7 June, p. 26.

Crosbie, J. (2007) 'Cities Shape up for Economic Challenge', *European Voice*, 19–25 July, p.18.

Czech Republic Government (1998) 'National Progamme for Adoption of the Acquis Communautaire', Prague: Ministry of Foreign Affairs.

Czech Republic Government (2002) Resolution No. 102/2002 on 'Completion of the Preparation of Programming Documents and Establishment of Managing and Paying Authorities for Use of the Structural and Cohesion Funds', Website: www.mmr.cz/cz/rdp/opprog/uv102.html.

Davis, S. *et al.* (2007) 'The Impact of Structural Funds Programmes in Scotland 1994–2006', European Policy Research Paper Number 60, Glasgow: European Policy Research Centre.

Delfi (2005a) *Lietuvos premjeras patenkintas pasiektu susitarimu dėl ES biudžeto,* 17 December, Website: http://www.delfi.lt/archive/article.php?id=8280700.

Delfi (2005b) *V.Uspaskichas atsistatydina iš ūkio ministro pareigų ir traukiasi iš Seimo.* 16 June, Website: http://www.delfi.lt/archive/article.php?id=6912992.

Delfi (2006) *ES lėšų skirstymą ragina atskirti nuo politinių peripetijų*, 14 February, Website: http://www.delfi.lt/archive/article.php?id=8779684.

Delfi (2007a) *Teismas dar kartą išteisino Z.Balčyčio sūnų*, 7 December, Website: http://www.delfi.lt/news/daily/lithuania/article.php?id=15248627.

Delfi (2007b) *Eurokomisarė D. Grybauskaitė kritikuoja Lietuvos gebėjimus panaudoti ES pinigus*, 13 October, Website: http://www.delfi.lt/archive/article.php?id= 14691996.

Delwit, P. (ed.) (2005) *Les parties régionalistes en Europe. Des acteurs en développement?* Editions de l'Université de Bruxelles, Bruxelles.

De Rynck, S. and McAleavey, P. (2001) 'The Cohesion Deficit in Structural Fund Policy', *Journal of European Public Policy*, vol. 8, no. 4, pp. 541–57.

Deutscher Bundestag (2006a) *Kürzung der Gemeinschaftsaufgabe 'Verbesserung der regionalen Wirtschaftsstruktur' im Jahr 2007*, Bundestag printed paper 16/3519, Berlin.

Deutscher Bundestag (2006b) *Bericht der Bundesregierung über die Entwicklung der Finanzhilfen des Bundes und der Steuervergünstigungen für die Jahre 2003 bis 2006 (20. Subventionsbericht)*, Bundestag printed paper 16/1020, Berlin.

Deutscher Bundestag (2007a) *Bestandsaufnahme der Bund-Länder-Finanzbeziehungen*, Bundestag printed paper 16/4304, Berlin.

Deutscher Bundestag (2007b) *Sechsunddreißigster Rahmenplan der Gemeinschaftsaufgabe 'Verbesserung der regionalen Wirtschaftsstruktur' (GA) für den Zeitraum 2007 bis 2010*, Bundestag printed paper 16/5215, Berlin.

DfT (2005) *Updated Mid-Term Evaluation of England Objective 1 and Objective 2 Programmes: Collation of Regional Analysis*, London : DfT.

DG Regio (2005) 'Partnership in the 2000–06 Programming Period – Analysis of the Implementation of the Partnership Principle', November, Brussels: European Commission.

DTI (2006) *United Kingdom National Strategic Reference Framework: EU Structural Funds Programmes: 2007–2013*, London: DTI.

ECOTECH (2003) 'Evaluation of the Added Value and Costs of the European Structural Funds in the UK', Final report to the Department of Trade and Industry (DTI) and Office of the Deputy Prime Minister (ODPM), London, DTI/ODPM.

EEDA (2007) *Management Arrangements for the ERDF Operational Transfer*, Resource Committee Paper 19 September, Cambridgeshire East of England Development Agency.

Enterprise Ireland (2006) *Annual Report and Accounts 2005*, Dublin: Enterprise Ireland.

Enyedi, G. and Tózsa, I. (eds) (2004) *The Region. Regional Development Policy, Administration and E-Government*. Budapest, Akadémiai Kiadó.

ETK (2006) *Ex Ante Evaluation of the Lithuanian Operational Programmes 2007–13: Final Ex-ante Evaluation Report*, Website: http://www.esparama.lt/ES_Parama/strukturines_paramos_2007_1013m._medis/veiksmu_programu_projektu_vertinimas/files/Final_Report_Ex_ante_integrated_2007_May.pdf.

Euractiv (2004a) 'Ministerstvo pro místní rozvoj je v přípravě na čerpání ze strukturálních fondů EU nejdále', Prague, 26 April, Website: http://www.euractiv.cz/strukturalni-politika/clanek/ministerstvo-pro-mstn-rozvoj-je-v-pprav-na-erpn-ze-strukturl.

Euractiv (2004b) 'Kraje kritizují MMR za nedostatky při zpracování žádostí o prostředky ze strukturálních fondů', Prague, 9 September, Website: http://www.euractiv.cz/print.cgi?cid=571&sid=27&pid=27.

Euractiv (2004c) 'ČR čerpá správně dotace z EU u dvou programů', Prague, 6 December, Website: http://www.euractiv.cz/print.cgi?cid=874&sid=27&pid=27.

Euractiv (2005) 'Asociace krajů kraje nebudou schopny spolufinancovat projekty podpořené ze strukturálních fondů EU', Prague, 27 June, Website: http://www.euractiv.cz/index?a=show&cid=1654&pid=27&sid=27.

Euractiv (2006a) 'Vláda schválila Národní rozvojový plán na období 2007–2013', Prague, 23 February, Website: http://www.euractiv.cz/strukturalni-politika/clanek/vlda-schvlila-nrodn-rozvojov-pln-na-obdob-2007--2013.

Euractiv (2006b) 'Martínek: čerpání evropských peněz v ČR se zvýší', Prague, 8 March, Website: http://www.euractiv.cz/strukturalni-politika/clanek/martnek-erpn-evropskch-penz-v-r-se-zv.

Euractiv (2006c) 'ČR dostatečně nevužívá prostředky ze strukturálních fondů', Prague, 22 September, Website: http://www.euractiv.cz/strukturalni-politika/clanek/r-dostaten-nevyuv-prostedky-ze-strukturlnch-fond.

Euractiv (2006d) 'Podle MMR Česká republika urychlila čerpání peněz z evropských fondů, Prague, 2 October, Website : http://www.euractiv.cz/strukturalni-politika/clanek/podle-mmr-esk-republika-urychlila-erpn-penz-z-evropskch-fond.

Euractiv (2008) 'New Members in EU Funds Spending Frenzy', Brussels, 13 February, Website: http://www.euractiv.com/en/innovation/new-members-eu-funds-spending-frenzy/article-170251.

Eurion (2006) 'Návrhy opatření ke zefektivnění čerpání prostředků v rámci operačních programů SF EU 2007–13', Brno, unpublished document, May.

Euro (2002) 'Lachnituv urad vyrostl v obra', No. 5, p. 25.

European Commission (1997a) 'Agenda 2000: For a Stronger and Wider Union', COM (1997) 2000, *Bulletin of the European Union*, Supplement, 5/97.

European Commission (1997b) 'Commission Opinion on the Czech Republic's Application for Membership of the European Union', Document drawn up on the basis of COM(97) 2009 final, *Bulletin of the European Union*, Supplement 14/97 Luxembourg: Office for Official Publications of the European Communities.

European Commission (1998) 'Czech Republic Accession Partnership 1998', Brussels: DG 1A.

European Commission (2001a) '2001 Regular Report on the Czech Republic's Progress Towards Accession', SEC (2001) 1746, Brussels: DG Enlargement, 13 November.

European Commission (2001b) *Phare 2000 Review – Strengthening Preparations For Membership*, Luxembourg: European Commission.

European Commission (2003) 'Comprehensive Monitoring Report on the Czech Republic's Preparations for Membership', November, Brussels: European Commission.

European Commission (2004) *A New Partnership for Cohesion: Convergence, Competitiveness, Cooperation. Third Report on Economic and Social Cohesion*, 18 February, Brussels: European Commission.

European Commission (2005a) *Third Progress Report on Economic and Social Cohesion*, COM (2005) 192 final, 17 May, Brussels: European Commission.

European Commission (2005b) *Romania 2005 Comprehensive Monitoring Report*, Brussels: European Commission.

European Commission (2006a) *Fourth Progress Report on Cohesion: The Growth and Jobs Strategy and the Reform of European Cohesion Policy*, Communication from the Commission, COM(2006) 281 final, Brussels, 12 June.

European Commission (2006b) 'Position Paper of the European Commission on National Strategic Reference Framework of the Czech Republic 2007–2013 (NSRF v. 4)', Brussels, September, Website: http://www.strukturalni-fondy.cz/uploads/documents/HSS_2007_2013/POSITION_PAPER_NSRF_CZ_2007_2013.pdf.

European Commission (2006c) *Sapard Annual Report 2004*, Brussels: European Commission.

European Commission (2006d) Inforegio Factsheet: Cohesion Policy 2007–2013 – Germany, DG Regional Policy, October, Website: http://ec.europa.eu/regional_policy/sources/docgener/informat/compar/comp_de.pdf.

European Commission (2006e) Inforegio Factsheet: Cohesion Policy 2007–2013 – Spain, DG Regional Policy, October, Website: http://ec.europa.eu/regional_policy/sources/docgener/informat/compar/comp_es.pdf.

European Commission, (2006f) Inforegio Factsheet: Cohesion Policy 2007–2013 – Ireland, DG Regional Policy, October, Website: http://ec.europa.eu/regional_policy/sources/docgener/informat/compar/comp_ie.pdf.

European Commission (2006g) Inforegio Factsheet: Cohesion Policy 2007–2013 – Greece, DG Regional Policy, October, Website: http://ec.europa.eu/regional_policy/sources/docgener/informat/compar/comp_el.pdf.

European Commission (2007a) 'Growing Regions, Growing Europe: Fourth Report on Economic and Social Cohesion', Luxembourg: Office for Official Publications of the European Community, May.

European Commission (2007b) 'Member States and Regions Delivering the Lisbon Strategy for Growth and Jobs through EU Cohesion Policy, 2007–13', Communication from the Commission, COM (2007) 798, Brussels, 11 December.

European Commission (2008a) *General Report on the Activities of the European Union in 2007*, Chapter 111, Solidarity.

European Commission (2008b) 'Communication form the Commission on the Results of the Negotiations Concerning Cohesion Policy Strategies and Programmes for the Programming Period 2007–2013', COM (2008) 301/4, Brussels, 14 May.

European Council (1999) 'Presidency Conclusions, Berlin European Council, 24 and 25 March 1999'. Website: http://ue.eu.int/ueDocs/cms_Data/docs/pressData/en/ec/ACFB2.html.

European Council (2005) Final Comprehensive Proposal from the Presidency on the Financial Perspective 2007–2013, No. 15915/05, CADREFIN 268, Brussels, 19 December.

European Court of Auditors (2004) *Special Report 2/2004*, Official Journal of the EU, C295/1.

European Court of Auditors (2006) *Special Report 4/2006 2006 Concerning Phare Investment Projects in Bulgaria and Romania, Together with the Replies of the Commission*, Official Journal of the EU, C174/1.

European Voice (2007) 'Delebarre Welcomes New Treaty Deal', 19–25 July, p. 17.

Europos socialiniai, teisiniai ir ekonominiai projektai (2007) *Viešinimo ir informavimo apie ES struktūrinių fondų paramą 2004–2006 m. vertinimo galutinė ataskaita*, Website: http://www.esparama.lt/ES_Parama/bpd_2004_2006m._medis/administravimo_sistema/bpd_igyvendinimo_vertinimas/files/Viesinimo_vertinimo_galutine_ataskaita.pdf.

Faragó, L. (2004) *The General Theory of Public (Spatial) Planning*, Pécs, Centre for Regional Studies, Discussion Papers, 43.

FCO (2008) *Consolidated Text of the EU Treaties as Amended by the Treaty of Lisbon*, Command 7310, January.

Featherstone, K. and Radaelli, C. (eds) (2003) *The Politics of Europeanisation*, Oxford: Oxford University Press.

Ferry, M. and McMaster, I. (2005) 'Regional Governance in Industrial Regions in Central and Eastern Europe: A Polish-Czech Comparison', in I. Sagen and H. Halkier (eds), *Regionalism Contested*, London: Ashgate.

Fine Gael (2006) *Cowen's Plans for the Next NDP Do Not Inspire Confidence – Connaughton*, Fine Gael National Press Office Press Release, 18 June.

Garmise, S. O. (1995) 'Economic Development Strategies in Emilia-Romagna', in M. Rhodes (ed.), *The Regions and the New Europe: Patterns in Core and Periphery Development*, Manchester: Manchester University Press, pp. 136–64.

GCSS (2006) *The Concept of the Spatial Policy of the State*, Governmental Centre for Strategic Studies, Warsaw, scientific coordination: G. Gorzelak.

Generalitat de Catalunya (2005) 'La posició de Catalunya devant dels nous reglaments financers 2007–13'.

Getimis, P. and Demetropoulou, L. (2004) 'Towards New Forms of Regional Governance in Greece: The Case of Southern Aegean Islands', *Regional and Federal Studies*, Special Issue, C. J. Paraskevopoulos and R. Leonardi (eds), 'Learning from Abroad (by Comparison): Regionalization and Local Institutional Infrastructure in Cohesion and CEE Countries', pp. 353–76.

Gilmartin, S. (2006) 'In Defence of Decentralisation', *Public Affairs Ireland*, Issue 27, February/March, Dublin: PAI Publications Limited.

Goetz, K. and Hix, S. (eds) (2001) *Europeanised Politics? European Integration and National Political Systems*, London: Frank Cass.

Gorzelak, G. (2007) *Rozwój – region – polityka (Development-Region-Policy)*, in G.Gorzelak and A. Tucholska (eds), *Rozwój, region, przestrzeń*, Ministerstwo Rozwoju Regionalnego and EUROREG UW, Warszawa.

Gorzelak, G. *et al.* (1999) *Dynamics and Factors of Local Success in Poland*, vol. 15. EUROREG-CASE, Warszawa.

Gorzelak, G. and Smętkowski, M. (2005) *Metropolia i jej region*, Scholar, Warszawa.

Government of Hungary (2003a) *Hungarian National Development Plan, 2004–2006*, Budapest, Prime Minister's Office, Office for National Development and European Funds.

Government of Hungary (2003b) *Community Support Framework 2004–2006, Republic of Hungary*, CCI No.: 2003 HU 161 CC 001, Website: http://www.nfu.hu/national_development_plan.

Government of Hungary (2006) *The New Hungary Development Plan, 2007–2013*, Budapest, Prime Minister's Office.

Government of Ireland (1999) *Ireland National Development Plan 2000–06*, Dublin: The Stationary Office.

Government of Ireland (2007) *National Development Plan 2007–13; Transforming Ireland: A Better Quality of Life for All*, Dublin: the Stationary Office.

Government of Lithuania (2007) *Annual Progress Report of the National Lisbon Strategy Implementation Programme*, Website: http://www.ukmin.lt/lisabona/lt/node/22.

Government of Poland (2003) *Poland. National Development Plan 2004–2006*, adopted by the Council of Ministers on 14 January, Website: http://www.funduszestrukturalne.gov.pl/NR/rdonlyres/07FACA74-E350-4A7B-869D-B20744987C20/0/npr_complete_final.doc.

Government of Poland (2004) *Narodowy Plan Rozwoju (National Development Plan)*, Council of Ministers, Warsaw.

Government of Poland (2006) *National Development Strategy*, Website: http://www.mrr.gov.pl/NR/rdonlyres/88134D68-A81E-4FC7-8475-6194F7B4E730/29991/SRK_ang_new.pdf.

Government of Poland (2007a) *National Strategic Reference Framework*, Warszawa http://www.mrr.gov.pl/NR/rdonlyres/A1A61D68-4528-499F-9199-5FE0E0533F0D/31941/NSRO_maj2007.pdf.

Government of Poland (2007b) Wykorzystanie funduszy strukturalnych i Funduszu Spójności – stan na sierpień 2007 (Utilization of the Structural Funds and Cohesion Fund – August 2007), Website: http://www.mrr.gov.pl/NR/rdonlyres/ D7A57AFC-F88C-4D78-A44C-2396AD6350C5/38135/notatkaprasowa_25wrzesnia2.pdf.

Government of Poland (2007c) *Informacja o stanie realizacji programów opera-cyjnych współfinansowanych z funduszy strukturalnych Unii Europejskiej za okres od 1 do 31 lipca 2007 r. (Implementation report on the programmes co-financed by the European Union)*, Website: http://www.mrr.gov.pl/NR/rdonlyres/019B8E2C-F771-46E2-AF9A-099D373CA745/37586/wdrazanie_fs_31072007.pdf.

Government of Poland (2007d) *Stan wdrażania ZPORR (IROP Implementation)*, July, Website: http://www.zporr.gov.pl/Stan+realizacji+ZPORR/.

Government of Romania and European Commission (1997) *Carta Verde. Politica de dezvoltare regională în România*, Bucureşti.

Government of Romania (2001) *National Development Plan, 2002–2005*, Bucureşti: Government of Romania.

Government of Romania (2003) *National Development Plan 2004–2006*, Bucureşti: Government of Romania.

Government of Romania (2006) *National Development Plan, 2007–2013*, Bucureşti: Government of Romania.

Government of Romania (2007) *The National Strategic Reference Framework 2007–2013*, Bucuresti: Government of Romania.

Grabbe, H. (2001) 'How Does Europeanization Affect CEE Governance? Conditionality, Diffusion and Diversity?' *Journal of European Public Policy*, vol. 8, no. 6, pp.1013–31.

Granados C. (2006) 'La actualización del Programa Nacional de Reformas para alcanzar los objetivos de la Estrategia de Lisboa: ¿Cumple España con Europa?', Real Instituto Elcano, ARI N° 116/2006.

Hart, J. (1985) 'The European Regional Development Fund and the Republic of Ireland', in M. Keating and B. Jones (eds), *Regions in the European Community*, Oxford: Clarendon Press, pp. 204–33.

Hayward, K. (2006) *A Marriage of Convenience: The EU and Regionalisation in Ireland*, paper delivered to PSAI Annual Conference, University College Cork, 21 October.

Héritier, A. *et al.* (2001) *Differential Europe: The European Union's Impact on National Policymaking*, Boulder, CO: Rowman & Littlefield.

HM Treasury and ODPM (2006) *Review of Government Offices*, London: HM Treasury. HM Treasury/DBERR/DCLG (2007) *Review of Sub-national Economic Development and Regeneration*, London: HM Treasury.

HM Treasury, DTI and ODPM (2003) *A Modern Regional Policy for the United Kingdom*, London: HM Treasury.

Hooghe, L. (1996) 'Building a Europe with the Regions: The Changing Role of the European Commission', in L. Hooghe (ed.), *Cohesion Policy and European Integration: Building Multi-Level Governance*, Oxford: Oxford University Press, pp. 89–126.

Hooghe, L. (ed.) (1996) *Cohesion Policy and European Integration: Building Multi-Level Governance*, Oxford: Oxford University Press.

Hooghe, L. and Marks, G. (2001) *Multi-Level Governance and European Integration*, Lanham, MD: Rowman & Littlefield.

Horváth, G. (2001) 'Consequences of the Interrelationship between Institutions of Regional Development and of Integration in Hungarian Regional Policy', *European Mirror*, Special Issue, pp. 119–54.

Horváth, G. (2005) 'Decentralization, Regionalism and the Modernization of the Regional Economy in Hungary: A European Comparison', in G. Barta, É. G. Fekete, I. Kukorelli Szörényiné and J. Timár (eds), *Hungarian Spaces and Places: Patterns of Transition*, Pécs, Centre for Regional Studies, HAS, pp. 50–63.

Hughes, J., Sasse, G. and Gordon, C. (2001) 'Enlargement and Regionalization: The Europeanization of Local and Regional Governance in CEE States', in H. Wallace (ed.), *Interlocking Dimensions of European Integration*, Basingstoke: Palgrave.

Hughes, J., Sasse, G. and Gordon, C. (2003) 'EU Enlargement, Europeanisation and the Dynamics of Regionalization in the CEECs', in M. Keating and J. Hughes (eds), *The Regional Challenge in Central and Eastern Europe: Territorial Restructuring and European Integration*, Brussels: P.I.E.-Peter Lang, pp. 69–88.

Hughes, J., Sasse, G. and Gordon, C. (2004a) 'Conditionality and Compliance in the EU's Eastward Enlargement: Regional Policy and the Reform of Sub-national Government', *Journal of Common Market Studies*, vol. 42, no. 3, pp. 523–51.

Hughes, J., Sasse, G. and Gordon, C. (2004b) *Europeanization and Regionalization in the EU's Enlargement to Central and Eastern Europe: The Myth of Conditionality*, Basingstoke: Palgrave.

Ianoş, I. (2006) Potential Strukturdynamik, Attraktivität der rumänischen Wirtschaft, in T. Kahl, M. Metzeltin and M.-R.Ungureanu (eds), *Rumänien. Raum und Bevölkerung. Geschichte und Geschichtsbilder. Kultur. Gesellschaft und Politik heute. Wirtschaft. Recht und Verfassung. Historische Regionen*, pp. 105–30. Lit Verlag, Wien, Berlin (Österreichische Osthefte, Sonderband).

Iara, A. (2005) *European Integration, Regional Structural Change and Cohesion in Romania*, EURECO Working Paper, Website: http://www.zei.de/zei_alt/eurec/WP3_Romania.pdf.

IDA Ireland (2006), *Ireland: Vital Statistics*, IDA Ireland: Dublin.

Illner, M. (2002) 'Thirteen Years of Reforming Subnational Governments in the Czech Republic', paper presented at the Conference on Reforming Local Government: Closing the Gap between Democracy and Efficiency, University of Stuttgart, 26– 27 September.

IIRPS (2006) *Lithuania's Participation in the European Union Open Method of Co-ordination Processes: Impact Assessment on Public Administration and Public Policy*, Institute of International Relations and Political Science, Website: http://www.euro.lt/lt/apie-lietuvos-naryste-europos-sajungoje/lietuva-ir-europos-sajunga/narystes-es-poveikis-lietuvai-/atvirojo-koordinavimo-metodo-itaka-viesajam-administravimui-ir-viesajai-politikai/.

Irish Regions Office (2006) *EU support for Irish Regions*, Brussels: Irish Delegation to the Committee of the Regions, Website: http://www.iro.ie/EU-structural-funds.html.

Jacoby, W. (2004) *The Enlargement of the European Union and NATO: Ordering from the Menu in Central Europe*, Cambridge: Cambridge University Press.

Jacoby, W. and Černoch, P. (2002) 'The EU's Pivotal Role in the Creation of Czech Regional Policy', in R. H. Linden (ed) *Norms and Nannies: The Impact of International Organizations on the Central and Eastern European States*, Blue Ridge Summit, PA: Rowman & Littlefield.

Jákli, Z. (1990) *Vom Marshallplan zum Kohlepfennig. Grundrisse der Subventionspolitik in der Bundesrepublik Deutschland 1948–1982*, Opladen: Westdeutscher Verlag.

Jeffery, C. (ed) (1997) *The Regional Dimension of the European Union: Towards a Third Level in Europe?* London: Frank Cass.

Jeffery, C. (2000) 'Sub-National Mobilization and European Integration: Does it Make Any Difference?', *Journal of Common Market Studies*, vol. 38, no. 1, pp.1–23.

Jones, B. J. and Keating, M. (eds) (1995) *The European Union and the Regions*, Oxford: Oxford University Press.

Jordan, P. (1998) 'Regionalisation and Decentralisation in Romania-Opportunities and Obstacles', in W. Heller (ed.), *Romania: Migration, Socio-economic Transformation and Perspectives of Regional Development*, Südosteuropa-Studie, 62, München.

Kafkalas, G. and Andrikopoulou, E. (2003) 'Greek Regional Policy in the Context of Europeanization: 1961–2000', in D. Dimitrakopoulos and A. Passas (eds), *Greece in the European Union*, London: Routledge, pp. 35–47.

Keating, M. (2003) 'Regionalization in Central and Eastern Europe: The Diffusion of a Western Model?' in M. Keating and J. Hughes (eds), *The Regional Challenge in Central and Eastern Europe: Territorial Restructuring and European Integration*, Brussels: P.I.E.-Peter Lang, pp. 51–67.

Keating, M. and Hughes, J. (eds) (2003) *The Regional Challenge in Central and Eastern Europe: Territorial Restructuring and European Integration*, Brussels: P.I.E.-Peter Lang.

Keating, M., Loughlin, J. and Deschouwer, K. (2003) *Culture, Institutions and Development: A Study of Eight European Regions*, Aldershot: Edward Elgar.

Kelleher, J., Batterbury, S. and Stern, E. (1999) *The Thematic Evaluation of the Partnership Principle: Final Synthesis Report*, London: The Tavistock Institute.

Keogh, D. (1994) *Twentieth Century Ireland: Nation and State*, Dublin: Gill and Macmillan.

Knill, Christoph (ed) (2001) *The Europeanization of National Administrations: Patterns of Institutional Change and Persistence*, Cambridge: Cambridge University Press.

Kohler-Koch, B. (1996) 'Catching up with Change: The Transformation of Governance in the European Union', *Journal of European Public Policy*, vol. 3, no. 3, pp. 359–80.

Kohler-Koch, B. (2004) 'Gobernanza Interactiva: Las Regiones en la Red de la Política Europea' in F. Morata (ed), *Gobernanza Multinivell en la Unión Europea*, Barcelona: Tirant lo Blanc.

Kok, W. *et al.* (2004) 'Facing the Challenge: The Lisbon Strategy for Growth and Employment, Report for the Commission', Brussels: European Commission.

Kozak, M. (2004) 'Ocena systemu wdrażania europejskiej polityki regionalnej w Polsce. Rekomendacje dla przebudowy systemu wdrażania po roku 2006 (Assessment of the European Regional Policy Implementation System in Poland)', in T. G. Grosse (ed.), *Polska wobec nowej polityki spójności Unii Europejskiej*, Instytut Spraw Publicznych, Warszawa.

Kozak, M. (2007) 'Problem strategii w dokumentach rozwoju regionalnego (Strategy Problem in the Regional Development Documents)', in G. Gorzelak and A. Tucholska (eds), *Rozwój, region, przestrzeń*, Ministerstwo Rozwoju Regionalnego and EUROREG UW, Warszawa.

Laffan, B. (1996) 'Ireland: A Region Without Regions – The Odd Man Out', in L. Hooghe (ed.), *Cohesion Policy and European Integration: Building Multi-level Governance*, Oxford: Oxford University Press, pp. 320–37.

Laffan, B. (2000) 'Rapid Adaptation and Light-Coordination', in R. O'Donnell (ed), *Europe: The Irish Experience*, Dublin: Institute of European Affairs.

Laffan, B. (2004) *Multi-level governance: The Dynamics of EU Cohesion Policy: A Comparative Analysis*, OEUE Phase II Occasional Paper 3–9 April, Dublin European Institute University College, Dublin.

Lenschow, A. (1997) 'Transformation in European Environmental Governance', EUI Working Papers, RSC No 97/61.

Leonardi, R. (2005) *Cohesion Policy in the European Union: The Building of Europe*, Basingstoke: Palgrave Macmillan.

Lietuvos laisvosios rinkos institutas (2007) *Valstybės biudžetas: geriau jokio nei toks*, Website: http://www.lrinka.lt/index.php/meniu/spaudai/pranesimai_spaudai/valstybes_biudzetas_geriau_jokio_nei_toks/4489.

Lietuvos rytas (2007) *Lietuva sugebėjo pasiimti tik trečdalį ES paramos*, 3 April.

Lyberaki, A. and Paraskevopoulos, C. J (2002) 'Social Capital Measurement in Greece', paper prepared for the OECD-ONS International Conference on Social Capital Measurement, London, 25–27 September.

Mapa pomocy Unii Europejskiej udzielonej Polsce w ramach programu PHARE 1990–2003, ISPA 2000–2003 and SAPARD (Map of EU Assistance to Poland within the PHARE 1990–2003, ISPA 2000–2003 and SAPARD programme) (2004) Urząd Komitetu Integracji Europejskiej, Warszawa, Website: http://www2.ukie.gov.pl/HLP/files.nsf/0/73C64711C4628031C1256EDA0034E6E4/$file/publikacja_mapa_pomocy_UE.pdf.

Marek, D. and Baun, M. (2002) 'The EU as a Regional Actor: The Case of the Czech Republic', *Journal of Common Market Studies*, vol. 40, no. 5, pp. 895–919.

Marks, G. (1992) 'Structural Policy in the European Community', in A. Sbragia (ed), *Euro-Politics: Institutions and Policymaking in the 'New' European Community*, Washington, D.C.: Brookings Institution.

Marks, G. (1993) 'Structural Policy and Multilevel Governance in the EC', in A. W. Cafruny and G. Rosenthal, G. (eds), *The State of the European Community, Vol 2: The Maastricht Debates and Beyond*, Boulder, CO: Lynne Rienner, pp. 391–411.

Marks, G. (1996) 'Exploring and Explaining Variation in EU Cohesion Policy', in L. Hooghe (ed), *Cohesion Policy and European Integration: Building Multi-Level Governance*, Oxford: Oxford University Press, pp. 388–422.

Marks, G. and Hooghe, L. (2004) 'Contrasting Visions of Multi-level Governance', in I. Bache and M. Flinders (eds), *Multi-Level Governance*, Oxford: Oxford University Press, pp. 15–30.

Marks, G., Hooghe, L. and Blank, K. (1996) 'European Integration since the 1980s: State Centric Versus Multi-Level Governance', paper presented at the American Political Science Association Meeting, Chicago.

Marks, G., Hooghe, L. and Blank, K. (1996) 'European Integration from the 1980s: State-Centric vs. Multi-level Governance', *Journal of Common Market Studies*, vol. 34, pp. 341–78.

Marks, G. *et al.* (1996) 'Competencies, Cracks and Conflicts: Regional Mobilization in the European Union', in G. Marks, F. W. Scharpf, P. C. Schmitter and W. Streeck (eds), *Governance in the European Union*, London: Sage, pp. 40–63.

Marshall, J. (2002) 'European Regional Policy and Urban Governance: Assessing Dublin's Experience', paper presented at the European Consortium for Political Research Joint Sessions, Turin, 22–27 March.

Matía Portilla, F. (2003) 'Las oficinas y Delgaciones en Bruselas', in Paloma Biligno Campos (ed), *La Politica Europea de las Comunidades Europeas*, Valencia: Tirant lo Blanc, p. 72.

McAleese, D. (2000) 'Twenty Five Years and Growing', in R. O'Donnell (ed), *Europe: The Irish Experience*, Dublin: Institute of European Affairs, pp. 79–110.

McMaster, I. (2004a) 'Spatial Development Policy in Ireland: Lessons for the New Member States?', paper at ECPR Workshop European 'Spatial Politics or Spatial Policy for Europe?', Uppsala, Sweden, 13–18 April.

McMaster, I. (2004b) 'From Regional Deficit to Institutional Overload? Regional Policy in the Czech Republic', European Policy Research Paper No. 52, European Policies Research Centre, University of Strathclyde, February.

McMaster, I. (2006) 'Evaluation Cultures in the EU Member States', paper presente at the Latvian Ministry of Finance conference 'The EU Funds Evaluation: Experience and Opportunities', Riga, Latvia, 3 March.

MDPH (2007) *Regional Operational Programme*, Bucureşti: Ministry of Development, Public Works and Housing.

Mendez, C., Wishlade, F. and Yuill, D. (2006) 'Conditioning and Fine Tuning Europeanization: Negotiating Regional Policy Maps under the EU's Competition and Cohesion Policies', *Journal of Common Market Studies*, vol. 44, no. 3, pp. 581–605.

Midland Regional Authority (2006) Website: http://www.midlands.ie/.

Ministerio de Economia y Hacienda (2002) *Marco Comunitario de Apoyo para las Regiones del Objetivo 1, Evaluacion Intermedia*. Madrid: Ministerio de Economia y Hacienda

Ministerio de Economia y Hacienda (2007) *Marco Estrategico Nacional de Referencia*. Madrid: Ministerio de Economia y Hacienda

Ministerium für Arbeit und Soziales Baden-Württemberg (2007) *Europäischer Sozialfonds (ESF). Operationelles Programm. Ziel 2: 'Regionale Wettbewerbsfähigkeit und Beschäftigung' in Baden-Württemberg 2007–2013*, as of 28 February 2007, Stuttgart.

Ministerium für Ernährung und Ländlichen Raum Baden-Württemberg (2007) *Operationelles Programm für das Ziel 'Regionale Wettbewerbsfähigkeit und Beschäftigung', Teil EFRE in Baden-Württemberg 2007*–2013, Stuttgart.

Ministerium für Wirtschaft, Arbeit und Soziales Mecklenburg-Vorpommern (2007) *Europäischer Sozialfonds ESF. Operationelles Programm des Landes Mecklenburg-Vorpommern. Förderperiode 2007–2013*, as of 5 March 2007, Schwerin: Ministerium für Wirtschaft, Arbeit und Soziales Mecklenburg-Vorpommern.

Ministry of Economy and Finance (2007a) *Framework Document for Implementing the SOP Increase of Economic Competitiveness*, Bucureşti: Ministry of Economy and Finance.

Ministry of Economy and Finance (2007b) *Disparităţile regionale la orizontul anului 2008*, Bucureşti: Ministry of Economy and Finance.

Ministry of Environment and Sustainable Development (2007) *SOP Environment*, Bucureşti: Ministry of Environment and Sustainable Development.

Ministry of Labour, Family and Equal Opportunities (2007) *SOP Human Resources Development*, Bucureşti: Ministry of Labour, Family and Equal Opportunities.

Ministry of Transport (2007) *SOP Transport*, Bucureşti: Ministry of Transport.

Mitsos, A. (2001) 'The Community's Redistributive and Development Role and the Southern European Countries', in H. D. Gibson (ed.), *Economic Transformation, Democratization and Integration into the European Union: Southern Europe in Comparative Perspective*, Basingstoke: Palgrave, pp. 306–42.

Morata, F. (1995) 'Spanish Regions in the European Community, in M. Keating and B. Jones (eds), *The European Union and the Regions*, Oxford: Clarendon Press.

Morata, F. (2004a) 'Gobernaza multinivel y cooperación subestatal en la Unión Europea', in F. Morata, G. Lachapelle and S. Paquin (eds), *Globalización, Gobernanza e Identidades*, Barcelona: Fundación Pi i Sunyer, d'Estudis Autonomic i Locals.

Morata, F. (2004b) 'Politicas de Cohesión y Gobernanza Europea', in F. Morata (ed), *Gobernanza Multinivel en la Unión Europea*, Barcelona: Tirant lo Blanc, pp. 155–88.

Morata, F. (ed) (2004) *Gobernanza Multinivel en la Unión Europea*, Barcelona: Tirant lo Blanc.

Morata F. and Muñoz X. (1996) 'Vying for European Funds', *Cohesion Policy and European Integration-building multi-level governance*, Oxford: Oxford University Press.

Moxon-Browne, E. and Kreuzbergová, E. (2001) 'The Ambiguous Effects of EU Regional Policy on the Applicant States: The Case of the Czech Republic', paper presented at the Conference on EU Regionalism, Georgia State University, Atlanta, GA, 20 April.

MRD (2001) 'Implementační opatření v programových dokumentech regionálního rozvoje: Varianta A – jeden společný ROP', unpublished government working document, Prague.

MRD (2002) 'Completion of the Preparation of Programming Documents and Establishment of Managing and Paying Authorities for the Use of the Structural and Cohesion Funds', Explanatory Report, Website: www.mmr.cz/cz/rdp/opprog/zprava. html.

MRD (2003) 'Community Support Framework Czech Republic 2004–2006', Prague, Website: http://www.strukturalni-fondy.cz/uploads/old/1074592072 communitysupportframework.pdf.

MRD (2005a) 'Výroční zpráva Rámce podpory Společenství za rok 2004', Prague: MRD, Website: http://www.strukturalni-fondy.cz/uploads/old/1125564614. vyrocni- zprava-rps-za-2004_pro-ek_final.pdf.

MRD (2005b) 'Fondy Evropské unie ve finanční perspektivě', Prague: MRD, December, Website: http://www.mmr.cz/index.php?show=001021348000209.

MRD (2006a) 'Nejvíce peněz z fondů EU je určeno na rozvoj dopravy – dokument „Evropské zdroje 2007 – 2013" prošel vládou', Prague: MRD, Website: http://www.strukturalni-fondy.cz/regionalni-politika-eu-2007–2013/evropske-zdroje-2007–2013.

MRD (2006b) 'Výroční zpráva Rámce podpory Společenství za rok 2005', Prague: MRD, Website: http://www.strukturalni-fondy.cz/uploads/documents/ Rizeni_fondu_EU/ Monitorovani/VZ_RPS_2005_26_06_06.pdf.

MRD (2006c) 'Evaluace střednědobého pokroku RPS', MRD *Structural Funds Newletter*, Prague: MRD, Website: http://www.strukturalni-fondy.cz/uploads/documents/Rizeni_fondu_EU/Dokumenty/NL_web_rocnik_2006_cervenec_srpen.pdf.

MRD (2006d) 'Přípravy na další čerpání z EU jdou do finále', Prague: MRD, October, Website: http://www.mmr.cz/index.php?show=001021542.

MRD (2006e) 'Vláda ČR schválila dokumenty klíčové pro čerpání 750 miliard z EU', Prague: MRD, November, Website: http://www.mmr.cz/index.php?show= 001021545.

MRD (2007) 'National Strategic Reference Framework of the Czech Republic 2007-2013', July, Website: http://www.strukturalni-fondy.cz/uploads/ documents/NOK/NSRF_en_170707_bez_zmen_db_fin.tablka.pdf.

MRD (2008) 'Čerpání evropských peněz z minulého programovacího období se úspěšnědaří', Prague, 8 January, Website: http://www.mmr.cz/cerpani-evropskych-penez-z-minuleho-programovaciho-obdobi-se-uspesne-dari.

Muraru, I. and Iancu, Gh. (1999) *Constituţiile Române*, Regia Autonomă Monitorul Oficial, Bucureşti.

Nacionaline regionų plétros agentūra (2002) *Europos Sąjungos regioninės politikos pasekmių ūvertinimas Lietuvos viešajai administracijai*, Vilnius, Nacionaline regionų plétros agentūra.

Nakrošis, V. (2003a) 'Managing EU Funds in the Candidate Countries: Administrative Organization and Resource Distribution' in B. Funck and L. Pizatti (eds) *European Integration, Regional Policy and Growth*, The World Bank, pp. 201–17.

Nakrošis, V. (2003b) *The Influence of the EU and Domestic change: Lithuania's Adaptation to the EU Cohesion Policy*, paper for the ECPR research session 'The Impact of EU Integration upon Public Administration in Central and Eastern Europe'.

Nakrošis, V. (2007) The Reform of Performance Management in Lithuania: Towards Result-Based Government, Policy study (unpublished paper).

Nanetti, R., Rato, H. and Rodrigues, M. (2004) 'Institutional Capacity and Reluctant Decentralization in Portugal: Case-study of the Lisbon and Tagus Valley Region', *Regional and Federal Studies*, Special Issue, C. J. Paraskevopoulos and R. Leonardi (eds), 'Learning from Abroad (by Comparison): Regionalization and Local Institutional Infrastructure in Cohesion and CEE Countries', pp. 403–28.

National Agency for Regional Development (1999) *National Development Plan, 2000–2002*, Website: http://www.mie.ro.

National Statistical Office (2006) *National Accounts, Hungary, 2004–2005*, Budapest: National Statistical Office.

Navarro, T. and Garrido, R. (2004) 'La politica Regional de la Unión Europea: Quo Vadis', Real Instituto Elcano, Documento de Trabajo (DT), 28/2004.

Navarro, A. and Viguerra, E. (2005) 'Las Perspectivas Financieras 2007–13 y la Posición de España', Real Instituto Elcano, Documento de Trabajo (DT), 22/2005.

OECD (2001) *OECD Territorial Reviews: Hungary*, Paris: OECD.

O'Donnell, C. M. and Whitman, R. G. (2007) 'European Policy under Gordon Brown: Perspectives on a Future Prime Minister', *International Affairs*, vol. 83, pp. 253–72.

O'Donnell, R. and Walsh, J. (1995) 'Ireland: Region and State in the European Union' in M. Rhodes (ed), *The Regions in the New Europe*, Manchester: Manchester University Press, pp. 200–28.

O'Hara, P. and Commins, P. (2002) 'Social Partnership and Regional Development' in S. Reynolds and S. Healy (eds), *Choosing a Fairer Future*, Dublin: CORI Justice Commission, pp. 29–63.

Oficina Económica de la Presidencia (2006) 'National Reform Plan-Progress Report', October, Madrid: Oficina Económica de la Presidencia.

OJEC (1999) Council Regulation (EC) No 1260/1999 of 21 June 1999, laying down general provisions on the Structural Funds, *Official Journal of the European Communities*. Brussels: Office for Official Publications of the European Communities.

OJEU (2006a) Council Regulation (EC) No 1083/2006 of 11 July 2006, laying down general provisions on the European Regional Development Fund, the European Social Fund and the Cohesion Fund and repealing Regulation (EC) No 1260/1999, *Official Journal of the European Union*. Brussels: Office for Official Publications of the European Communities.

OJEU (2006b) Council Regulation (EC) No 702/2006 of 6 October 2006, on Community strategic guidelines on cohesion, *Official Journal of the European Union*. Brussels: Office for Official Publications of the European Communities.

Olsen, J. (2002) 'The Many Faces of Europeanization', *Journal of Common Market Studies*, vol. 40, no. 5, pp. 921–52.

Open Europe (2005) 'Briefing Note: The EU Budget: A Historic Missed Opportunity – Executive Summary', London: Open Europe.

Pálné Kovács, I., Paraskevopoulos, C. J. and Horváth, G. (2004) 'Institutional "legacies" and the shaping of regional governance in Hungary', *Regional and Federal Studies*, vol. 3, pp. 430–60.

Paraskevopoulos, C. J. (1998) 'Social Capital, Institutional Learning and European Regional Policy: Evidence from Greece', *Regional and Federal Studies*, vol. 8, no. 3, pp. 31–64.

Paraskevopoulos, C. J. (2001a) 'Social Capital, Learning and EU Regional Policy Networks: Evidence from Greece', *Government and Opposition*, vol. 36, no. 2, pp. 251–75.

Paraskevopoulos, C. J. (2001b) *Interpreting Convergence in the European Union: Patterns of Collective Action, Social Learning and Europeanization*, London: Palgrave.

Paraskevopoulos, C. J. (2005) 'Developing Infrastructure as a Learning Process in Greece', in K. Featherstone (ed), 'The Challenge of Modernisation: Politics and Policy in Greece, *West European Politics* – Special Issue, vol. 28, no. 2, pp. 445–70.

Paraskevopoulos, C. J. (2007) 'Social Capital and Public Policy in Greece', LSE Hellenic Observatory Papers on Greece and Southeast Europe, GreeSE Paper No 9, December.

Paraskevopoulos, C. J. and Leonardi, R. (2004) 'Introduction: Adaptational Pressures and Social Learning in European Regional Policy: Cohesion (Greece, Ireland and Portugal) vs. CEE (Hungary, Poland) Countries', *Regional and Federal Studies* vol. 14, no. 3, pp. 315–54.

Paraskevopoulos, C. J. et al. (eds) (2006) *Adapting to EU Multi-Level Governance: Regional and Environmental Policies in Cohesion and CEE Countries*, Aldershot: Ashgate.

Pasquier, R. (2005) 'Cognitive Europeanization and Territorial Effects of Multilevel Policy Transfer: Local Development in French and Spanish Regions', *Regional and Federal Studies*, vol. 15, no. 3, pp. 295–310.

Pérez Tremps, P. (ed) (1999) 'La participación Europea y la Acción Exterior de las Comunidades Autonomas, Madrid: Marcial Pons.

Pollack, M. A. (1995) 'Regional Actors in an Intergovernmental Play: The Making and Implementation of EC Structural Policy', in C. Rhodes and S. Mazey (eds),

The State of the European Union, Vol. 3: Building a European Polity? Boulder, CO: Lynne Rienner, pp. 361–90.

Polverari, L. *et al.* (2005) *Strategic Planning for Structural Funds in 2007–2013: A Review of Strategies and Programmes,* IQ-Net Thematic Paper No. 18 (2), Glasgow: European Policies Research Centre.

Potluka, O., Pĕlucha, M. and Halámek, P. (2005) *Hrozby a příležitosti strukturálních fondů EU v ČR,* Prague, Transparency International Czech Republic, Website: http://www.transparency.cz/pdf/TIC_SF_sesit2.pdf.

Popescu, C. (2000) *Industria României în secolul XX. Analiză geografică,* Editura Oscar Print, București.

Public Policy and Management Institute (2008) Evaluation about the Implementation of the Horizontal Priorities during the Absorption of the European Union Structural Assistance: Final report (unpublished report).

Pyszkowski, A. and Kozak, M. (eds) (1999) *Pilotażowy program rozwoju regionalnego Phare-STRUDER (Pilot Regional Development Phare-STRUDER Programme),* Polska Agencja Rozwoju Regionalnego, Warszawa.

Radaelli, C. (2000) 'Whither Europeanization? Concept Stretching and Substantive Change', *European Integration Online Papers,* vol. 4 , no. 8.

Radaelli, C. (2004) 'Europeanisation: Solution or problem', *European Integration Papers Online,* vol. 8, no. 16.

Redeco (2006) 'Evaluace střednědobého pokroku RPS', Prague: MRD, May, Website: http://www.strukturalni-fondy.cz/uploads/documents/Rizeni_fondu_ EU/ Evaluace/MTE_RPS_fin.pdf.

Rees, N., Quinn, B. and Connaughton B. (2004) 'Ireland's Pragmatic Adaptation to Regionalization: The Mid West Region', *Regional and Federal Studies,* Special Issue, C. J. Paraskevopoulos and R. Leonardi (eds.), 'Learning from Abroad (by Comparison): Regionalization and Local Institutional Infrastructure in Cohesion and CEE Countries', pp. 377–402.

Rees, N., Quinn, B. and Connaughton, B. (2006) 'The Challenge of Multi-Level Governance in Ireland', in C.J. Paraskevopoulos, *et al. Adapting to Multi-Level Governance,* Aldershot: Ashgate, pp. 53–77.

Regeneris (2006) 'Good Practice Guide for English ERDF and ESF Programmes 2007–13 : Case Study Evaluations of Wider Impacts of English Objective 1 and 2 Activities: Final Report', London: Department for Communities and Local Government.

Respekt (2008) 'To nejlepší, co jsem pro Evropu udělala', Prague, 12 January, Website: http://www.respekt.cz/clanek.php?fIDCLANKU=141&fIDROCNIKU=2008.

Rey Martinez, F. (2003) 'La participación a través del Estado, Conferencias Sectoriales y Conferencia para Asuntos Relacionados con las Comunidades Europeas', in Paloma Biligno Campos (ed.), *La Politica Europea de las Comunidades Europeas,* Valencia: Tirant lo Blanc.

Risse, T., Cowles, M. and Caporaso, J. (2001) 'Europeanization and Domestic Change: Introduction', in M.G. Cowles, J. Caporaso and T. Risse (eds), *Transforming Europe: Europeanization and Domestic Change,* Ithaca: Cornell University Press, pp. 1–20.

Sandu, D. (1999) *Spatiul social al tranzitiei,* Editura Polirom, București: Editura Polirom.

Sapir, A., *et al.* (2004) *An Agenda for a Growing Europe: Making the EU Economic System Deliver,* Report of an Independent High Level Study Group (Chairman:

Andre Sapir), Oxford University Press (originally published online by the EU Commission, 2003).

Schmidt, V. A. (1997) 'European Integration and Democracy: The Differences Among Member States', *Journal of European Public Policy*, vol. 4, no. 1, pp. 128–45.

Scottish Executive (2006) *Scottish Executive Consultation: Future European Structural Funds Programmes in Lowlands and Uplands Scotland 2007–2013*, Scottish Executive, Website: http://Scotland.gov.uk/Publications/2006/10/201 55513/3.

Scottish Government (2006) *Scottish Executive Consultation: Future European Structural Funds Programmes in Highlands and Islands 2007–2013*, Edinburgh: Scottish Government, Website: http://www.scotland.gov.uk/ [accessed 27/9/07].

Sloat, A. (2002) *Scotland in Europe: A Study of Multi-Level Governance*, Oxford: Peter Lang.

Smith, J. (2001) 'Cultural Aspects of Europeanization: The Case of the Scottish Office', *Public Administration*, vol. 79, no. 1, pp. 147–65.

Smith, J. (2006) 'Government in Scotland', in I. Bache and A. Jordan (eds), *The Europeanization of British Politics*, Hampshire: Palgrave Macmillan, pp. 67–81.

Smyrl, M. (1997) 'Does European Community Regional Policy Empower the Regions? *Governance*, vol. 10, no. 3, pp. 287–309.

Southern and Eastern Regional Assembly (2007) *Draft Southern and Eastern Regional Operational Programme for 2007–2013*, Southern and Eastern Regional Assembly: Waterford.

Sosvilla, S. and Herce, J. (2004) 'La Política de Cohesion Europea y la Economía Española: Evalución y Prospectiva', Real Instituto Elcano, Documento de Trabajo (DT), 142/2004.

Sotiropoulos, D. (1993) 'A Colossus with Feet of Clay: The State in Post-authoritarian Greece', in H. Psomiades and D. Thomadakis (eds), *Greece, the New Europe and the Changing International Order*, New York: Pella.

Sotiropoulos, D. A. (2004) 'Southern European Public Bureaucracies in Comparative Perspective', *West European Politics*, vol. 27, no. 3, pp. 405–22.

Spanou, C. (2001) Ελληνική Διοίκηση και Ευρωπαϊκή Ολοκλήρωση (Greek Administration and European Integration), Athens: Papazisis.

Sturm, R. (1991) *Die Industriepolitik der Bundesländer und die europäische Integration. Unternehmen und Verwaltungen im erweiterten Binnenmarkt*, Baden-Baden: Nomos.

Sturm, R. and Pehle, H. (2005) *Das neue deutsche Regierungssystem. Die Europäisierung von Institutionen, Entscheidungsprozessen und Politikfeldern in der Bundesrepublik Deutschland*, 2nd edition, Wiesbaden: Verlag für Sozialwissenschaften.

Tavistock Institute (1997) *Thematic Evaluation of the Partnership Principle, Report to DGXVI*, European Commission, London: Tavistock Institute.

Taylor, S. (2006a) 'Budget Deal Leaves Regions with Plenty of Opportunities', *European Voice*, 1–7 June, p. 23.

Taylor, S. (2006b) 'Trouble for Commission's 'Lisbonisation' project', *European Voice*, 1–7 June, p. 24.

Thielemann, E. (2000) 'Europeanisation and Institutional Compatibility: Implementing European Regional Policy in Germany', *Queen's Papers on Europeanization*, No. 4/2000.

Torreblanca, J. (2005a) 'Farewell to Funds? Keys to Understanding Spain's Position When Negotiating the 2007–13 EU Budget', Real Instituto Elcano, WP 21/2005.

Torreblanca, J. (2005b) 'The European Financial Perspective 2007–13: A Good Agreement for Spain' (II), Real Instituto Elcano, ARI 155/2005.

Torreblanca, J. and Sorroza, A. (2006) 'España y la Unión Europea: Actualización del EU-25 Watch', Real Instituto Elcano, ARI Nº 28/2006.

Transparency International (2006) *Europos Sąjungos struktūrinių fondų paramos Lietuvai paskirstymo skaidrumas*, Website: http://www.transparency.lt/new/images/es%20parama_tils_tyrimas.pdf.

UK House of Commons (2004) 'The EU's Financial Perspective for 2007–13 and Reform of the Structural and Cohesion Funds', European Scrutiny Committee, Fifteenth Report of Session 2003–04, HC 42-xv.

Veidas (2008) *Šie metai – paskutinis šansas panaudoti 1,2 mlrd. Lt ES paramos*, No. 3. Verslo žinios (2005) *Verslas nusileido*, 28 January, Website: http://vz.lt/DefaultArchive.aspx.

Vigvári, A. (2005) 'Competitiveness, absorption ability and sub-national governments', in A. Ágh (ed), *Institutional Design and Regional Capacity-Building in the Post-Accession Period*, Budapest, Hungarian Centre for Democracy Studies, pp. 227–59.

Waele, J.-M. De (ed) (2004) *Les clivages politiques en Europe centrale et orientale*, Editions de l'Université de Bruxelles, Bruxelles.

WEFO (2007a) *West Wales and the Valleys Convergence Programme: Operational Programme for the European Regional Development Fund 2007–2013*, Carmarthen: Welsh European Funding Office.

WEFO (2007b) *East Wales Regional Competitiveness and Employment Programme: Draft Operational Programme for the ERDF 2007–2013*, Carmarthen: Welsh European Funding Office.

Zahradník, P. and Jedlička, J. (2006) *Úspěšnost čerpání ze strukturálních fondů EU do února 2006*, Prague: EU Office České spořitelny, March, Website: http://www.csas.cz/banka/content/inet/internet/cs/FondyEU_cerpani.pdf.

Index

294   *Index*